DIGITAL MEDIA AND THE GREEK CRISIS

DIGITAL ACTIVISM AND SOCIETY: POLITICS, ECONOMY AND CULTURE IN NETWORK COMMUNICATION

The *Digital Activism and Society: Politics, Economy and Culture in Network Communication* series focuses on the political use of digital everyday-networked media by corporations, governments, international organizations (Digital Politics), as well as civil society actors, NGOs, activists, social movements and dissidents (Digital Activism) attempting to recruit, organise and fund their operations, through information communication technologies.

The series publishes books on theories and empirical case studies of digital politics and activism in the specific context of communication networks. Topics covered by the series include, but are not limited to:

- the different theoretical and analytical approaches of political communication in digital networks;
- studies of socio-political media movements and activism (and 'hacktivism');
- transformations of older topics such as inequality, gender, class, power, identity and group belonging;
- strengths and vulnerabilities of social networks.

Series Editor
Dr Athina Karatzogianni

About the Series Editor
Dr Athina Karatzogianni is an Associate Professor at the University of Leicester, UK. Her research focuses on the intersections between digital media theory and political economy, in order to study the use of digital technologies by new sociopolitical formations.

Published Books in this Series:

Digital Materialism: Origins, Philosophies, Prospects by Baruch Gottlieb
Nirbhaya, New Media and Digital Gender Activism by Adrija Dey
Digital Life on Instagram: New Social Communication of Photography by Elisa Serafinelli
Internet Oligopoly: The Corporate Takeover of Our Digital World by Nikos Smyrnaios
Digital Activism and Cyberconflicts in Nigeria: Occupy Nigeria, Boko Haram and MEND by Shola A. Olabode
Platform Economics: Rhetoric and Reality in the "Sharing Economy" by Cristiano Codagnone
Communication as Gesture: Media(tion), Meaning, & Movement by Michael Schandorf

Forthcoming Titles:

Journalism and Austerity: Digitization and Crisis During the Greek Memoranda by Christos Kostopoulos
Chinese Social Media: Face, Sociality, and Civility by Shuhan Chen and Peter Lunt

DIGITAL MEDIA AND THE GREEK CRISIS: CYBERCONFLICTS, DISCOURSES AND NETWORKS

BY

IOANNA FERRA
University of Leeds, UK

emerald
PUBLISHING

United Kingdom – North America – Japan – India – Malaysia – China

Emerald Publishing Limited
Howard House, Wagon Lane, Bingley BD16 1WA, UK

First edition 2020

British Library Cataloguing in Publication Data
A catalogue record for this book is available from the British Library

ISBN: 978-1-78769-328-9 (Print)
ISBN: 978-1-78769-327-2 (Online)
ISBN: 978-1-78769-329-6 (EPub)

Printed and bound by CPI Group (UK) Ltd, Croydon, CR0 4YY

ISOQAR
REGISTERED
ISOQAR certified Management System, awarded to Emerald for adherence to Environmental standard ISO 14001:2004.

Certificate Number 1985
ISO 14001

INVESTOR IN PEOPLE

Contents

List of Figures

List of Tables

List of Abbreviations

ACTA	Anti-Counterfeiting Trade Agreement
AN.EL.	Independent Greeks
ANT1	Antenna Television Network
BBC	British Broadcasting Corporation
CCF	Conspiracy of Cells of Fire
CEO	Chief Executive Officer
CH.AY.	Golden Dawn
CLP	Coalition of the Left and Progress
DIKKI	Democratic Social Movement
DIMAR	Democratic Left
EAM	National Liberation Front
E.AR	E.AR-Greek Left
EC	European Commission
ECB	European Central Bank
EIR	Hellenic Radio Foundation
EIRT	Hellenic Radio-Television Foundation
ELA	Revolutionary Popular Struggle
EL. STAT	National Statistical Service of Greece
ERT	Hellenic Radio Television
ET-1	Hellenic Television, Channel 1
ET-2	Hellenic Television, Channel 2
ET-3	Hellenic Television, Channel 3
EU	European Union
EYP	National Intelligence Service
FB	Facebook
FLOSS	Free/Libre and Open Source Software
GSEE	General Confederation of Greek Workers
ICT	Information Communication Technology
IMF	International Momentary Fund
ISIS	Islamic State in Iraq and Syria
KKE	Communist Party
LAOS	Popular Orthodox Rally

MEGA	Mega Channel
M15	May 15, Spanish Movement of Indignados
ND	New Democracy
NERIT	New Hellenic Radio, Internet and Television
NSM	New Social Movement
NWO	New World Order
ODG	Observatory for Digital Greece
OTE	Hellenic Telecommunications Organizations
OWS	Occupy Wall Street
PAK	PanHellenic Liberation Movements
PASOK	Pan-Hellenic Socialist Movement
PIGS	Portugal, Iceland, Greece, Spain
RMT	Resource Movement Theory
RS	Revolutionary Struggle
RT	Russia Today
rt	retweet
SE	Solidarity Economy
SMI	Social Movement Industry
SMO	Social Movement Organization
SMT	Social Movement Theory
SMS	Social Movement Sector
SNA	Social Network Analysis
SYNASPISMOS (SYN)	Coalition of Left, Ecology and Movements
SYRIZA	Coalition of Radical Left
TA	Thematic Analysis
Troika	IMF, European Commission and European Central Bank
US	Unites States
WSJ	The *Wall Street Journal*
WWII	World War II
WWW	World Wide Web
YENED	Armed forces Information Centre
17 November (17N)	Revolutionary Organization, 17 November

Introduction

This project examines the influence of digital media on the contentious politics in Greece, as well as the political-economic sphere's impact on the formation of the digital mediascape. The research concentrated on the parallel evolution of the (debt) crisis and the digital communications in Greece, by examining four different online media platforms and covering a seven-year period (2008; 2011–2012; 2015). The research employed cyberconflict theory to situate online mediated conflict (sociopolitical and ethnoreligious cyberconflict) in a geosociopolitical and historical context, indicating the dynamic relation between the online media and the offline world. This research suggests the use of online data for the examination of cyberconflict and updates the framework so as to efficiently support the study of social media platforms.

The research reflected the evolution of the sociopolitical debates and the political transformations that emerged in the Greek crisis context (anti-/pro- austerity debate to the euro-vs-drachma/or grexit discussion, the anti-/pro-governmental debate, and the anti-/pro-European discourse). The pre-crisis era and discourse online had already indicated the debates, which later, shaped the crisis discourse online and offline. Then, the SYRIZA network rides the mobilisation wave of Aganaktismenoi, offering a platform and promising representation of all the included actors. During the referendum. polarisation helped in the formation of less fluid identities online and offline, which further developed focusing on the division between the political Us and Them. In the crisis context, the Internet used a magnifying glass, pointing out conflict, opposition and supporting polarisation.

Chapter 1

Digital Media in Greece: A Cyberconflict Approach

From the Internet Evolution to the Global Recession and Greek Digital Media

Since the 1990s, the development of the Internet and its potential use in activism, social movements and protest (Van Aelst & Walgrave, 2002), the impact on politics (Castells, 2000a), on democracy (Coleman & Blumler, 2009; Morozov, 2012), on the formation of identity, community and networks (Bennett, 2003; Castells, 2015; Rheingold, 2000; Turkle, 1997), on the public sphere (Dahlberg, 2006; Habermas, 1991; Nguyen, 2016; Papacharissi, 2002) and digital activism (Joyce, 2010; Karatzogianni, 2015) has grown. While there are many approaches to understanding the growth of the Internet, Karatzogianni (2015) discusses its association with activism, social movements and conflict, concentrating on four waves until 2015, in collocation with the historical and theoretical developments in digital activism in the last two decades (Karatzogianni, 2015).

The first phase concentrated on the period 1994–2001 (Karatzogianni, 2015, pp. 5–24) and according to Curran (2016), it was cloaked in romance, as it was characterised by optimism, and the Internet's potentiality for a social, political and cultural revolution. In this era, the story of the Internet is told as a Western story (2016, p. 48), while it is dominated by debates over anonymity, the notion of multiple selves (Turkle, 1999) and the rise of countercultures and gaming culture, which altogether with the FLOSS movement designating the emergence of the so-called Internet culture (Karatzogianni, 2015, p. 1). The Internet of that era promised the uncensored and multidirectional flow of communication, the equal and free access to information, the democratisation of communication and society (McChesney, 2013, p. 96). The Internet optimism of that period was criticised by many scholars, who highlighted dangers and limitations of this new technology by focusing on the 'digital divide' argument and inequality, on the centralisation of power, as well as on issues related to privacy and surveillance (Hesmondhalgh, 2013, Morozov, 2012, Mosco, 2014).

While the Internet had already transformed the mainstream mediascape, the second period came with the 2000s and the rise of social media, and in extension, debates around self-representations (Goffman, 1959), and user-generated content (Curran, 2016, p. 49). Focusing on the period 2001–2007, Karatzogianni (2015, pp. 25–64) explores the use of ICTs in war and conflict, as also the impact of the Internet on activism, which is now challenging the dominant structures providing alternative imaginaries and structures for mobilisation (Karatzogianni, 2015, p. 2). Some of the most significant examples in this period included the use of ICTs in the 9/11 and the war in Iraq and Afghanistan. At the same time, after the commercialisation of the Internet during the 1990s, this period leads to debates on the power of data, surveillance and later, digital capitalism (Curran, 2016).

The third period starts in the late 2010s and is characterised by the diffusion of smartphones, the power of data and the impact of digital media in every aspect of contemporary life (Curran, 2016). The use of ICTs by social movements, dissidents and non-state actors, indicated the impact of digital media on mainstream politics (Karatzogianni, 2015, pp. 66–120). Among others, some of the indicative examples of that era included the Obama campaign, the Green Movement and the origins of the anti-austerity movement, as it appeared in the context of the EU debt crisis and the southern EU countries (Karatzogianni, 2015, pp. 66–120). The fourth phase ran from 2010 to 2014 (Karatzogianni, 2015), after the WikiLeaks collateral damage release encompassing a wave of social media-enabled mobilisations, such as the so-called Arab Spring, the Occupy movement, the Indignados all the way through to the Snowden revelations, which considerably influenced the debates surrounding surveillance and privacy, raising concerns about the use of ICTs by digital activists (Karatzogianni, 2015, pp. 2–4). These phases describe how the Internet developed, promising to revolutionise contemporary society and the political environment, the rise and spread of digital activism and the mainstreaming of digital activism during the anti-austerity protest wave in the global recession era. Later on, Facebook scandals and the Cambridge Analytica case raised further questions on privacy, surveillance, the power of data and the impact on contemporary democracy (Berghel, 2018; Fuller, 2019).

Starting from 2008, the global crisis was characterised transnationally by several cycles of social and political turmoil starting with the OWS (Occupy Wall Street) in the US, which was spread and adapted in different countries and contexts, to the Arab Spring and the Spanish Indignados, and digital media indicated multiple ways in which they supported the development of collective actions and networks of resistance. At the same time, dissent events in Iran, Egypt, Tunisia, Libya, Palestine, China and elsewhere (Christensen, 2011) displaced the focus from the use of Internet and its potential role in politics, communication and so on, to online conflict, digital activism, the emergence of the i-culture and the networked individual in the networked society (Castells, 2000a). The use of social media in events of dissent, revolts and occupations indicated the role of digital media and social media as an organisational and communication tool, locating the theoretical debates on the issue within the framework of social movement and public sphere theory.

While there is a very rich literature as regards the causes and the impact of the global recession and the capitalist crisis of 2008 (Douzinas, 2013; Katsikas, 2012; Plender, 2003; Posner, 2011), in Greece this resulted to what became known as the debt crisis. Later, in the Greek context, the debt crisis was also discussed in political and social terms (Douzinas, 2013; Michael-Matsas, 2010). Therefore, throughout this study, the term crisis, as regards the Greek context, is used to describe the multidimensional 'crisis', which started after the global recession as a debt crisis, but soon, further evolved and developed as multiple manifestations of 'the crisis', which altogether developed with new crisis events up to 2015, deeply affecting every social and political structure in Greece. In this context, digital and social media has been examined as a tool of everyday use, which promotes the formation of online and offline networks, complementing offline everyday communicational practices and focusing on communities and networks. Beginning with the global recession, and later the Eurozone crisis of 2008 to the migration or refugee crisis of 2014 and so on, digital media are understood as having a significant impact on the transformation of digital networks into a digital public sphere (Karatzogianni, Nguyen & Serafinelli, 2016). While the debate on public sphere and the digital public sphere is not new (Dahlberg, 2006; Habermas, 1991; Nguyen, 2016; Papacharissi, 2002), the way that networks influence crisis, migration, culture and conflict in the digital public sphere are some of the most contemporary research considerations (Karatzogianni et al., 2016).

The global recession of 2008 brought the discussion as regards capitalism into the spotlight (Plender, 2003; Posner, 2011), while the so-called Arab Spring, the Occupy movement and the movement of the squares, in Mediterranean countries, expressed the necessity for democracy while the rise of far-right politics, highlighting the dangers raised by neoliberal politics (Gould-Wartofsky, 2015, pp. 212–3). In this frame, radicalisation and violence, the rise of extreme or populist politics as observed both in the online and the offline space, are not unexpected phenomena and can be historically predicted and justified. Nonetheless, in this context, the use of digital media is an interesting point of investigation, especially focusing on the advantages and disadvantages of such technologies, as well as on the linkage between capitalism and the information society (Fuchs, 2014a; Tsatsou, 2014). At the same time, the evolution of social media, and their contribution on the radicalization of politics, the rise of populism and far-right politics in EU and US, as well as the rise of religious and white extremism, further highlighted concerns regarding the use of social media. The global recession indicated that the impact of digital media in contemporary social movements and collective actions should be understood by focusing not only on the digital media per se but also on the context in which these are used.

Greece was among the most notable examples of countries affected by the global recession, which had a significant impact on the rise of unemployment, poverty and social exclusion (Malkoutzis, 2011; Mylonas, 2014), and the collapsed political system, resulting in intense reconfiguration of the social and political environment. At the same time, the intensification of resistance and solidarity networks, the development of the third civil society sector as well as the radicalisation of politics, indicated the potentiality of digital media in the Greek context, pointing out the necessity for further research into the issue. During the last years there were several researches that concentrated on the

Greek digital media environment, focusing on the use of digital and social media platforms (Theocharis, 2011), on political parties, communication and voting (Coursaris & Papagiannidis, 2009; Papagiannidis, Coursaris & Bourlakis, 2012; Papagiannidis & Manika, 2016), on the crisis and the media (Kaitatzi-Whitlock, 2014; Mylonas, 2014; Touri & Rogers; 2013, Tzogopoulos, 2013) on digital divide (Georgopoulou, 2014), surveillance (Samatas, 2015) or even protests and mobilisations (Theocharis, Lowe, & Van Deth, 2014). However, while the Greek digital media environment has been extensively examined, concentrating on different issues and sub-themes, there is still a need for an extensive research linking the media background environment, as this shaped according to the sociopolitical and historical background, to the transition to the digital media era, and its development in the crisis context.

Starting from this point, this project aims to provide a longitudinal and in-depth examination of the digital media in Greece. The aim of this research is to investigate digital media in Greece within the crisis context, and at the same time, to contribute to the contemporary debate regarding the influence of digital media on contemporary social movements (Della Porta & Diani, 2006; Karatzogianni, 2006, 2015; Melucci, 1980; Stekelenburg & Klandermans, 2009). Another major aim of the project is to evaluate the contribution of digital media to the 'democratic function' in contrast to the crisis limitations and the global recession (Fuchs, 2011). The project examines whether and up to which level the usage of digital media has challenged the dominant (mainstream and traditional) media system, and by extension the dominant discourse. The objectives of this study embrace the in-depth examination of the usage of digital media and the impact of the so-called anti-austerity movement. The study focuses on cyberconflict, digital activism and the use of digital media in Greece between 2008 and 2015, by looking into key digital platforms using digital research methods. The research was developed through the study of Indymedia and YouTube, using thematic analysis, so as to identify sociopolitical tensions and conflicts that pre-existed in the crisis context. Further, this research applies Social Network Analysis (SNS) and studies the dominant actors, online coalitions and discourses as these were posted in Facebook during the Greek Indignados, or the so-called Aganaktismenoi. Finally, through social network and semantic analysis, the study developed an in-depth look at the use of Twitter during the Greek Referendum.

Finally, an overall objective of the research is to contribute to the field both by looking at a single case study in depth and longitudinally over a long period of time across multiple digital platforms and, also, by using a combination of research techniques and extending cyberconflict as a framework. One of the goals of this research is to update and enrich the cyberconflict theory so as to efficiently support the study of social media mediated conflict. At the same time, taking into consideration the latest discussion and critiques as regards digital research methods, another goal of this research is to test the use of such methods for researching cyberconflict. Until now, the use of these digital research methods' material is unprecedented in previous applications of this framework.

Overview of the Project

Greece, as a significant empirical case affected by the global recession, is potentially well set as a case study to examine the contributions of digital media and their use in the crisis context. The analysis of digital media here concentrates on the individual, on the collective actions and social movements, and finally, on socio/political/economic cyberconflict and its linkage to the offline world. At the final stage, the project provides an insight into the digital media impact on political polarisation and radical politics.

The main questions on which the research concentrate focus on how the digital media influence contentious politics and the political transformations in Greece between 2008 and 2015 and, also, on how the political-economic sphere, and the crisis context, influence the formation of the digital mediascape. Looking on the use of digital media in the crisis context, the study examined specific periods and waves of protest, concentrating on the use of digital media platforms by individuals, groups and political movements. Then, looking on digital media and social movements, the study investigates how cyberconflict and digital activism evolved in Greece, by examining and identifying online networks, online coalitions to the offline world and vice versa.

The research of digital media in Greece is developed under the theoretical umbrella of cyberconflict theory, starting with a review of the theoretical framework (Chapter 2). Following the cyberconflict framework, a review of the historical and sociopolitical background of Greece is provided (Chapter 3), before proceeding to the methodological design of the project (Chapter 4). Then, the next three chapters concentrate on the empirical data and the findings (2008 Indymedia and YouTube in Chapter 5; 2011–2012 Facebook and Twitter in Chapter 6; 2015 Twitter in Chapter 7). The findings from the three studies are discussed comparatively in the final and concluding chapter of the research (Chapter 8).

In more detail, the first chapter, the introductory chapter of this project, provides the contextualisation of the research (Chapter 1). The first step in this process was to locate the study of the case of Greece into the debate on digital media and their association/use in the global recession context, before providing an overview of the research. The second chapter presents cyberconflict theory and additional theoretical debates, based on which the research developed. This theoretical framework borrows elements from three overlapping theories and supports the examination of online mediated conflict (Karatzogianni, 2006). However, this framework was created for the examination of pre-social media events, and therefore this research was enriched further so as to support the examination of social media usage in the examined cases. Thus, starting from the basic components of cyberconflict, the social movement theories and the framework are enriched with additional theoretical debates on contemporary forms of collective action, *concentrating on the transformation of collective action to connective action by using Bennett's theory of connective action.* Then, the next component of cyberconflict, media theory, is discussed focusing on digital media, elaborating on the way that online data can be utilised, before drawing conclusions on the way that this framework is applied for the study of the Greek case.

In Chapter 3, a review of the historical and sociopolitical background of the examined case is provided. This includes an overview of both the mainstream political parties, as these were shaped before and during the development of the crisis, an insight into the most significant social movements in Greece and the extra-parliamentary left and right, with reference to the examination of the anti-austerity movement developed. It should be noted that these points were discussed in the same section for reasons of structure, offering an insight into the non-mainstream or parliamentary politics of the examined case. To preclude additional concerns, this is a structural decision to enable the discussion of extra-parliamentary groups, and it does not imply any ideological association between the extreme left and right. Finally, the understanding of the Greek case is completed through an overview of the Greek mediascape, including a review of the evolution of both the traditional and digital media sectors. Chapter 4 presents the research design and how the research was conducted. The research design of the project was built focusing on digital research methods and associative characteristics with the cyberconflict framework. Next, the research lays out the techniques and the research tools used in the project, providing a justification for the theoretical and computational tools, and a timeline relating to the selection of the analysed cases and platforms.

The empirical examination of digital media in Greece starts with the case of the December Riots and data collection from two different online media platforms (Chapter 5). This chapter provides an understanding of the early days of digital media and its association with collective action, and at the same time, it analyses the use of digital media during the December Riots, as a prelude to the crisis that was about to break out. Next, the research focuses on digital media in the crisis context, examining the usage of Facebook in the anti-austerity mobilisations of 2011 (Aganaktismenoi) and the SYRIZA Online Diaspora, as shaped until 2015, January elections when SYRIZA came to power (Chapter 6). After giving the sociopolitical and historical contexts of the two examined cases, the methods, sampling and the analysis techniques are provided. What follows is the overall understanding of the two examined cases, focusing on the identified networks and the overall graph metrics. At this point, the overall graph statistics of the two networks are discussed in the same section, for structural purposes, without suggesting any comparison between the two cases. Instead, what is provided here is a more general descriptive and statistical-oriented understanding of the two networks. Then, each of the two cases is discussed separately culminating in the analysis and the findings of each case. The third and lastly examined platform of the project is Twitter and the so-called 'Greferendum' in June/July 2015 (Chapter 7). Following the same pattern, as the previously analysed platforms, the study of Twitter begins with a description of methods, sampling and analysis techniques used for the specific platform. Next, the examination of Twitter concentrates on the two conflicted ideological and political fronts and the review of the examined case with the analysis of online data and the identification of networks and discourse. In Chapter 8, I offer a discussion of the main findings of the research, the contribution to the field of digital activism, and the limitations and suggestions for future research.

Chapter 2

Theoretical Approaches on Cyberconflict and Digital Media

The theoretical framework is a combination of cyberconflict (Karatzogianni, 2006, 2015) and connective action (Bennett, 2012). In this chapter, I first explain what the core elements of cyberconflict theory are (e.g. environment, social movement, media and conflict theories), and then proceed, analysing social movement theories (SMTs) in more depth, extending the frame to connective action and updating it in line with social media-enabled mobilisations. Then, I discuss the next important element of the theory – digital media theory.

The Rationale for Employing Cyberconflict Theory and Extending to Connective Action

According to Della Porta and Diani (2006, pp. 2–3), the beginning of the millennium was the first time after 1968, when movements (e.g. the global justice movement, etc.) combined the characteristics new social movements and class, while, at the same time, were characterised by a degree of radicalism, influencing the political processes (Della Porta & Diani, 2006, pp. 2–3). Globalisation, together with technological revolution, deeply influenced contemporary society (Fenton, 2007, p. 225), promising the consolidation of 'democracy around the world' (Diaz Romero, 2013). Digital media emerged promising as regards their contribution to the political and social mobilisations, as well as the rise of social movements and collective action. Therefore, the intersection between the two was understood as a response to the 'dominant capitalist communication' and its limitations, indicating the potentiality to overcome the privatisation of 'information and culture' (Fenton, 2007, p. 225). Hence, Fenton rather optimistically, argues that the Internet invokes 'a cultural politics that resists, transforms, or presents alternatives to the dominant virtual and real worlds' (Fenton, 2007, p. 232).

The significant growth of the Internet in the new millennium and the first examples of its impact on politics and society pointed to the necessity of a theoretical framework, able to evaluate the use and the impact of digital media in different cases of cyberconflict, which refers to conflict in computer-mediated environments (Karatzogianni, 2006). The theoretical framework of cyberconflict provides a theoretical and practical path based on which the researcher is able to situate conflict in computer-mediated environments (digital media platforms) in a geosociopolitical, historical and communication context, borrowing elements from three overlapping theories; Social Movement Theories (e.g. RMT/NSM), Media Theory (e.g. networks, new media and traditional media elements) and Conflict Theory (e.g. international conflict analysis) (Karatzogianni, 2006). This theoretical framework suggests two major types of online mediated conflict (Sociopolitical and Ethnoreligious) (Karatzogianni, 2006). This is among the basic assets of this theoretical framework as it manages to study conflict, without categorising/labelling the type of actions or events, which are examined (e.g. social movements and collective actions, type of movements and activism, terrorism). Instead, the theoretical framework focused on the study of the two different types of conflict, each of which assign different characteristics and features on the examined cases and events.

Up to now, cyberconflict theory has been used in various studies that concentrated on computer-mediated conflict (e.g. anti-rape movement in India, Boko Haram in Nigeria and MEND); still this theoretical framework was not used for the study of conflict in social media platforms. While this framework was developed before the rapid growth of social media, this study considers how it could be used for the in-depth study of social media, proposing an 'extended' or 'enriched' version of the theory, so as to efficiently support the study of cyberconflict in social media platforms concentrating both on networks and discourse. In this research, Cyberconflict theory, which is composed of three overlapped theories, will be 'combined' with a fourth theoretical element, Bennett's connective action (2012). Connective action, which focuses on the organisational dynamics of contemporary contentious politics and the contribution of digital media, will be an interesting addition to cyberconflict, pointing out the evolution of organisational dynamics, the framing processes and finally the struggle for political change, as this emerges in the digital terrain, and more precisely in social media platforms, which are understood here as the space of conflict.

In terms of research methods and methodology, this framework applied in various researches by conducting and studying in-depth interviews and CDA. For example, Dey's research using cyberconflict theory on the anti-rape movement in India (2016) and Olabode's cyberconflict analysis of Boko Haram, Occupy Nigeria and MEND in Nigeria (2016), use CDA and in-depth interviews. Therefore, the second innovative component of using Cyberconflict theory in this research is that this will be now supported by a very rich toolkit and the use of digital research methods, which supports the study of social network or semantic analysis, involving thousands of networks and threads that this study sets out to deliver. Focusing on the earlier two points, the extended version of Cyberconflict, so as to examine social media, and the use of digital research methods, this research could provide a helpful example for other researchers on how to use the cyberconflict theory for social media research, how to use digital research methods in this framework, and also the limitations of difficulties that might arise. While the combination of the two is not a requirement, still it is suggested as an interesting research approach, both theoretically and methodologically.

Starting with the original version of the theoretical framework, Karatzogianni indicated the following parameters, which decode cyberconflict, or computer-mediated conflict (Karatzogianni, 2006, p. 88, 2015, pp. 16–17):

- *Environment of conflict and conflict mapping (real and virtual)*: this focuses on the concept of 'networks connected horizontally and lacking a hierarchical centre (Deleuze & Guattari)', as well as on the structure of the Internet and the alternative provision of an experience of governance, time, space, ideology and identity in contrast to surveillance, control, boundaries and apparatuses.
- *Sociopolitical cyberconflict*: this refers to the ICTs impact on mobilising structures, on framing processes, on political opportunity structure and hacktivism.
- *Ethnoreligious cyberconflict*: this focuses on ethnic/religious affiliation, chauvinism and national identity, on discourses (inclusion-exclusion) and on conflict resolution.
- *The Internet as a medium*: this point refers to the analysis of discourses, on control of information, on the political contest model among antagonists and the media effect on policy (e.g. strategic, tactical and representational).

Through this theoretical lens, the Internet is a postmodern medium (opening up a new space of flows and potentialities altogether), which nevertheless is used for the achievement of traditional modernist goals (e.g. democracy, power, participation, community and identity), mostly reproducing offline hierarchies (Karatzogianni, 2006). The first area of focus points out the importance and the necessity for a detailed study of the environment of cyberconflict – the context, by looking on the historical and sociopolitical background. In the second area of focus in sociopolitical terms, cyberconflict is extensively concentrated on the debates and the theoretical considerations of SMTs, including Resource Mobilisation Theory and NSM Theory. Starting with the RMT, Karatzogianni (Karatzogianni, 2006, p. 134) suggested that the Internet could be understood as a form of resource, and therefore, concentrating on three central factors of analysis as provided by McAdam, Tarrow, and Tilly (1996, p. 2): '(1) the structures of political opportunities and constraints confronting the movements'; (2) 'the forms of organisation (informal as well as formal) available to insurgents'; and (3) 'the collective processes of interpretation, attribution, and social construction that mediate between opportunity and action'. Therefore, the examination of mobilising structures (e.g. participation, recruitment, tactics and goals), framing processes (e.g. issues, strategy and identity), as well as the concept of political opportunity structure (Zald, McCarthy, & McAdam, 1996), develop an insight into the usage of digital media in contemporary social movements and collective actions (e.g. anti-capitalist, anti-globalisation and anti-austerity) (Karatzogianni, 2006).

These points are used to decode mainly the sociopolitical type of conflict, in which digital media are used to support social or political change. In contrast to this form of conflict, ethnoreligious cyberconflict examines the use of digital media as a weapon, which is used either for propaganda or as a means to support domination of one group/side over the other. In this study, there is not a strong case or a typical example of ethnoreligious conflict, as can be observed in other countries and case studies (e.g. Israel/Palestine). Still though, the rise of far-right, as observed lately in many European countries, merely falls under this category of conflict, focusing on issues that are associated with ethnic/religious affiliation, chauvinism and national identity, as well as discourses of inclusion and exclusion. Karatzogianni highlights the dual modality of cyberconflict, as rhizomatic and hierarchical (Karatzogianni, 2006, p. 88). Ethnoreligious formations tend to be more hierarchical relying on reactive affect with fixed and closed identities, even when they are networked, while sociopolitical formations are horizontal/rhizomatic, relying on open fluid identities stemming from an active desire for change (Karatzogianni & Robinson, 2013).

Then, looking on the revolutionary period of 2010–2012, Karatzogianni and Schandorf (2015), discuss the 'order of dissent', which can be used to locate and evaluate the order of concerns and goals of a collective action or a social movement, in national, transnational or global order. This scheme adds an additional layer to the agent-structure problem in the analysis of cyberconflict, especially when this is located in a complex sociopolitical environment (e.g. global recession, EU crisis and debt crisis in Greece). The first order, the local order of dissent, concentrates on the basic human liberties and rights and such examples can be found in the case of an ethnic minority group's right to housing, health, education and so on (Karatzogianni & Schandordf, 2015). The second order of dissent, the national, is focused on democracy, equality, the distribution of power and resources, etc., and an interesting example here is the EU crisis, concentrating on the national effect and protests against national governments implementing EU anti-austerity policies. Elsewhere in the Arab Spring, national-level protests demanding democratisation and the ousting of dictatorial and corrupt regimes are also some indicative examples. The third order of dissent, the transnational, is focused on the failing of the capitalist order and is understood through examples, such as anti-Iraq war mobilisations, the anti-globalisation movement and, later on, the Occupy Movement. An important consideration with regard to the order of dissents concentrates on how different cases can be categorised and evaluated within more than one of those orders, pointing out the complex system and tensions at the interfaces of the local, national and transnational/postnational.

Cyberconflict's social movement component is further discussed in great detail in the following section, in order to extend the framework to connective action, which will prove useful for the examination of social media's use in mobilisations.

Social Movement Theories

The French philosopher Le Bon was among the first who concentrated on the theorising of collective actions and mobilisations, examining social unrest in France during the 1890s (Stekelenburg & Klandermans, 2009, p. 18). Le Bon's approaches on collective action and mobilisation were reflected in breakdown theories, which perceived the 'participation in collective action as an unconventional, irrational type of behaviour' associated with the concept of contentious politics (Stekelenburg & Klandermans, 2009, p. 18). Later, most of the classical approaches to social movements were cultivated based on the notion of contentious politics (Stekelenburg & Klandermans, 2006, p. 22). The history and the basic concepts of SMT gradually appeared by the end of the 1940s (Della Porta & Diani, 2006, p. 1). However, the dramatically sociopolitical transformations of the late 1960s and 1970s, 'the most vigorous areas of sociology' (Marx & Wood, 1975, in Della Porta & Diani, 2006, p. 1), pointed to the necessity for intensive research in the field, based on a synthetic and comparative approach (Zald et al., 1996).

A major theoretical debate here is raised by the contrasts between the European approach to the issue, which focuses on the identity-oriented paradigm and post-industrial capitalism (e.g. SMT and New Social Movement Theory), and the American approach, which concentrates on mobilising structures, the framing processes, the political opportunity and media (e.g. Resource Mobilisation Theory). There are essential differences between the European and the US approach to collective actions and social movements, with the first concentrating on the linkage between new forms of social conflict and post-industrial capitalism, and the second one concentrating on resource mobilisation (Karatzogianni, 2006, p. 126). Alongside the differences between the European and the US perspectives on collective actions and social movements, Tilly (1973 in Melucci, 1980, p. 212) has pointed out that, in most of the theories, social movements emerge because of the breakdown of the social system, with the development of new interests, or because of the formation of collective identity and solidarity. However, in Melucci's words, most of the theories 'tell us *how* collective action is manifested but not *why*' (Melucci, 1980, p. 212). Change – naturally or not – either as an external cause/variable or an internal one, leads to the breakdown or restructure of the social system, or to the development of new interest and so on, before, finally, resulting in the creation of social movements. Melucci explains that it is the notion of change, which, in most cases, is pre-supposed, and does not allow the examination of the real origin of the social movement through a more structural analysis, but leads to a diachronic analysis (Melucci, 1980, p. 213). Concentrating on the contrast between breakdown and solidarity models on collective actions and social movements, Melucci (Melucci, 1980, p. 202) explains the distinction between these two, highlighting the basic conditions that diversify them:

> I define *Collective actions* in the strict sense as the *ensemble of various types of conflict-based behaviour in a social system. A collective action implies the existence of a struggle between two actors for the appropriation and orientation of social values and resource, each of the actors being characterised by a specific solidarity.*

Melucci explains that in the aforementioned, the first condition, describes conflict-based collective actions. Then, he explains the second one. When the first and the second conditions are fulfilled then these define the social movements: 'Collective action also includes all the types of behaviour which transgress the norms that have been institutionalized in social roles which go beyond the rules of the political system and/or which attack the structure of society's class relations' (Melucci, 1980, p. 202). However, the definition of social movements and collective actions is not only a complicated process but, in most cases, these concepts are used to describe specific cases or examples and therefore, they cannot be applied or define all social movements or collective actions successfully. According to Touraine, social movements can be understood focusing on conflict formed 'around social control of the main cultural patterns' (1985, p. 760). Crossley (2002, pp. 2–9), suggests that the commonly shared characteristics of collective actions and movements could be used to define social movements. However, Crossley indicates that a major characteristic of movements is that all of them are understood as 'collective ventures', although the way that collective is defined should be considered (Crossley, 2002). Crossley discussed some of the main definition of social movements of the literature, that concentrate on different features and conceptualisation of movements (2002, pp. 2–6).

Starting with the first one, Blumer defined social movements as 'collective enterprises'[1], emerging due to the shared interest/project of individuals seeking to establish a different form of life (Crossley, 2002, p. 3). Eyerman and Jaminson (1991) added two additional points to Blumer's approach (1969), and perceived social movements as a source of creativity, which result in the creation of identities, ideas, etc., while they also make a reference to 'public spaces', which should be perceived as an equivalent reference to the notion of the 'public sphere'[2] (cited in Crossley, 2002, p. 4). On the other hand, Tarrow (1998) indicates the distinctions between social movements and singular protest events, highlighting through the linkage between social movements and protests[3] (cited in Crossley, 2002, p. 4). Tarrow inserts the concept of '*social networks*', as well as concerns that not only related to the content and causes of social movement but also the way that these emerge. Moreover, Tarrow explains the creation of identities, ideas etc., as also suggested by Eyerman and Jamison, indicating that this point should be linked to the notion of struggle (Crossley, 2002, p. 4). Della Porta and Danni expand on Tarrow's point about 'shared beliefs and solidarity' and additionally focus on the concept of

---

[1]Blumer (1969, p. 99): Social movements can be viewed as collective enterprises seeking to establish a new order of life. They have their inception in a condition of unrest, and derive their motive power on the one hand, from dissatisfaction with the current form of life, and on the other hand, from wishes and hopes for a new system of living. The career of a social movement depicts the emergence of a new order of life. (in Crossley, 2002, p. 3)

[2]Eyerman and Jamison (1991, p. 4): 'Social movement [...] best conceived of as temporary public spaces, as moments of collective creation that provide societies with ideas, identities and even ideals'. (in Crossley, 2002, p. 4)

[3]Tarrow (1998, p. 2): Contentious Politics occurs when ordinary people, often in league with more influential citizens, join forces in confrontation with elites, authorities and opponents...When backed by dense social networks and galvanised by culturally resonant, action-oriented symbols, contentious politics leads to sustained interaction with opponents, the result is social movement. (in Crossley, 2002, p. 4)

networks, protests and conflict[4] (Crossley, 2002, pp. 6–7); although, Tarrow recognises the issue of internal disagreements within social movements, parallel to a homogenised view of the movement via an external aspect. Finally, Crossley refers to Melucci's analysis and stresses the new social movements and the cultural extensions of the issue (Crossley, 2002, p. 5).

Consequently, according to Crossley's points on the aforementioned definitions, social movements could be conceived as being 'collective enterprises' able to support the creation of ideas, identities and ideals. At the same time, social movements should be linked to the concept of the public sphere and to the concept of contentious politics. The formation of social networks and the minimum share of beliefs and solidarity among them have been recognised as some of the major characteristics of social movements. Nevertheless, could these characteristics define every case of 'collective enterprise', and what are the additional arguments raised by such an examination? Opp (2009, p. 33–44) analyses some additional definitions of social movements, explaining how the definition of social movement could be fluid and based on abstract concepts, which are not always applicable in the real world, while the distinction between social movements and protests could be indistinguishable and overlapping. Opp (2009, p. 35) looking on the notion of protest, discussed various definition of social movements[5] and suggested that protests could be perceived as 'action or

[4]Della Porta and Diani (1996, p. 16): Social movements are (1) informal networks, based on, (2) shared beliefs and solidarity, which mobilise about (3) conflictual issues, through (4) the frequent use of various forms of protests'. (in Crossley, 2002, p. 6)

[5]McCarthy and Zald: (1) 'A "social movement" is "a set of opinions and beliefs in a population which represents preferences for changing some elements of the social structure and/or reward distribution of a society" (McCarthy & Zald, 1977)' (Opp, 2009, p. 35); (2): "A social movement organization is a complex, or formal organization which identifies its goals with the preferences of a social movement or a countermovement and attempts to implement those goals" (McCarthy & Zald, 1977)' (Opp, 2009, p. 35); (3): 'Social movements are voluntary collectivities that people support in order to effect changes in society. Using the broadest and most inclusive definition, a social movement includes all who in any form support the general ideas of the movement. Social movements contain social movement organization, the carrier organizations that consciously attempt to coordinate and mobilize supporters' (McCarthy & Zald, 1973). Zald and Ash: 'A social movement is a purposive and collective attempt of a number of people to change individuals or societal institutions and structures' (Zald & Ash, 1966). Tarrow: (1) '[The term] Social movement "I reserve for those sequences of contentious politics that are based on underlying social networks and resonant collective action frames and which develop the capacity to maintain sustained challenges against powerful opponents' (Tarrow, 1998, p. 2).; (2): 'Social movements "are better defined as collective challenges, based on common purposes and social solidarities, in sustained interaction with elites, opponents, and authorities"' (Tarrow, 1998, p. 4). McAdam, Tarrow and Tilly: '"Social movements have traditionally been defined as organized efforts to bring about social change" (Jenkins & Form, 2005)' (Opp, 2009, p. 35).

behaviour' and the context of SMTs, protests are being perceived as 'joint actions' (Opp, 2009, p. 34). Individuals participate in joint actions, having at least one common goal/target, and like this, often unconventional or irregular goal/target is not achievable by themselves, thus, they put pressure on third parties (Opp, 2009, p. 35).

Opp (2009, pp. 36–38) continues the same argument and extends on social movements, which are conceived as being 'collectivities of individuals' – yet different definitions refer to different kind of collectivities. While the definitions agree on the concept of 'collectivises of individuals', McCarthy and Zald perceive the social movement as a 'set of opinions and beliefs' (2009, p. 36), inserting the concept of 'social movement organisation' (Opp, 2009, p. 36). Parallel to the concept of 'collectivities/individuals', social movements are also defined as 'organisations' or simplified as a 'number of people' who are involved in 'sequences of contentious politics', having a common goal (Opp, 2009, p. 36). Some suggest that the goal is 'to seek for mobilisation' or others that the goal is to solve a problem (Opp, 2009, p. 36). But, at the same time, they have an antagonist, which means that they are not able to change things alone, they need to pursue and influence someone else to bring about this change for them (i.e. third parties or antagonists 'outside the constituency').

In a slightly different approach, Diani and McAdam (2003, p. 1) describe social movements as 'strings of more or less connected events, scattered across time and space', while the organisation, the patterns of communication and action, and interaction varies from centralised to decentralised (Diani & McAdam, 2003, p. 1). Here, individuals might participate as atomised individuals, sharing common values and ideas, budding collective actions and creating complicated 'webs of exchanges' (Diani & McAdam, 2003, p. 1). In this sense, 'social movements are in other words, complex and highly heterogeneous network structures' (Diani & McAdam, 2003, p. 1).

In a different approach, Opp, highlights Snow and Oliver's definition, which conceptualises social movements based on whether these include the following elements: 'some degree' of different things – changed oriented goals; some degree of organisation; some degree of temporal continuity; some extra-institutional (e.g. protests in the streets) and institutional activity (e.g. political lobbying) (Opp, 2009, p. 37). While these definitions create an insight into social movements, there are many issues for further investigation, including the usage of different terms, the introduction of different concepts/ideas, as well as the multidimensional content and application of SMTs, resulting in a variety of arguments among theorists, who fail to come up with a single universal definition of social movements. Melucci (1980) points out the necessity of a theoretical framework for the analysis of social movements and collective actions, which would be able to link together actors, systems, class and conflict, while, the conditions in which collective actions and social movements emerge is suggested as another interesting point of investigation.

New Social Movement

The European approach in understanding social movements, the New Social Movement, concentrated on the Marxist viewpoint, and highlighted that the 'preconditions of revolution' (Melucci, 1980, pp. 199–201) determine the way that the collective action, which in most cases is underestimated, will turn to a class movement in the capitalist context. During the 1970s, this approach reassessed basic theoretical foundations identifying the 'crisis' as a mode of capitalist production. This suggests a clear distinction between the analysis of the system and the actors creating additional theoretical difficulties for the analysis of social movements. Later, Melucci (1980, p. 200) notes that a Marxist approach to social movements should move towards an analysis of class and political action, instead of concentrating on a structural analysis, which focuses on class relations and the capitalist system.

NSM was enriched by borrowing elements from Melucci's approach on social movements and the concept of identity, as well as Tarrow's approach on the issue, giving an insight into the relationship between social movements and post-industrial society (Flynn, 2011, p. 88). In a simplified analysis, Flynn explains that social movements could be defined as 'a voluntary organisation of individuals who act in concert to make or block a change' (2011, pp. 88–89). Thus, collective actions or movements act serving the common interest/goal of the group/organisation and do not concentrate on individual interests. Collective actions and social movements come about mainly within open and democratic societies (Flynn, 2011, pp. 88–89), where the idea of social change exists as an acceptable concept and an achievable goal. In opposition to Flynn's approach, contemporary examples indicate that social movements emerge in different contexts and do not always result in social or political change.

NSM are straightforwardly linked to the post-industrial/post-materialistic society and the middle-class argument (Karatzogianni, 2006, pp. 54–55). Therefore, their linkage to post-industrial capitalism (Melucci, 1980, p. 210), to globalisation (Castells, 2004a; Fenton, 2007; Tarrow, 2011) and cosmopolitanism (Castells, 2004a) are some of the major points to be debated. Some of the strongest critique of NSM raised by the questions related to the genuineness of these movements/actions (Karatzogianni, 2006, p. 124). In other words, how new are indeed these movements or actions. Buechler sums up the strongest debates/concerns about NSM discussing four different points (Buechler, 1995, p. 447). The first concern raised by the validity of the distinction among "new" and "old" movements. The second point questions if indeed new social movements are 'primarily or exclusively a defensive, reactive response to larger social forces', or whether they can also emerge having a proactive and progressive nature (Buechler, 1995, p. 447). Next, a major concern raised by the distinction between political and cultural movements, with the latter being apolitical. The last point questions, whether what here is understood as the social base of new social movements, could also be described focusing on social class (Buechler, 1995, p. 447).

Similarly, with social movements as discussed earlier, NSM cannot be defined using a strict definition applied in every examined case of collective action, social movement or mobilisation and protest. Instead, NSM should be understood via the examination of its basic characteristics and its application in different socio-political environments/contexts, in which the examined cases emerge. Melucci suggests that the following characteristics, which are commonly shared by contemporary collective actions, are able to provide a sufficient description of the NSM's concept (1980, pp. 219–222):

- end of the separation between public and private spheres;
- superposition of deviance and social movements;
- movements that are not focused on the political system;
- solidarity as an objective; and
- direct participation and rejection of representation.

While Melucci (1980, pp. 219–222) explains that these characteristics can be observed in different contemporary social movements, still, there are specific characteristics, which arise based on each examined case and the context in which this emerge, influencing the way that these characteristics can be developed and recognised each time.

Through a more Marxist viewpoint, NSM refers to actions that 'displaced the old social movements of proletarian revolution associated with classical Marxism' (Buechler, 1995, p. 442). New social movements are fostered based on the concept of 'politics, ideology and culture' and therefore, collective actions and collective identity emerge for different reasons and in a different context than the old social movements (e.g. ethnicity and gender instead of class). However, contemporary cases as raised in the global recession context have highlighted that the context and the reasons, due to which new and old social movements rise, might not be clearly distanced with traditional approaches of social movements, bringing the notion of the class into question. NMS links to the 'new middle class', concentrating on the 'Weberian' approach in which groups are created based on strategies of 'inclusion and exclusion' (Karatzogianni, 2006, p. 126). However, according to Kriesi's argument (1989), the idea of 'new middle class' and its linkage to social movements can be 'too narrow […] and too broad'. While the working class supports 'unexpectedly' strong movements, the new middle class does not equally participate and support them (Kriesi, 1989, pp. 130–132).

Buechler (1995, p. 442) underlines that NSM is widely adopted by theorists for the analysis of contemporary examples, pointing out some of its most significant characteristics, which are not always compatible with the traditional approaches of social movements: 'Cohen and Melluci suggest that NSM indicates the 'symbolic action in civil society or the cultural sphere as a major arena for collective action alongside instrumental action in the state or political sphere; According to Habermas and Rucht, NSM highlights the 'importance of processes that promote autonomy and self-determination instead of strategies for maximising influence and power'; Inglehard and Dalton, Kuechler and Burklin, note that NSM examines the 'post materialist values in much contemporary collective action, as opposed to conflicts over material resources'; Hunt et al and Johnston et all suggest that NSM's theorists often emphasise the 'fragile process of constructing collective identities and identifying group interests, instead of assuming that conflict groups and their interests are structurally determined'; additionally, according to Klandermans, and Johnston et al, NSM points out the 'socially constructed nature of grievances and ideology, rather than assuming that they can be deduced from a group's structural location; finally, Buechler (1995) stresses that NSM identifies 'a variety of submerged, latent, and temporary networks that often underdog collective action, rather than assuming that centralised organisational forms are prerequisites for successful mobilisation' (Melluci, 1993, p.442).

The notion of 'new middle class', 'autonomy', the 'cultural sphere' and 'identity', are components that should be understood in linkage with the information media society, which dominates the '(post-) modern world' (Buechler, 1995, p. 446). By extending the 'new middle class' argument, Melucci (1980) stresses that the examination of NSM should, among others, aim, to change the system of production, which leads to the creation of 'new class conflict', indicating the structure and the features of the post-industrial and advanced societies (Melucci, 1980, p. 217). NSM emerged in the post-industrial society aiming at a structural reform and not revolution (Flynn, 2011, p. 89), while, it also suggests new forms of conflicts highlighting the importance of the notion of identity, as shaped in the post-industrial system of production. In Melucci's words, 'the personal and social identity of individuals' is turned into the 'product of social action', which finally results in the emergence of new conflicts (1980, pp. 217–218). Habermas notes that NSM conflicts are no longer related to 'material reproduction' but, instead, they focus on 'cultural reproduction, social integration and socialization' (Buechler, 1995, p. 445), highlighting the displacing point of conflict.

Among the major critiques of NSM raised by the distinction between traditional/old SMT and NSM, as well as by the relationship between NSM and the movements, which emerged after the beginning of the new millennium (Flynn, 2011, pp. 96–97), a basic argument about NSM, as mentioned earlier, suggests that NSM and traditional/old SMT coexisted during the post-industrial society and there is no true difference or clear distinction between them (Flynn, 2011, pp. 96–97). Then, the concern that arose concentrated on the association of NSM and contemporary waves of movements and collective actions after the 2000s, starting from the anti-war and anti-globalisation movements, to the civil rights-related movements, environmental movements or contemporary examples of anti-fascist movements, anti-austerity and anti-authoritarian movements.

Another important critique of NSM is that this approach does not focus on organisational and structural procedures/features of the movements and the analysis of the 'mechanics of collective action' (Karatzogianni, 2006, p. 132). Hence, due to the limitations of the NSM approach, Resource Mobilisation Theory (RMT) is suggested as an alternative or supplementary approach to the in-depth examination of social movements. RMT does not concentrate on the content or the context of social movements, but it provides an 'understanding of organization dilemma' as this is raised within contemporary examples of social movements (Karatzogianni, 2006, p. 233).

Resource Mobilisation Theory

Resource Mobilisation Theory conceptualises social movement as 'a set of opinions and beliefs' in a population, which 'represents preferences for promoting or preventing social change' (Stekelenburg & Klandermans, 2009, p. 24). RMT extensively focuses on groups which 'overcome prevailing patterns of resource inequality' and act for 'social change goals' (Edward & McCarthy, 2004, p. 118). Overall, the notion of material and non-material resources here is understood as a principle cause of change (Edward & McCarthy, pp. 116–120). The resource types (e.g. moral, cultural, socio-organisational, human and material) and the 'pre-dominant-modes of access on resources' (e.g. movement, self-production, resource aggregation, resource appropriation and patronage) decode structural procedures of social movements, in regard to individuals and participation, or even groups/networks, etc. (Edward & McCarthy, p. 118). RMT conceptualises social movements as an extension of politics, and, similar to other forms of political struggle, social movements should be analysed based on the concept of conflict (Buechler, 1993, p. 218). However, among the critiques of RMT, while this is an approach that successfully explains the 'social movement participation on the individual level', the theory underestimates 'the significance of grievances and ideology as determinants of participation in a social movement' (Klandermans, 1994, p. 584), failing to examine both the meaning and orientation of social movements. Stekelenburg and Klandermans (2009, pp. 5–26) have pointed out that the 'vocabulary of economics', in combination with the underestimation of indigenous resources are some basic limitations of this approach.

On the other hand, the American sociologists perceived the concept of collective actions and social movements as an issue of collective behaviour (Klandermans, 2009, pp. 5–26). The concept of collective behaviour does not emphasise on class relations, but it concentrates on the analysis of the different types of collective behaviour, whose goal is the restoration of stability. Turner and Killian formulated this concept, looking on 'short terms – as spontaneous actions' and thereby this approach on social movements could not be used for the examination of 'ongoing, organised and political forms of protests', mobilisations, etc. (Buechler, 1993, p. 218). As mentioned earlier, RMT examines the way in which groups 'overcome prevailing patterns of resource inequality', looking on different resource types[6]. Therefore, the 'pre-dominant-modes of access

[6]Resource types: moral, cultural, socio-organisational, human, material (Edward & McCarthy, 2004, p. 118). Different approaches to the issue describe different typologies of the issue. However, all of them are based on the same concept (Edward & McCarthy, 2004, p. 144).

on resources'[7] are basic factors of the RMT analysis, which develops an insight into the participation of atomised individuals or even of groups and networks, (Edward & McCarthy, 2004, p. 118). Karatzogianni (2006, p. 134) highlights that RMT had a pivotal impact on SMT; however, while RMT successfully explained the 'social movement participation on the individual level', important critiques of the theory point out that RMT underestimates 'the significance of grievances and ideology as determinants of participation in a social movement' (Klandermans, 1994, p. 584). Cohen points out the following RMT features (Cohen, 1985, p. 675):

- Social movements must be understood in terms of a conflict model of collective action.
- There is no fundamental difference between institutional and non-institutional collective action.
- Both entail conflicts of interest built into institutionalised power relations.
- Collective action involves the rational pursuit of interests by groups.
- Goals and grievances are permanent products of power relations and cannot account for the formation of movements.
- This depends instead on changes in resources, organisation, and opportunities for collective action.
- Success is evidenced by the recognition of the group as a political actor or by increased material benefits.
- Mobilisation involves large-scale, special-purpose, bureaucratic, formal organisation.

(Cohen, 1985, p. 675)

The aforementioned points suggest an insight into RMT and are also associated with critics and limitations of RMT. Karatzogianni (2006, p. 134) explains that this theoretical approach is heavily criticised as being too narrow, while, according to Melucci, it fails to examine both the meaning and the orientation of social movements. Touraine, adding to that, explains that RMT emphasises the economic rationality, which is raised by the independent examination of goals, social relations or actors (Karatzogianni, 2006, p. 134). Stekelenburg and Klandermans (2009, pp. 25–26) notes that this results in a 'vocabulary of economics' and in combination with the underestimation of indigenous resources, these are the basic limitations of RMT.

However, this theoretical approach is extensively used for the analysis of contemporary social movements, which has emerged in the information society context, understanding, at least in the first instance, the Internet as a resource for mobilisation (Karatzogianni, 2006). Thereby, if the Internet is perceived as a

[7]Mode of access on resources: movement self-production, resource aggregation, resource appropriation, patronage (Edward & McCarthy, 2004, p. 118).

type of resource, then the usage of RMT could provide the following three central factors of analysis as noticed by McAdam et al. (1996, p. 2): (1) 'the structures of political opportunities and constraints confronting the movements', (2) 'the forms of organization (informal as well as formal) available to insurgents' and (3) 'the collective processes of interpretation, attribution, and social construction that mediate between opportunity and action'. Karatzogianni (2006, p. 136) suggests that these factors could support the analysis of contemporary examples/cases (e.g. anti-capitalist and anti-globalisation movements, and the 2008 recession's mobilisations), focusing on the contribution of Internet technology to the emergence of social movements, mobilisations or collective actions.

Stekelenburg and Klandermans (2009) create an overview of the basic approaches to the analysis as these emerged during the last sixty years both in Europe and in the US, and highlighted the singularity of each examined case, based on context and on the physical/historical environment in which each mobilisation movement has emerged, suggesting that the future approaches on examining social movements should be based on the 'synergizing structural and social constructivistic approaches' (2009, p. 43). Social constructivistic approaches have four key themes, which could support the examination of movements: the construction of the meaning, identity, emotions and motivation. These, together with a comparative studies analysis focused on the sociopolitical context, would be able to provide a circumstantial theoretical framework for the analysis of different cases of mobilisation (Stekelenburg & Klandermans, 2009, pp. 34–43). However, the critique of the social constructivistic approaches concentrate on the fact that these approaches 'run the risk of fragmentation and de-contextualization' (Stekelenburg & Klandermans, 2009, p. 35) and in most cases, as is required, they are applied in a different context, through different approaches and based on the individual examined case's characteristics.

While the analysis of contemporary cases of social movements could be achieved by focusing on different theoretical approaches and aspects on the issue, a major consideration raised by the contemporary examples, which illustrated the significant contribution of Information and Communication Technology (ICT). While the contribution of technology in social movements is not a new phenomenon, the frequency, the scale and the dispersion, by which movements were dominated by ICT's features during the examined period is significant. Therefore, while the influence of ICT is a factual element of contemporary mobilisations or movements, the way that these elements influence the growth and nature of the mobilisation should be the subject of an in-depth investigation. Contemporary analysis of social movements concentrates on the in-depth understanding of mobilising structures, framing processes and the concept of political opportunities (McAdam et al., 1996). Karatzogianni (2006) suggests that a comprehensive theoretical framework, which supports the examination of digital media in social movements, collective action, as well as social or political turmoil, should not solely focus on media theories but instead, should combine principles from both conflict theory and SMT (e.g. both NSM and RMT).

Collective Versus Connective Actions: Networks

Concentrating on contemporary social movements, especially as these appear during the global recession in opposition to political, social or economic oppression, Castells (2015) discusses the notion of networked social movements, pointing out the importance of context, by analysing cases both from the EU and US, from Brazil to Turkey and Chile, including examples, such as the Occupy movement, the Indignados or the Arab Spring. In all these examples, Castells notes that the most commonly shared characteristic is the crisis of the political system and its legitimacy, as well as, corruption (Castells, 2015, p. 222). After a brief examination of the core characteristics of these examples, he discusses about the rise of the movements, the most common characteristic that relates to the use of digital media, which contributes to the development of an autonomous communicative capacity and communicative networks. In this new communicative capacity, digital social networks and wireless communication are suggested as being equally important as the Internet, having a strong impact on the way that contemporary movements evolve. Digital media overcomes the limitations of time and space, while, at the same time, change the organisational procedure of movements (Karatzogianni, 2006).

Digital media contributes to the successful organisation of contemporary social movements, which in most cases, tend to isolate political parties, unions and other similar institutions, targeting them as part of the problem and a distance from the movements' struggles (Bennett, 2012). While in the previous examples of social movements, traditional media had an important impact on the communication process both internally and externally, digital media rapidly changed that process. First, digital media provided the opportunity for communication, participation, while also transformed processed of recruitment, organization and representation. In contemporary social movements, the communication process is shaped mainly by the younger population, who tends to question and reject the existing social order and at the same time is heavily using the Internet and is famliarised with different technologies and platforms (Bennet, 2012, p. 223). At the same time, social technology supports both the public engagement as well as the personalised actions, as users expand the communication process also to their personal networks (Bennet, 2012, p. 223).

Following the debates that arose during the 1960s and the discussion on new social movements and the notion of personalised politics, Bennett and Segerberg (2012) have brought forward some of these considerations, situating the discussion in the context of the global economic crisis and neoliberalism, taking into consideration the impact of digital media technologies. Bennett (2012) focuses on the notion of personalised politics, highlighting the importance of diversity and networks, while Bennett and Segerberg (2012) identify three major conditions based on which personalised politics emerge:

> An ethos of diversity and inclusiveness defined by tolerance for different viewpoints and even different issues linked across loosely bounded political networks. The rise of crowd-sourced

> inclusive *personal action frames* (e.g., 'We are the 99%') that lower the barriers to identification. These easily personalised frames contrast with more conventional collective action frames (e.g., 'Eat the rich') that may require more socialisation and brokerage to propagate in large numbers. Participation is importantly channelled through often dense social networks over which people can share their own stories and concerns—the pervasive use of social technology enables individuals to become important catalysts of collective action processes as they activate their own social networks.
>
> (Bennett, 2012, p. 22)

The origins of the personalised politics are traced in the financial crisis of the 1970s and the neoliberal regime, which back them, strongly influenced the production, consumption, labour and overall politics, while Bennett (2012), highlights that neoliberalism influenced everything; from the global economy and markets to daily personal life. A focus on the notion of individualism and fragmentation, suggests a postmodern approach, with personalised politics providing an insight into the complex interrelationship between digital media, social movements and politics. The individualised collective action settles new patterns of political consumerism, establishing 'more entrepreneurial and less centrally manageable relations' between individuals and civic organisations (Bennett, 2012, p. 27), and therefore is also changing the communication processes of the formation of collectivities. This is the point when Bennett and Segerberg introduce the logic of connective action, which focuses on the individuals' self-interest and the participation in e-contentious politics. Here, the motivation for participation depends on the need for personal expression and therefore, the engagement arises by sharing this expression across social networks and by extension linking participants with protest networks (Bennett, 2012, p. 28). Bennett explains that this concept is linked to Castells and his work on networks, as this process results in the emergence of collectivities, which are understood as multi-layered networks, having no hierarchical organisation. In a network lens, Bennett (2014) points out once again that communication denotes something more than just the exchange of messages, as it can also transform organisational processes.

Tarrow (2014) strongly criticises Bennett and Segerberg's discussion on the logic of action, focusing on the conservative and utopian approaches to digital media and the debate on digital media potentiality; how new, new and digital media are? Will digital media revolutionise every aspect and structure of society? These questions have cultivated a well-established and much-analysed debate (Coleman & Blumler, 2009; Morozov, 2012), which has also a philosophical content and spectrum of analysis. Tarrow suggests that digital and, especially, social media indeed contributed to contemporary social movements and activism; however, that happens in a similar way as previous technology and different forms of media did in the past, by 'sharing the work of mobilizing and organizing contention, and, in some cases, do more of this work than formal organizations do' (2014, p. 468). On the other hand, Bennett (2014) explains that previous technologies were linked to the already existing organisations of all sorts, and the content of communication depended on and was controlled by them. However, what is happening now is that organisations emerge as the 'outcomes of patterns of communication-technology use' (Bennett, 2014, p. 470). At the same time, Bennett (2014) further explains the logic of connective action, highlighting the notion of Durkheim's anomie, which here indicates the distance of the individual from traditional society as shaped in post-industrial society.

Bennett and Segerberg (2012) cultivate the concept of connective action as opposed to classic collective action, as a framework, which supports the investigation of the organisational dynamics of contemporary contentious politics, highlighting the contribution of digital media. This concept suggests that the political content can be converted from a general framework into a more personalised framework (Bennett & Segerberg, 2012). In contrast to traditional organisation models, the individuals here reinterpret and recreate meanings in their social media networks (Bennett & Segerberg, 2012). Additionally, personal communication technologies give the users the opportunity to 'share cognitive resources and diffuse them across trusted social networks without formal ties or commitment to organisations or other forms of group membership' (Anduiza, Cristancho, & Sabucedo, 2013, p. 753). While in traditional resource mobilisation theory organisation has a central role, Anduiza highlights that in Bennett's connective action, this has changed:

> While collective action on a large scale depends on brokered organizations 'bearing the burden of facilitating cooperation', connective action networks 'self-organize' without central or 'lead' organizational actors, using technologies as important organizational agents.
>
> (Anduiza et al., 2013, p. 753)

Therefore, the examination of digital and especially social media could provide an insight into the change and the evolution of organisational dynamics, of the framing processes and finally the struggle for political change. While the importance of online social networks is already indicated, at the same time, the conceptualisation of the Internet should be focused both on the Internet as a space of conflict (Karatzogianni, 2006), having a new communicative capacity as well as on the Internet as a 'network of networks' (Castells, 2015). Castells (2000a) highlights the linkage between technology, history and society, highlighting that from the industrial age we have now proceeded to the information age. This results in the transformation of the community-based structure that now transformed into a network-based structure (Castells, 2000a).

Networks can be conceptualised and discussed looking on various different theoretical approaches and examples. Brieger goes back to Marx and Montesquieu, explaining that the network metaphor has a very long tradition (2004, pp. 505–506): 'society is not merely an aggregate of individuals; it is the sum of the relations in which these individuals stand to one another' (Marx, [1857] 1956, p. 96 in Brieger, 2004, p. 505). In networks, individuals or edges and nodes have a significant importance, and according to the social or sociological pragmatism, Cooley refers to the self-consciousness within which an individual is understood as the 'point of intersection of an indefinite number of lines representing social groups, having as many arcs passing through him as there are groups' (Cooley, [1902] 1964, p. 184 in Brieger 2004, p. 505). From a different point of view, this is also linked to Radcliff-Brown's notion of social structure, which, describes the complex social relations arising around each individual or node (Brieger, 2004, p. 506). Digital media and online data provide the opportunity for the examination of the abstract notion of social structure and networks through the usage of various tools and software, while, visualisation of networks help on the understanding of social structure and social networks, either when is used as a method or supplementary to other research methods and techniques.

Social networks are important to the process of individual participation in social movement and play a crucial role in the emergence of identities (Passy, 2003). Hensby (2014) highlights that contemporary research is much focused on participation, and especially, on the understanding of individual decision-making, on moral and emotional engagement, as well as, on the emergence and maintenance of collective identities. In this context, participation in collective action is understood as an identification process of the individuals with the notion of collective, based on common identity and values. This procedure is reinforced by social networks, which support the formation of common political consciousness and an ideological space that individuals will be identified with (Passy, 2003). Then, individuals will participate in both formal and informal networks, online or offline, and will be part of interactive structures, contributing to the framing processes, the formation of identities, as well as to the emergence of political consciousness (Passy, 2003). In a closer look, Hensby discussed Crossley's idea of 'activist habitus', which suggest that the sustained engagement with movements and participation has its roots in personal networks and background, starting with family and the social networks built in adult life (Hensby, 2014, p. 97).

Social networks, including online networks, support the participation of individuals to collective action (Passy, 2003), but most importantly, support the convention of political consciousness into action. Networks are having a mediating role, supportive of the framing and mobilisation processes, through which action occurs. What Passy points out here is that individuals who are having many ties with a movement or network are more likely to actively participate in the movement or network; the network is having a 'structural-connection function' before the individual be part of the movement (Passy, 2003, p. 24). Nonetheless, there are many different important factors, in the complex procedure, through which individuals will decide to be part of the collective and participate in a movement. The rationalistic approach to understanding this process uses sophisticated models able to decode the individual decision-making process as a behaviour, among the universal human attributes (Passy, 2003, p. 25). In contrast, the structuralist approach concentrates on the enabling and restricting character of structural factors on human behaviour (Passy, 2003, p. 25). On the other hand, concentrating on Oliver Marwell, and Teixeira (1985) critical mass theory, Passy (2003) points out the linkage between the social networks and the decisional model, stressing the importance of social networks, which describes the decision-shaping function. For Passy, a social network defines the final stage of individual participation and shapes the individual's preferences and perceptions; this determines the decision-making process and to an extent, the individual's participation in collective action (Passy, 2003, p. 27). This process not only defines the pro-participation process of the individual, but it also brings to the fore the notion of structure and agent, and up to a point, the structuralistic and rationalistic approach to the issue (Passy, 2003).

At a later stage, questions about how the emergence of political consciousness is transformed into participation and then action, should also be considered. This is also associated to the online radicalisation, and the debates on the issue as appeared from the 'war on terror' context and onwards. The most indicative examples here can be found in ethnoreligious-driven polarisation and its different manifestations (e.g. ISIS, and far-right movements). Other considerations on the issue are related to the notion of radicalisation per se, the notion of extremism, as well as on the discussion on de-radicalisation including debates on surveillance, freedom of speech and human rights. This latter debate falls outside the scope of the Greek case to a certain extent but will be elaborated further in the chapter outlining the socio-political context.

Digital Media Theory and Globalisation

The third component of the cyberconflict toolkit requires the use of elements of new/digital media theory and this is where we turn to next. The first analogue computer, the Differential Analyser, appeared in the late 1920s (Naughton, 1999, p. 54), while the Internet developed a few decades later, during the 1960s, as an experimental network to connect remote computers. The Internet is understood as the culmination of the technological growth of almost two centuries (McChesney, 2013), while its evolution from the days of Usenet to smartphones and social media was long (Hafner & Lyon, 1998; McChesney, 2013; Ryan, 2010), raising strong debates on its impact on every aspect of contemporary society. Due to the emergence of the Internet, the twentieth century was characterised by the rapid changes in the mediascape, with the Internet providing the opportunity for communication both to mass audiences and individuals, who can now communicate without knowing each other (Coleman & Blumler, 2009). This new mediascape provides new public, virtual spaces which, for a while, promised the emergence of more democratic structures. The limitation of this idea is that instead of concentrating on the relationship between citizens and politics, the Internet and especially the concept of e-democracy is understood as a non-dependent and non-contextualised procedure (Coleman & Blumler, 2009). Nonetheless, during the 1980s and 1990s, the debates on the growth of the Internet concentrated on an optimistic perspective and ambiguity relating to its potential influence on the democratisation of communications and censorship, which according to McChesney, at that point were unthinkable (Fuchs, 2014b).

Apparently, up to a point, new technology and digital media has challenged the traditional media structures of communication and the media system, which were structured following the principles of globalisation, constructing a global commercial market dominated by a few media conglomerates (McChesney, Wood, & Foster, 1998, pp. 12–15). Thus, the already existing debate on the necessity of a more democratic media system enriched and escalated by the growth of the Internet, and, then, digital media. Later, the political economy of communication concentrated on democracy and its multidimensional linkages to the media, while the notion of the public sphere came under question as well. In this context, the political economy of communication should not only foster critiques on the mainstream media system, which is perceived as being an element of globalisation, but should also cultivate a framework in which the media will directly serve the 'democratic function' (McChesney et al., 1998, p. 8). McChesney explained that for the first time in history, genuine democracy seemed to be possible (McChesney et al., 1998).

In contrast to the ambiguous predictions relating to the Internet's potentiality, still, the Internet didn't manage to support the establishment of the so-called open government, the end of corruption, inequality and conflict with hierarchical capitalist powers (McChesney et al., 1998, pp. 96–97). Instead, McChesney draws on Curran's argument, which explained that the Internet indeed didn't manage to influence capitalism, but the opposite, illustrated the capitalist colonisation of the Internet. While, originally, the Internet developed as a non-commercial institution, later, it contributed to the emergence of even closer and monopolistic markets, governmental corruption, the private sphere and to the enormous and profound expansion of contemporary capitalism (McChesney et al., 1998). Therefore, in opposition to the so-called cyber-utopianism, Morozov (2012) critically discussed the Internet's impact on contemporary society and democratisation, introducing the notion of cyber-realism, which should replace the idea of cyber-utopianism and Internet-centrism (Morozov, 2012). Instead of trying to answer the abstract question on how the Internet could change closed societies, a more realistic and measurable question should concentrate on how the Internet might be able to affect specific policies, in different contexts (Morozov, 2012, p. 319). Through this approach, technology should not be understood as the solution to political and social problems, able to promote freedom or democratisation, but instead, these issues should still be understood within the traditional debates. A critical analysis of media and especially the Internet should be situated in a historical and social context, and not examined in transcendental or ahistorical contexts (Morozov, 2012, p. 319).

At the same time, in juxtaposition to the capitalistic colonisation of the Internet, and to, the corporate colonisation of social media (Fuchs, 2014b), the notion of globalisation should also be considered. In a similar way, that globalisation has a significant impact on cultures and identities (Kegley & Blanton, 2009, pp. 322–323), taking into consideration concepts, such as space, time, or even individualism, the Internet indicated a potentiality as regards the multiple usages that this could have, supporting bottom-up communication, activism and social movements. Nonetheless, Stiglitz (2002) points out that that the notion of globalisation became very controversial, as illustrated by the contrast between the prospects and its actual application and effects. The optimistic perspective on globalisation and neoliberal theory concentrated on the cultural overlap between geopolitical boundaries and concepts such as 'national identity', creating the so-called 'global citizen' (Kegley & Blanton, 2009, p. 322). This approach illustrates some of the advantages of globalisation, in terms of prosperity, financial growth, international aid and de-isolation of the developed world as some of the benefits of globalisation (Stiglitz, 2002).

However, globalisation, in juxtaposition to the evolution of the Internet, hasn't brought the promised growth and economic prosperity but instead has escalated inequality (Stiglitz, 2002). Instead, globalisation indicated that the common interest among people is not strong enough to expound homogenised environments; people will protect their sovereign independence, creating competition and resulting in the division of the world into wealthy/stable countries and poorer/fragile countries (Kegley & Blanton, 2009), with the West dominating this relationship (Stiglitz, 2002). The Internet emerged from and accelerated by globalisation, and it was exploited as offering a brave new world: a cherry on the cake of globalisation. Yet, the Internet, already from the Zapatistas in the mid-1990s, contributed to the emergence of an anti-globalisation and anti-capitalist front. This does not mean that digital media should be understood as a tool able to automatically result in a better and radically new world (Fuchs, 2014b). Contemporary examples indicate that digital information communication technology can be extensively used in the formation and coordination of social movements, supporting at the same time communicational and organisational processes. This late 1990s discussion settles around the notions of cyberactivism, cyberprotest or online activism (Fuchs, 2014b).

The online world, alongside online mobilisation and radicalisation, or even extremism, extensively discussed after 2008 and the so-called global recession, the enormous crisis following the second world economic crisis of the 1970s (Fuchs, 2008). Already since the 1970s' crisis, the role of the state and the pattern of society have been transformed from a so-called post-Fordist society, with the neoliberal state replacing the Keynesian state (Žižek, 2012). While different schools and paradigms describe this historical moment focusing on various secondary points and debates, an important issue on this discussion is the change on the balance between state and the capital, resulting in an uncontrolled influence of the markets on society. After the 1970s' crisis, the state stopped acting as an intervening institution within the capitalistic structure but transformed into an antagonistic and competitive neoliberal state (Žižek, 2012). However, this new condition shaped by the contemporary social practices and struggles, has a strong impact on the rise of the neoliberal state and society (Fuchs, 2008, p. 108). Within this context, it is interesting to examine the use of digital media in the emergence of contemporary social movements. Focusing on the 2008 crisis, Fuchs (2014b) draws on Graeber (2013) explaining that, among others, what neoliberalism achieved in this phase was to break the linkage between productivity and wages, resulting in phenomena, such as the Arab Spring, the Occupy Movement, the UK riots, the Spanish indignados and the Greek indignados or even Breivik's case and the rise of the far-right (Žižek, 2012). At this point, Žižek explains that an effective approach for understanding the crisis is not by concentrating on the capital, but, referencing to Badiou, by concentrating on democratic illusion, which limits the possibilities for radical transformations in the capitalist structure (Žižek, 2012, p. 87).

While the social practices and struggles are suggested as being able to influence and shape the emergence of the neoliberal state and society, what is observed by the examples emerging after 2008 is that contemporary social movements and struggles were characterised by an abstract and fragmented ideological frame, without suggesting an actual alternative. Žižek (2012) discusses the 'zero level' protests, which in most cases, are described by the violence that is used as a means of expression, without entailing meaning or any kind of alternative suggestion and without involving specific demands. This could be relevant to the December Riots in Greece, which while it started as an expression of discontent, demanding end of police violence and justice for Grigoropoulos, soon extended its purview, and as a result, the characteristics of the riots overshadowed the original demands of the protests. Therefore, the way that the riots unfolded, in some occasions, were misleading as regards the original demands and goals and overshadowed by violence. These limitations were fulfilled by religion (Žižek, 2012) and/or national identity, which used to produce meaning and suggest an alternative form of violence.

According to Žižek, globalisation should be understood as the mechanics and structure that has a detotalised meaning, formulating truth without meaning, which is the only truth within the capitalist and globalised structure (Žižek, 2012, p. 55). The political economy of the so-called post-Fordism, or advanced capitalism, is characterised by the attempt to create alternative discourses and a fragmented, postmodernist culture (Wood, 1995), in which the contemporary Western left emerged. In this fragmented and postmodernist culture, the totalising knowledge is not only impossible but also undesirable, and consequently so is politics (Wood, 1995); this results in the inevitable confrontation with capitalism, as the most totalising system which, though, cannot be confronted without totalising knowledge (Wood, 1995, p. 2). Later, this relationship is reassessed and Žižek (2012) notes that the Western left indeed rediscovered capitalism as a problem, concentrating on struggles and subtopics raised from contemporary capitalism and can be understood as being more fragmented; as Žižek puts it, the 'class-struggle essentialism' for the plurality of anti-racist, feminist, and other struggles, 'capitalism is now clearly reemerging as the name of the problem' (Žižek, 2012, p. 17). As is pointed out here, the conflict is concentrated directly between the non-society and society, 'those who have nothing to lose and those who have everything to lose' (Žižek, 2012, p. 60).

The usage of the digital media in this conflict is decisive. Fuchs highlighted that social technology supports the establishment of offline and online relationships, as well as the emergence of non-hierarchical protest networks (2014b). The Internet features support both the globalisation of movements and at the same time, facilitate the emergence of counter-public spheres indicating cyberspace as a new battlefield or space of conflict (Karatzogianni, 2006). Starting from the anti-globalisation movement and the pre-social media era, up to the Occupy movement and the Arab Spring, the Internet has demonstrated its multiple uses and the globalised effect on movements. For Žižek (2012), the spread of digital media usage is linked to the contemporary crisis, contributing both to the expansion of globalisation as well as the struggle against it. According to Fuchs, while the Internet introduced as a space of conflict, a medium of communication able to facilitate social movements and revolution, still, the fundamental requirement for these to emerge is the material basis and the objective conditions and contradictions, based on which the necessity for collective action arises. Even in the case in which these conditions are realised, Žižek explains that the media mechanism confines the radical potentiality of contemporary movements and revolutions; therefore, contemporary movements examined within the global recession context should be situated in the central antagonism of contemporary capitalism (Žižek, 2012, p. 1). Nonetheless, the Internet indicates the necessity of humanising technology and points out the potentiality of the commons, highlighting the importance of the artificial commons in juxtaposition to the natural ones (Fuchs, 2008, p. 108).

Fuchs (2011, pp. 17–19) discussed the critical theory, as the 'analysis and questioning of domination, inequality, societal problems and exploitation in order to advance social struggles and the liberation from domination so that a domination less, co-operative, participatory society can emerge', while Harvey concentrates on 'a mode of investigation and inquiry that can uncover the deep structure of capitalism and suggest alternative value systems based on radically different kinds of social and material relations' (2010; cited in Fuchs, 2011, p. 20). Through a more Marxist approach, critical theory is 'radical, which means that it questions the root causes of domination and that it is a critique of domination and, therefore, of dominative societies' (Fuchs, 2011, p. 20). In that sense, critical theory is described as 'intellectual class struggle' (Fuchs, 2011, p. 14) and as a materialistic approach, which tends to decode social phenomena based on the idea of 'resource distribution and social struggles' (Fuchs, 2011, p. 21). In this materialistic approach, media and information are described 'neither as purely subjective nor as purely objective, but as attributes of matter' (Fuchs, 2011, pp. 98–99). In other words, information can only be discussed in terms of 'subject-object dialectic' (Fuchs, 2011, pp. 98–99), while Fuchs also highlights that the information is contradictory, pointing out the way that in society 'antagonism of capitalism' is embedded (Fuchs, 2011). Media, both digital and offline, act as a mirror for societal problems, while at the same time also suggest solutions (Fuchs, 2011, p. 99).

The contemporary digital era, in contrast to the traditional paradigms and the academic disciplines, is characterised by blurred disciplines and genres, which borrows intellectual traditions from different areas and does not follow the traditional strict boundaries (Lincoln, 2004, pp. 52–57). Lauk (2014) described the global recession as the 'triple crisis of western capitalism', focusing on democracy, banking and currency. Greece came to international attention as a significant example of the global recession, concentrating both on the crisis impact at the national level and the multidimensional character of the crisis' impact at a European level (Mavroudeas, 2015, p. 1). At the same time, the period of global recession, characterised by the wave of mobilisations and protests, indicated the significant and multidimensional contribution of ICTs to the formation of contemporary social movements. Taking into consideration the importance of digital media, especially in the latest global recession as well as in other crisis periods, the study of digital media in Greece is situated in the aforementioned framework, examining the interaction linkage between online conflict and the offline world. In this context, this study situates the Greek case in the global 'taxonomy' of contemporary movements and their linkage to ICTs (Della Porta & Diani, 2006; Stekelenburg & Klandermans, 2009).

After the understanding of the environment of the conflict as described earlier, the examination of different types of conflict (e.g. sociopolitical/ethnoreligious) will explore the debates of the crisis and how they have transformed and manifested online and offline during the crisis era. This will develop an insight into the evolution of the anti-/pro-austerity discourse and its transformation into an anti-/pro-governmental discourse, before, finally, being transfigured into an anti-/pro-European discourse. This will lead to the study of how digital media has challenged, or not, the dominant system and discourse, both focusing on politics and media processes, evaluating the contribution of digital media to the democratic function in contrast to crisis limitations and the global recession. The examination of digital media usage must concentrate firstly on the individual and the processes of participation, then on collective actions (e.g. collective identities, ideology and communities) and finally on conflict and its linkage to the offline world (e.g. politics and offline media). This will lead to an understanding of the impact of digital media on political polarisation and radical politics, alongside the foundation of collective actions, movements and changes in sociopolitical cohesion.

Chapter 3

The Historical and Sociopolitical Background of Greece

Starting with the Greek political landscape, the review concentrates on the mainstream political parties as these were formed after the fall of the dictatorship and before the crisis erupted. Later, the review focuses on the impact of the crisis on political formations. Then, the review examines non-parliamentary politics and focuses on the background/origins of two of the most significant social movements (students and labour) on the non-parliamentary left and far-right. Next, the discussion of the historical and sociopolitical background of Greece is completed by focusing on the evolution of the political economy of the media industry and the digital communications in Greece. This is accomplished with a review of traditional media, focusing on the early days of radio and television, on the impact of the crisis on the media and the problem of media ownership. Finally, the review looks at the development of digital media in Greece and the association of digital media with contemporary social movements and activism in the Greek context.

Mainstream Politics and Political Parties

> Although Greece is not a Constitutional Monarchy, historians of the future would probably benefit from the terminology used in this type of state in order to describe Greek politics of the last half century.
>
> E. Dinas (2010, p. 389)

Political Parties: From Metapolitefsi to the Greek Crisis, 1974–2012

After the so-called December Riots that took place in 2008, which are later discussed in detail, Fouskas (2009) suggests the end of the Third Hellenic Republic, after the fall of the Junta (Metapolitefsi). While this seems to be an ambitious perspective on the impact of the December Riots on the Greek political scene, the Greek crisis, which began almost simultaneously to the December Riots, reordered the fundamental structures of the Greek societal and political environment.

A discussion of the Greek crisis and the impact on the sociopolitical structure of Greece could not be developed without first going back to some of the most significant points in contemporary Greek history. Starting with the Greek Junta (1967–1974), the Metapolitefsi (fall of the Junta), or in other words the transition to multi-party democracy, has acted as a political reference for 'generations of politicians, voters and young people' (Kassimeris, 2005, p. 745), shaping political identities up to the present day (Asimakoulas, 2009, pp. 1–3). The fall of the dictatorship was inaugural to the establishment of a new political context, which was characterised by a three-block structure (Lyrintzis, 2007, pp. 242–243), which was built based on the axis of the Left-Right spectrum, following the tradition of the first decades of the twentieth century (Lyrintzis, 2007, p. 243). While the origins of this three-block structure can only be understood with reference to the pre-dictatorship period, still, its development after the fall of the Junta determines the Greek political system until the outbreak of the crisis and the restructuring of the political environment.

In 1974, after the fall of the dictatorship, Konstantinos Karamanlis returned from exile to lead Greece into Democracy (Pappas, 2008, p. 1124). Karamanlis, who represented the right block, tried to create a pluralist order (Pappas, 2008, p. 1124) which was later expressed by the newly established party New Democracy (ND). In an attempt to democratise the Greek political environment, the Communist Party (KKE), which, after the civil war and during 1950s–1960s was banned, was now recognised as a legitimate force representing the left block, possessing 10% of the votes (Lyritzis, 2007, p. 243, Pappas, 2008, p. 1124). In the same year, the Pan-Hellenic Socialist Movement (PASOK) was founded by Andreas. Papandreou, son of the centrist politician Georgios Papandreou who had previously served as prime minister three times (Siani-Davies & Katsikas, 2009). PASOK was founded as a radical-Marxist party and managed to win state power in 1981 representing the Centre-Left (Pappas, 2008, p. 1126) and dominating the Greek political scene in the years to follow.

There were several attempts to establish different political parties, which were intended to either fill the ideological gap between the existing parties, or to situate themselves on the edges of the political spectrum, expressing more radical political views. However, only SYNASPISMOS, a leftist party, which later came to the forefront of Greek politics, was a viable attempt gaining around 3% of the votes, before transforming into SYRIZA in 2004 and then, coming to power in 2015. The fall of the dictatorship, only a few decades after the civil war, provided the opportunity and the necessity not only for reform but also for the establishment of a new sociopolitical reality as well. However, apart from some small breaks, PASOK (1981–1989, 1993–2004) and ND (1974–81, 1990–1992, 2004–2009) alternated in state power until 2012. During the period 1974–2004, Greece became the 10th member of the European Common Market. The country adopted a simpler version of the Greek language in education and administration, solving the so-called language question, which overlapped with the discrimination and stereotypes raised by civil war, and adopted the European currency in 2001.

While the fall of the dictatorship resulted in the radical change of the political landscape, another important period of political restructures started in the mid-1990s and was signed by the new leadership in both ND and PASOK

(Pappas & Dinas, 2006). In 1996, A. Papandreou resigned from the PASOK leadership and was replaced by Costas Simitis (Pappas & Dinas, 2006, p. 481). In the same year, after the 1996 elections and the defeat of ND, the party's leadership passed to Kostas. Karamanlis, nephew of the ND founder, Konstantinos Karamanlis. During the same period, Costas Simitis, who was presented as a technocrat, became PASOK's leader, and later was characterised by his vision of the country's modernisation, which though was overshadowed by the big financial and political scandals of those days. In contrast, K. Karamanlis' profile was constructed based on the image of the young politician whose intention was to reestablish ND's political identity and reunite the party, leading the ND to power again. The new leadership in the two antagonistic parties highlighted a new era of Greek politics. Pappas and Dinas (2006) discussed the way that this new era in politics was reflected in public opinion, quoting Loulis who notes:

> (a) a marked decline of statism, most notably in the belief that economic growth should not be left entirely to the state; (b) the ascendancy of political pragmatism over the radicalism and ideologization that had prevailed in the past; (c) the growth of the centre vote and the dramatic reduction in voters placing themselves on the left; (d) widespread disillusionment with politics, which resulted in the tendency of the electorate to vote, not for the 'best' party, but for the 'least bad'; and (e) high vote volatility, which severed past electoral alliances and caused significant shifts in political allegiances from one election to the next.
>
> (cited in Pappas & Dinas, 2006, p. 483)

This new era of the Greek politics was a point of transition for the political programmes of 'neo-liberalism and financialisation (globalisation)' which, in the case of Greece, illustrated the problematic and unsuccessful adaptation of such programmes by the 'periphery' of Europe (Fouskas & Dimoulas, 2012). Already, since the early 1990s, the Greek political system had changed orientation and concentrated on the deliberation of the markets as well as on the privatisation of banks and companies. This process was later completed under the Semites neo-revisionist PASOK, during 1996–2004 (Michael-Matsas, 2010).

The crowning moment of this new era, which at the same time signalled its end, came a decade later, after the 2004 elections and the Olympic Games. The year 2004 was a significant year for Greece. The completion of the Olympic Games, which cost millions of Euros, was considered a huge success in terms of governmental goals; at the same time, the parliamentary elections indicated that 'PASOK's Monopoly Ends' (Kassimeris, 2004). The socialist party, which, at that point, had been in power for nineteen out of twenty-two years of the multiparty democracy since the fall of the Junta, was blamed for the 'spiralling prices, persistent unemployment and perceived corruption within the governmental party' (Kassimeris, 2004, p. 243).

Just before the elections of 2004, C. Semites passed PASOK's leadership to G. Papandreou, son of the PASOK's founder, who, at the time, was serving as the minister of foreign affairs. This denoted the beginning of PASOK's crisis era (Kassimeris, 2004). G. Papandreou, who was strongly criticised for his US citizenship and lack of Greekness (Kassimeris, 2004, p. 249), followed the Semites vision of modernisation. However, he didn't manage to unite the party or to create a new political vision to inspire a new generation of voters (Kassimeris, 2004). PASOK had a tradition of establishing new political identities and inventing new or innovative political visions. This was the main element that brought the socialist party into power only a few years after its foundation, during the 1980s. Back then, PASOK managed to encompass the 'old divisions between conservatives and liberals, communists and anti-communists' and created a new conceptualisation of the 'right wing and anti-right-wing forces'; it presented itself as the 'third road to socialism', promising to stand for all the 'non-privileged' Greeks (Lyrintzis, 2007, p. 246). From A. Papandreou's calling for 'change' (Αλλαγή), PASOK moved to C. Semites' 'modernisation' (Εκσυγχρονισμός) and ended with George Papandreou, who was characterised by the well-known and much-criticised phrase 'The money exists' (The Guardian, 2011), binging the party to power after the 2009 elections (Pappas, 2014). Later, this phrase denoted the dispute of public opinion against PASOK, as expressed after the outbreak of the crisis.

In the 2004 parliamentary elections, K. Karamanlis and ND were elected with 45.4% of the vote. In juxtaposition to the new era of PASOK (Kassimeris, 2004), a new era for ND began. The changes between the two antagonists' party dynamics were also translated into ideological and political changes, which resulted in the emergence of ideological gaps that not only became noticeable in the crisis context but were also filled by new political parties. Indeed, ND under K. Karamanlis' headship was very different from the ND of the Mitsotakis' period of 1990–1993 (Kassimeris, 2004), or later, the Samaras period. While ND had been searching for a new political identity since 1993 (Lyrintzis, 2007, p. 245), after 2004, the party managed to appeal to a 'broad cross-section of voters' (Kassimeris, 2004) by adopting a not so strictly neo-liberal, right-wing rhetoric. This rapidly changed in the context of the crisis when ND moved from centre-right rhetoric to a more right-wing populist position. At that point, in 2004, ND was a party promising to 'reconstruct the state, to fight the corruption as well as the rising of the prices' (Gemenis, 2008, pp. 95–96). In doing so, ND successfully followed PASOK's example (Lyrintzis, 2007, p. 246), which started as a radical left party but eventually moved to a more centre-right position on the traditional political axis.

Nonetheless, ND, which remained a conservative party, came into power under K. Karamanlis' leadership, who at the age of 47 became the youngest prime minister in Greece (Kassimeris, 2004, p. 950). In the 2004 elections, the same year that witnessed the Olympic Games and the European parliament elections, ND was re-elected for the first time after 1993 and therefore, enjoyed an 'unprecedented honeymoon period' (Dinas, 2008, p. 601), with PASOK presented as being responsible for most of the problems occurring in the first period of the new government (Dinas, 2008). Later, disaffection with ND's attempt to reform the organisation of Greek universities, as well as the corruption-related political scandals, brought under consideration the issue of early elections (Dinas, 2008, pp. 601–602) before 2007 and prior to the outbreak of wildfires across Greece. In August 2007, the wildfires across Greece resulted in one of the most dramatic environmental catastrophes of contemporary Greek history and the death of 70 people. In statements, K. Karamanlis pointed out the extent of the political crisis as it emerged, by adapting a rhetoric commonly used for terrorism-related issues, characterising the wildfires as an 'asymmetric threat' that supported a 'conscious strategic plan', which intended to harm both the government and the country (Dinas, 2008, p. 603).

In September 2007, ND was re-elected with 41.8 % of the votes, after the shortest pre-election period in decades and with a new electoral system (Gemenis, 2008, p. 605). The 2007 elections indicated the weaknesses of the two opposing political parties, ND and PASOK, which were no longer able to maintain the existing two-party system (Gemenis, 2008) and therefore, the potential for the rise of smaller parties became obvious. The Coalition of Left, Ecology and Movements (SYNASPISMOS) converted to the Coalition of the Radical Left (SYRIZA), and Alekos. Alavanos passed the presidency to Alexis Tsipras (Gemenis, 2008, p. 96). SYRIZA managed to gain 5.7% of the votes, up from the 3.2% of the votes that SYNASPISMOS gained in the elections of 2000 and 2004. The Communist Party, KKE, gained 8.1% of the votes in contrast to the 5.9% in the elections of 2004, and the 5.5% in 2000. LAOS (Popular Orthodox Rally), a far-right populist party, which constantly denied its far-right orientation but maintained its nationalistic rhetoric, gained 3.8% of the votes in contrast to 2.19% in 2004.

In 2009, the outbreak of the global recession had already strongly influenced the Greek political and social context, while financial and other governmental scandals indicated that the viability of the government was doubtable. Tsalikidis and the so-called Vodafone case, which refers to the wiretapping of high-ranking public servants and politicians including the prime minister (Bamford, 2015; Galpin, 2006; Petropoulos, 2015), the suicide attempt of the Secretary-General of the Ministry of Culture (Moustaka, 2008), the Siemens scandal (Pappas, 2010; TVXS, 2011), the Grigoropoulos case and the so-called December Riots (Karamichas, 2009) were only some of the most striking scandals that led to the 2009 elections. PASOK came to power with its legendary 'The money exists' slogan of A. Papandreou (The Guardian, 2011), illustrating once again that the political environment as shaped since 1974 was about to change. While the dispute between the two main parties was clear, the potential and rise of the smaller parties could not be interpreted as a true political change, but rather as the expression of disaffection with PASOK and ND policies.

After the elections of 2009, when crisis had rapidly emerged, PASOK came to power and realised that the 'projected fiscal deficit was going to be more than double' compared to what ND had estimated (Katsikas, 2012, p. 50). Due to the estimations of the public debt, the competitiveness limitations and the credit ratings, the Greek financial system was shown not to be viable, with Greece becoming unable to 'access funding from the financial markets' (Katsikas, 2012, p. 50). Under G. Papandreou's government, Greece sought a loan request from the EU and the International Momentary Fund (IMF). Greece signed a bailout agreement for three years (Katsikas, 2012, p. 50) through which the country accepted supervision from the so-called Troika (IMF, European Commission and the European Central Bank) on the adoption of the 'comprehensive policy programme (memorandum)' (Katsikas, 2012, p. 50). At the same time, the Dubai crisis in 2009 had already indicated the 'symptoms of the globally propagated disease' and the 'Greek tragedy', which was about to follow (Michael-Matsas, 2010, p. 460), highlighting the so-called 'Greek crisis' as one of the most notable examples of the EU austerity politics of the last decade.

After the chaotic progress of the crisis, at the national and European level, the three-year bailout agreement was followed by many other agreements and memoranda, which resulted in the collapse of the social and political fabric and structures. G. Papandreou announced his resignation in November 2011. PASOK, ND and LAOS formed a 'government of national unity', led by P. Papademos, former head of the Bank of Greece (Vasilopoulou & Halikiopoulou, 2013, p. 4). This governmental scheme didn't change policy on the memorandum and the austerity agreements and remained in power until the double elections of 2012, which took place in May and June, marking the shortest period between elections since 1974 (Vasilopoulou & Halikiopoulou, 2013).

The first round of the 2012 elections demonstrated the breakdown of the traditional governmental two-party system with PASOK and ND together gaining less than 32% of the votes. SYRIZA gained 16.8%, the second-highest percentage of votes, while Golden Dawn, a neo-Nazi party, which was later accused of organised violence and associated, among others, to the murder of Pavlos Fyssas (Killah P), an anti-fascist musician, gained 10.6% of votes, entering the Greek parliament for the first time. After the May elections, the creation of a coalition government was not possible and therefore Greece entered a six-week pre-election period, leading to the second round of elections in June 2012. The dominant political debate, as shaped by the mainstream parties and the mainstream media at that time, concentrated on the theory of extreme politics, focusing on the rise of SYRIZA and Golden Dawn. At the same time, EU politicians and media constantly supported the mainstream political parties, with the discussion around the so-called Grexit being intense and raising strong criticism and questions regarding national sovereignty and the meaning of elections in democratic societies (Vasilopoulou & Halikiopoulou, 2013, pp. 6–7). The outcome of the June elections was perceived as a confirmation to the EU that Greece would comply with the EU and Troika's demands, giving a vote to the mainstream political parties, which supported the memorandum. ND gained 29.6 % of the votes, PASOK 12.28% and together with DIMAR, which gained 6.25% created a coalition government. At the same time, SYRIZA became the main opposition party (26.9%), and Golden Dawn gained 18 seats in the parliament (6.9%).

Admittedly, the 2012 elections indicated the end of the political era which started after 1974, and at the same time it highlighted the fact that 'the legitimacy of the political system was seriously damaged' (Lyrintzis, 2011, p. 22). The Greek crisis, which started as a financial one, had now converted into a political and, consequently, social crisis. The collapse of the traditional political parties, including the political and ideological identities, which developed after 1974 and remained constant for decades, resulted in the segregation of political and social structures. Society was struggling to respond to the crisis, and at the same time, the new political environment did not manage to generate any substantive political debate or vision as regards the future of the new sociopolitical environment. In this context, the rise of the far-right and Golden Dawn in Greece, as well as the rise of far-right groups in other EU countries, indicated the strong impact of austerity politics on the fragile European democratic society. The global recession, especially as it emerged in the EU context, indicated a new era of extreme politics, highlighting the danger raised by conservative and extreme politics in financial and sociopolitical terms, reminding the EU that in periods of great recession, the rise of far-right and conservative politics, as well as the rise of extreme politics, is still a real threat (Table 3.1).

Social Movements, Far Right and the Left

The Evolution of the Student and Labour Movement in Greece

The history of the Greek student movement began in the late nineteenth century. Only six years after the foundation of the first Greek university in 1843, academia showed itself to be a place of strong politicisation and social struggles (Psacharopoulos & Kazamias, 1980, pp. 128–129). At the beginning of the twentieth century, the student movement had a conservative orientation, with students protesting both against new policies and the adoption of the simplest version of the Greek language (Psacharopoulos & Kazamias, 1980, pp. 128–129). The Metaxas

Table 3.1. Results of the Greek Parliamentary Elections 2000–2012.

%	2000	2004	2007	2009	2012 (May)	2012 (June)	2015 (Jan)	2015 (June)
PASOK	43.79	40.55	38.10	43.92	13.18	12.28	4.68	6.29
ND	42.74	45.36	41.84	33.47	18.85	29.66	27.81	28.09
KKE	5.52	5.90	8.15	7.54	8.48	4.50	5.47	5.55
SYN/SYRIZA	3.20	3.26	5.04	4.60	16.78	26.89	36.34	35.46
DIKKI	2.69	1.79						
EN.KENTROON	0.34	0.26				0.28	1.79	3.44
LAOS		2.19	3.80	5.63	2.90	1.58	1.03	
Golden Dawn (GD)					6.97	6.92	6.28	6.99
DIMAR					6.11	6.25	0.48	
Ecologist Greens (Oikologoi Prasinoi)				2.53	2.93	0.88		
AN.EL.					10.61	1.59	4.75	6.69
ANTARSYA						0.33	0.64	0.85
POTAMI							6.05	4.09

Source: Ministry of Interior, ypes.gr, n.d.

fascist dictatorship crushed most of the student organisations, which only re-emerged after the civil war, during 1950s–1960s, with one of its most significant moments being the Lambrakis affair (Psacharopoulos & Kazamias, 1980, p. 129). The student movement's contribution to the fall of the Junta until 1973 was significant. The fall of the Junta and the Metapolitefsi were characterised by the promise of change, while the transition to multi-party democracy was marked by the monumental uprising, which was overshadowed by the student movement and the university occupations.

The occupation of the Athens University Law School and the Athens Polytechnic lasted for three days and began as part of the student protests against the 'authoritarianism of the educational system' (Kassimeris, 2005, p. 746), before turning to a general political revolt against the dictatorship. The Greek student movement and its role in 1973 could be examined in juxtaposition to other movements, such as those in Chile and Italy (Kassimeris, 2005, pp. 746–748). At the same time, the French May '68 ideals were an aspiration, influencing the social and student movements, which were struggling for social and political change, parallel to the cultural revolution of those days (Kassimeris, 2005, pp. 746–748). The Greek uprising of 1973 developed an anti-authoritarian rhetoric, rejecting the political system, because it was seen as built on values, ideas and concepts, all originating in the attempt to re-establish the state after the civil war. Rigos (2007) explains that, during 1973, the student movement became the 'sole vehicle of collective expression of solidarity and public revulsion against oppression, injustice and limited freedom, gaining for itself autonomous political maturity and universal popular recognition' (cited in Karamichas, 2007, p. 749).

The Metapolitefsi highlighted that the student movement had a significant impact on contemporary political identities as shaped after the fall of the Junta, influencing the Greek political landscape to the present time. However, the student movement's vision for the establishment of a new republic and the expectations of movement supporters and participants were not fulfilled and efficiently represented by any political parties and the policies of the multi-party democracy after the uprising (Karamichas, 2007, p. 745). Various activist groups formed during the dictatorship and represented the revolutionary Left, in order to fill this ideological and political gap. Maoist, Trotskyist or Anarchist groups were some of the groups, which remained active after the dictatorship and were associated with the European Movement (Karamichas, 2007, p. 751), focusing on political reform and democratisation. The political pluralism that developed after 1974 supported not only the development of extra-parliamentary and revolutionary left groups but also resulted in the development of neo-fascist groups. Such groups focused mainly on terrorist acts and campaigns, with one of the most noteworthy and common examples being cinema bombings (Karamichas, 2007, p. 751).

Both the left-wing and non-fascist groups founded during the mid-1970s emerged parallel or in confluence with the student movement. In 1974, the labour movement, which already had a long tradition in Greece, alongside the student movement, equally contributed to the uprising, shaping the post-Junta political environment. The origins of the Greek Labour Movement can be found in the late nineteenth century and early twentieth century, when strikes took place in different urban centres across Greece. In 1918, and after the cycles of Syros strikes started in 1879, the 'General Confederation of Workers of Greece' (GSEE) was founded, signalling a new era for the labour movement, which developed at a distance from the European example (Ioannou, 1999).

Both the student and the labour movement were shaped in juxtaposition to the political developments of Greece and deeply influenced by civil war, occupation and the dictatorship. After the civil war, social and political conflicts were raised by the contrast between communism and anti-communism, transmuted to fanaticism and sociopolitical division (Kassimeris, 2013a), which lasted for decades. Governmental policies and control over this issue were various, having a strong impact both on the student and labour movements, which in most cases, were associated with left-wing oriented groups. During dictatorship and the Metapolitefsi, the labour movement strongly associated with the student movement, supporting democratisation. While both the student and the labour movement have been characterised by violent conflicts with the police and the state, the incidents at the Athens Polytechnic – National Technical University (Polytechneio) were a momentous example for both the two movements, standing against state oppression and violence. This uprising ended with the violent intervention of the army, which resulted in many casualties and, eventually, a change of regime (Psacharopoulos & Kazamias, 1980). The state's determination to control politicised spaces and the communist peril, associated the left-wing political identity to the danger of unemployment, political persecution or even physical torture.

Ioannou (1999) examined the Greek labour movement focusing on five periods following the social and political turmoil of contemporary Greek history. The first period began with the Syros strikes and the foundation of GSEE (1879–1918); the second period is between the creation of GSEE and the end of Metaxas' dictatorship (1919–1940); the third period ran parallel to WWII, the Occupation and the Civil War (1940–1949); and the fourth period encompassed the end of civil war and the end of dictatorship (1950–1974). Finally, according to Ioannou, the fifth period started with the end of dictatorship and is still in progress now. However, considering that Ioannou's study was written before the Greek crisis of 2008, it would be reasonable to perceive the period after 2008 as a new period for the Greek labour movement. The significant changes in both working conditions and the extremely high percentages of unemployment bring to light additional questions about the role of the movement and its dynamic in the crisis context.

The Extra-parliamentary Left and Revolutionary Groups

The 1973 uprising was a struggle for democratisation and political modernisation which created the proper conditions for the emergence of a radical communist utopianism, which reinforced debates on 'class, social structure and revolutionary strategy' (Kassimeris, 2013a, p. 134). At the same time, the uprising was a turning point for the conception of political identities, ideologies and parties, creating the grounds for political fermentations, which were later associated with the rise of radical politics, including examples of revolutionary left and far-right groups, both intensively active during that period. After the Civil War, the attempt to create an anti-communist state was intense (Kassimeris, 2013a, p. 133), and this resulted in political discrimination against the Left, even after the fall of the dictatorship. During that period, Greece followed the Western Europe example with the extra-parliamentary left and different revolutionary groups intensively active, resulting in the most active political-oriented terrorist movement on a global scale (Kassimeris, 2004, p. 260). In the opposite approach, during the same period, the far-right was strengthened as well in a way reminiscent of the political debates and conflict raised during and after WWII.

The dictatorship can be understood as an era of intense political violence both by the state and left and right-wing extra-parliamentary groups. Violence among sub-state groups and the state, alongside the environment of political instability, contributed to the emergence of revolutionary and extra-parliamentary groups (Xenakis, 2012), suggesting a political and social alternative in which violence was both inevitable and justified (Kassimeris, 2005, p. 748). During the first years of Metapolitefsi, more than 95 revolutionary and resistance groups were active (Kassimeris, 2013a, p. 135), while until 2007, more than 250 such groups have claimed responsibility for various acts (Karyotis, 2007).

After the fall of the dictatorship and in opposition to the government attempt to create an anti-communist state, left politics became a strong political trend, reinforcing the political polarisation between Left and Right, which had a long historical tradition. The inadequate representation of the Left in parliament further contributed to the rise of the extra-parliamentary Left as well as anarchist and revolutionary groups (Xenakis, 2012). The Communist Party's position on this political trend did not support the creation of a strong unified movement (Xenakis, 2012). It is indicative that the KKE strongly criticised the Athens Polytechnic occupation, as having limited capabilities and potentiality and being organised by naive students (Kassimeris, 2013b, p. 15), while it accused the various extra-parliamentary left groups of being provocateurs, strongly associated with the Right (Xenakis, 2012, p. 441). This approach highlighted the distance between the KKE and the new radical-left, as well as the distance between what later became the parliamentary and extra-parliamentary left.

Some of the most influential groups, which were active until recently, were the 17 November (Revolutionary Organisation 17 November/17N) and ELA (Revolutionary Popular Struggle), which were characterised as Marxist–Leninists and started their activities in 1975 (Kassimeris, 2013b) having a rich record of activities. Another interesting example of anti-dictatorship and revolutionary groups which supported the legitimacy of the armed struggle is the case of PAK (Pan-Hellenic Liberation Movements), which later transformed to PASOK, one of the two governmental parties for decades (Kassimeris, 2013b, p. 440). These groups were founded after the fall of the dictatorship and understood Metapolitefsi as a trick, a 'democratic façade' (Kassimeris, 2013b, p. 135), or even a 'dynastic change of the regime' (Kassimeris, 2013b, p. 64). These groups formed as a response to the inefficient way that systemic actors and institutions, which came to power after the fall of the dictatorship, tried and failed to reform the state according to the uprising's ideals.

While these groups emerged in the national political context, they soon linked their actions to the international political context and social movements. Following the political utopianism of those days, the extra-parliamentary left and revolutionary groups justified their actions as 'a logical and inevitable political consequence of national and constitutional processes' (Kassimeris, 2004, p. 261), rationalising the use of violence as a response to 'right wing pressure' and 'a vital instrument of the social war against bourgeois democracy' (Kassimeris, 2004, p. 262). At the same time, such groups identified themselves as part of the anti-capitalist struggle, or as 17 November puts it, the struggle against the 'American military imperialism', which had a significant impact globally (Kassimeris, 2013b, p. 25).

While it would be interesting to have a more in-depth review of the extra-parliamentary left in Greece, this brief overview still succeeds in developing an insight into how different political parties, movements and groups developed, supporting an understanding of the contemporary political landscape. Therefore, the way that the state historically treated these groups as well as their relationship to the media, are some of the points that should be under examination. Nomikos divides the way that the examined groups have been perceived and treated into three periods/categories:

> (1) 1974–1989: the rise of the Greek leftish terrorism, which was characterised by the failure of the political elites to recognise the roots, the level and the significance of the terrorist threat.
> (2) 1989–1999: this period was defined by the politicisation of terrorism as well as the inclusion of the issue in the party politics debate.
> (3) 1999–onwards: this period was characterised by the impact of the security services on terrorism.
>
> (Nomikos, 2007, p. 66)

While this categorisation explains the way that such groups have been perceived and treated by political elites and the state, Xenakis (2012) makes a different categorisation based on generations, dividing such groups into two categories, the old and the new generation of revolutionary groups, or terrorists (1974–2002 and 2002 onwards).

Even if the extra-parliamentary left and revolutionary groups – or even terrorist groups – were created with a different structure to other European ones, the general movement was not independent of European and global events. The 9/11 in the US, the Olympic Games in Athens and the anti-globalisation protests changed the connotation of terms like terrorism, threat and security, not only in the international context but in Greece as well, having a strong impact on the Greek security agenda (Nomikos, 2007, pp. 72–73). In the Greek case, the abstract conception of terrorism was shaped by American-Greek international relations and Greek membership of the EU. During the Olympic Games, security became a high priority issue and the arrests of ELA and 17 November members were, not surprisingly, perceived as a great success at an international level. The new Greek anti-terrorism law and the cooperation between Greek and foreign police experts on terrorism contributed to the safe and successful organisation of the Olympic Games.

During the same period, surveillance programmes, including the NSA Athens-affair, the Vodafone wiretapping of politicians and the Greek Prime Minister, which related to the Tsalikidis murder (Bamford, 2015; Galpin, 2006; Petropoulos, 2015), illustrated how the national debate on terrorism contributed to the adoption of controversial policies in the Greek context. While this is an indicative example of the use of technology both by mainstream and non-mainstream politics, the extra-parliamentary and revolutionary groups already had a long tradition in the way that they used traditional media as a communication channel with society throughout the different phases and decades in which these groups were active. For decades, traditional media and especially the press were the main tools for communication with the public, through which such groups presented their ideas, published manifestos and claimed responsibility for attacks and actions. In Greece, the relationship between the media and such groups is structured on a completely different rationale in comparison to most European countries (Kassimeris, 2013b). The Greek state had several attempts at controlling this relationship, however, the media used both by revolutionary groups and the state. The emergence of new and social media dramatically changed the dynamic of the relationship between media and extra-parliamentary groups, revolutionary and activist groups.

While many contemporary political groups and initiatives have some strong ideological linkages, common concerns, inspiration and ideas focusing on democratisation, justice and so on, it should still be considered whether such groups manage to express all these in a more effective and influential way in the crisis context. The last generation of revolutionary and extra-parliamentary groups was marked and reinforced by the so-called December riots, in 2008. Kassimeris (2013b) explains that this generation of groups didn't develop concentrating on the left, following the national tradition and debates, but instead linked in with stronger ideological and political references to international movements, including the anti-capitalist and anti-war movements. Revolutionary Struggle (RS), which was founded around 2003, and the CCF (Conspiracy of Cells of Fire), which was founded after 2008, are the most notable groups of the contemporary period. Following the previous generation's paradigm, the December riots and the Grigoropoulos case had an equivalent impact on the movement, as the Kaltezas case did during the 1980s (Kassimeris, 2013b).

In this generation of groups, the struggle against capitalism, imperialism and so on was updated according to neoliberalism and the context of global recession. The 'New World Order to Terrorism International' manifesto by RS, published in 2004, closely developed along the lines of the 17November ideals, justifying violence as a medium of struggle and change against a variety of issues, including 'the Greek political establishment', 'globalisation', '9/11', 'the US-led war on terror', 'the wars in Iraq and Afghanistan', 'the Arab-Israeli conflict', as well as the

'US hegemonic plans in the Balkans' (Kassimeris, 2013b, p. 78). RS critically discussed the democratic illusion and the sociopolitical structures which were expected to lead to great poverty, unemployment, inequality and social exclusion (Kassimeris, 2013b, p. 80). Finally, such groups extensively expressed opposition to the rise of racism, xenophobia and the advance of far-right groups.

The Evolution of the Far-right in Greece: From Metaxas Dictatorship to Golden Dawn

Similar to the extra-parliamentary and revolutionary groups of the left, the efficient use of terms such as far-right, extreme-right, radical or ultra-right is arguable, raised strong debates on their use in the literature (Tsiras, 2012). In the Greek context, the term 'right' was used during the 1920s, without denoting a specific ideology, but instead, it just expressed opposition to the left (Tsiras, 2012). During the inter-war years and following the European example, Greece was searching for a third way, between neoliberalism and Marxism (Tsiras, 2012). In the late 1920s Thessaloniki was an urban centre with various ethnic groups marked by strong class and ideological turmoil which, among others, was expressed by the foundation of two conflicted ideological organisations, the Federation and the National Union of Greece (Εθνική Ένωση Ελλάδος). The Federation later transformed to the KKE, while the National Union of Greece became one of the most noteworthy and active fascist organisations of the period (Tsiras, 2012, p. 75).

The Metaxas dictatorship overshadowed the fascist, far-right groups and organisations, although that period is still a reference point for right-wing groups and is understood as a moment of glory for both the far-right and right groups and parties (Tsiras, 2012, pp. 75–77). During WWII, the triple occupation of Greece by Germany, Italy and Bulgaria, found many collaborators, members of the right-wing spectrum, expressing their affinity with fascism and Nazism (Tsiras, 2012, pp. 75–77). During the occupation, the far-right idealised the idea of the Great Greece; far-right wing and collaborationist military organisations such as Security Battalions (Tagmata Asfaleias) and Organisation Chi (X) were very active during occupation, while they also had a significant impact on the Dekemvriana and the Battle of Athens, in 1944[1] (Tsiras, 2012, pp. 75–77).

[1]The Battle of Athens, the Dekemvriana, was an event with noteworthy impact both in terms of national unity as well as international relations and political coalitions of that era (Vulliamy and Smith, 2014). After the occupation, the influence of the resistance movement, which was dominated by the National Liberation Front (EAM) and the Communist Party, was continually growing (Vulliamy and Smith, 2014). This was in opposition to Britain's plan, which, still being in conflict with Germany, wanted to restore the pro-war political conditions bringing the king back to power (Vulliamy and Smith, 2014). Therefore, during the demonstration on the 3rd of December 1944, Britain, alongside local Nazi collaborators, decided to open fire against demonstrators and EAM members, sowing the seeds for the outbreak of the Civil War and the rise of the far-right in Greece (Vulliamy and Smith, 2014).

The Dekemvriana was followed by a period of White Terror (Panourgiá, 2009, pp. 78–80; Tsiras, 2011, p. 79) and the Civil War. During the so-called White Terror, extreme policing and surveillance practices took place, altogether to the formation of the National Guard (Ethnofylaki) (Panourgiá, 2009, p. 78). White Terror came about in opposition to the Red Terror, which referred to the Communist Peril, while after the Treaty of Varkiza and the disarmament of the left, the right-wing groups started forming the first political parties, which obtained a presence in the parliament (Tsiras, 2011). While the KKE was still banned, some of the most noteworthy far-right parties of that period were the Chi (X) Party and the National Political Union, which comprised smaller far-right groups and parties, as well as the National Rally, led by Papagos[2] (Tsiras, 2011, p. 79). After the end of the Civil War, the enemy of the state continued to be on the left and in favour of communism (Panourgiá, 2009; Tsiras, 2011). Papagos founded the KYP, an equivalent to the CIA, whose mission was to engage in international espionage acts, and in the end, together with the CIA, strongly influenced Greek politics (Panourgiá, 2009, p. 122). The outcome of such procedures was the establishment of the so called Parakratos (parastate) (Panourgiá, 2009, p. 122), which was a shadow far-right state, operating next to the formal one (Tsiras, 2011, p. 83).

In 1967, colonel members of the Chi (X) organisation and the Tagmata Asfaleias established the dictatorship (Panourgiá, 2009). The years of dictatorship were characterised by political and social violence, with the pattern of conflict between the left and the right, evolving in the same way as in previous decades. In 1974, Karamanlis came back from years of exile in Paris to lead a government of national unity. He attempted to divide the far-right and the centre-right ideology and policies, with his party seeking to represent the second – the centre-right (Tsiras, 2011). However, while Karamanlis' party concentrated on the centre-right of the political spectrum, in the following decades his party was associated with the far-right. After Metapolitefsi, neo-fascist groups began terrorist campaigns with a series of bomb explosions and other attacks designed to create a climate of tension and instability. Most of the neofascists and far-right groups of that era were associated with political crimes, including the Panagoulis case, bombings or even attacks on migrants (Theofilopoulos, 2008, p. 116). Some of the most noteworthy groups of that era included the National Alignment (Εθνική Παράταξις- ΕΠ), the United Nationalist Movement (Ενιαίο Εθνικιστικό Κίνημα – EN.E.K.) as well as the National Student Novelty (Εθνική Φοιτητική Πρωτοπορία) and National Political Union (Εθνική Πολιτική Ένωσις (ΕΠΕΝ) (Theofilopoulos, 2008, p. 116).

During the 1980s, many neo-fascist organisations related to sports and more especially football emerged with one of the first examples being the

[2]Papagos was already a representative political figure of right-wing politics before the end of the civil war, whose ideology after the war focused on political oblivion, bringing and maintaining the right-wing parties into power until 1963, attracting all the far-right wing support of the previous decades (Tsiras, 2011, p. 79).

Panathinaikon Nazi-Organisation (Ναζιστική Οργάνωση Παναθηναϊκών Οπαδών – ΝΟΠΟ) and the Ypovrixios (Υποβρύχιος) associated with the Olympiakos football Club (Theofilopoulos, 2008, p. 116). In the following decades, and especially during the crisis, Greek football was, in several cases, related to the far-right. During this period, this included Golden Dawn, which became active after 1993 with the demonstrations about the so-called Macedonian Issue. During the same decade the far-right LAOS filled the political gap which arose when New Democracy re-identified as a centrist party (Ellinas, 2014). As the crisis unfolded, Golden Dawn entered the Greek Parliament, while LAOS collapsed. However, many LAOS MPs joined New Democracy and obtained high governmental positions, while New Democracy re-occupied the political space between the centre-right and the far-right.

After 2008, the outbreak of the crisis resulted in sociopolitical turmoil which was characterised by political debates on the crisis, ideological and political conflict, as well as a struggle for change. However, the rise of the far-right highlighted another area of conflict dominated by ethnoreligious characteristics (Karatzogianni, 2006). The rise of far-right and nationalistic discourse, together with the austerity/anti-austerity debate, blurred the boundaries of sociopolitical conflict, which here was enriched by elements of ethnic and religious content/conflict (discourse of inclusion/exclusion, racist discourse and national identity, etc.). In the Greek crisis context, the sociopolitical conflict had been transformed by and had adopted ethnoreligious characteristics, and the opposite. At the same time, the way that this is observed offline and online will be examined later focusing on empirical data.

The Greek Mediascape

The first decade of the twenty-first century was characterised by the adoption of the technological revolution, which supported the development of media in Greece. While the development of the press has a long tradition, the development of the Greek media sector, concentrating on broadcasting, began in the late 1930s. A milestone in this development was the broadcasting deregulation and privatisation, which took place in 1989, while the period after deregulation indicated the vulnerabilities of the sector, as the political sphere became hostage to media ownership by elites and corporate interests.

Traditional Media: From the Early Days of Radio and Television to the Traditional Media in the Crisis Era

During the early 1920s, the Greek government was not supportive towards the public development of the radio; however, until 1926, the Ministry of Navy and the Union of the Greek Amateur Wireless Operators were in charge of regulating the broadcasting of the new medium by licensing the owners of each radio receiver (Zaharopoulos, 2002). Since the early days of Greek media, television and radio were used as the 'arms of the state' (Papathanassopoulos, 1997, p. 352).

Although even before 1928 there were some noteworthy attempts at radio broadcasting, the first regular radio station was founded in 1928 in Thessaloniki by Ch. Tsigiridis, with the first broadcast programme having only two listeners (Mpintelas, 2009). This station was one of the first in the Balkans and broadcast for more than twenty years (Kounenaki, 1995, p. 3). In 1936, the Metaxas' dictatorship took advantage of technology and established a state broadcasting system (Zaharopoulos, 2002). Greece was one of the last European countries to have a broadcasting system, that only established after 1936. The early days of the Greek media sector and the development of radio in Greece were marked by the intensive interest of technological equipment supplier companies. Both British and German companies pushed for the project (Kounenaki, 1995, pp. 10–11). I. Voulpiotis[3] who was involved in the trade of equipment for many other state projects (e.g. telecommunications, etc.) arranged to cooperate with Siemens' subsidiary Telefunken (Papadimitriou, 2013).

On the 27th of March 1941, the radio station of Athens announced the German invasion of Greece, with the well-known phrase, 'this radio will no longer be Greek' (Mpintelas, 2009). During the war, the only radio station allowed to broadcast was the radio station of Athens, under strong censorship rules (Zaharopoulos, 2002), although many listeners continued to stay tuned to European stations and especially the radio station of London (Mpintelas, 2009). After the war, the Greek state established the Hellenic Radio Foundation (EIR) according to a new legal framework (Zaharopoulos, 2002). During the civil war, there were many stations set up by the armed forces, while the US Pentagon assisted in the establishment of the Central Radio Station for the Greek Armed Forces in 1949 (Zaharopoulos, 2002). Later the US Pentagon supported the government with the foundation of two more radio stations whose aim was to inform society about the 'Communist peril' (Zaharopoulos, 2002). In 1952, EIR established a new service called the 'Second Programme', and two years later, in 1954, the 'Third Programme',[4] both of which were the subject of strong censorship (Zaharopoulos, 2002). By 1961 there were already five private radio stations, twelve EIR stations and twelve stations of the Armed Forces (Zaharopoulos, 2002). During the Colonels' dictatorship, which started in 1967, the EIR building was seized by the military and was forced to broadcast the programme of the Armed Forces Channels (Doulkeri & Terzis, 1997, p. 118). In

[3]Decades later Voulpiotis was accused of links with the Nazis and his role during the war was examined, while he was also accused of involvement in the first case of state corruption and Siemens (Papadimitriou, 2013). Almost a century later, another scandal of corruption between the Greek state and Siemens would end in court too (Papadimitriou, 2013).

[4]The First Programme of EIR focused on broadcasting news, educational programmes or programmes related to fine arts and it didn't broadcast any advertisements, while the Second Programme was more commercial, broadcasting popular music. The Third Programme broadcast classical music and programmes related to the arts (Zaharopoulos, 2002).

1968, the military services created the Armed Forces Information Service (YENED), which controlled the Armed Forces Channels, while a year later, in 1969, the first national television channel[5] and the state-run EIR started broadcasting regular television programmes.

The fall of the dictatorship in 1974 was followed by changes to the Constitution (1975) which defined the role and nature of public television and radio, transforming EIRT to ERT (Hellenic Radio Television) (Doulkeri & Terzis, 1997, p. 119). Under the new regulations, television and radio was required to be 'under the immediate control of the state' and should be 'assured in consideration to the social mission and the cultural development of the country' through the objective transmission of information, news, literature and art', and therefore, no commercial broadcasting was allowed (Doulkeri & Terzis, 1997, p. 119). In 1978, YENED merged with ERT and a few years later, in 1982, YENED transformed to ET-2, while ERT was transformed to ET-1 (Doulkeri & Terzis, 1997, p. 119).

The socialist government of PASOK and its concept of modernisation and 'change' were not translated into significant changes in the media sector. In 1987, ERT was recognised as a public company based on the example of the BBC, having two television channels and six radio stations. In 1989, the third channel of ERT, ET-3, started to broadcast based in northern Greece (Papathanassopoulos, 1990, p. 393). In the same year, the changes in the legal framework relating to media allowed the creation of private radio stations, creating the proper conditions for the deregulation and privatisation of television too (Doulkeri & Terzis, 1997, p. 120). Before the elections of 1989, the government set up an inter-parliamentary commission responsible for analysing the feasibility of the private television stations (Papathanassopoulos, 1990, p. 394), a debate still strong until today. After the elections of 1989, the concept of the 'free market' dominated the political landscape completing the full deregulation and privatisation of the media sector, which could also be understood as a late response to the European development of the media industry (Petrakis, 1999). The coalition government of New Democracy and Coalition of the Left changed the legal framework again, allowing the development of commercial TV stations, while at the same time the National Broadcasting Council (NBC), an institution that would help the state to control and regulate the commercial media sector, was also founded (Doulkeri & Terzis, 1997).

While the privatisation of the media sector was a turning point for Greek society and the Greek political environment, it was conducted based on an insufficient legal framework, which is still not clearly enacted. Petrakis (1999) suggests that the development of the Greek media sector has many similarities with the media sector in Italy, which developed a decade earlier during the 1970s and 1980s. He also observes some similarities with the Turkish media sector, as the

---

[5]The first television programme was an experimental programme which intended to advertise the products of the Thessaloniki International Fair (Zaharopoulos, 2002).

poor legal framework and the limitations on the market resulted in a chaotic media sector similar to the case of Greece. In less than a decade, the media market, which consisted of two television channels and four radio stations, turned into an overcrowded market of 160 private channels and 1,200 radio stations, with the press developing in a similar way (Papathanassopoulos, 1999). The Greek media sector was enlarged based on private interest, which was strongly associated with politics and the state, indicating both the vulnerabilities of the mainstream media as well as the extent of corruption. Investors and businessmen, including shipping tycoons, were strategically involved in the media sector as a method of gaining political and economic power (Doulkeri & Terzis, 1997). The issue of cross-ownership has come under question and criticism, since the early stages of the growth of the Greek media sector until the present day, and there have been several attempts at the foundation of a regulatory framework which will protect media from turning into a tool of political pressure (Doulkeri & Terzis, 1997).

The background of the public media sector, as well as the inaccurate regulation upon which the private media developed, indicated notable limitations and dilutions about the potential of media features. Public television was marked by political patronage (Doulkeri & Terzis, 1997, p. 124) while the deregulation by the state's monopoly of media was shaped by political circumstances and private groups' pressure, creating an 'ill-planned' deregulation[6] (Papathanassopoulos, 1990, p. 396). At the same time, radio, newspapers and the press developed under in the same way as television[7] (Sims, 2003, p. 213). Up to the present day, the issue of ownership and its relationship to the sociopolitical structures of Greece has been a thorny politico-economic issue. After the end of the state's monopoly of the media, the sector continued to be monopolised by businessmen or well-financed investors (Kelly, Mazzoleni, & McQuail, 2004, p. 92) who, in most cases, were related to the most integral industries of the Greek economy (e.g. shipping, etc.). Whether this helped or not with the democratisation of the media, or pluralism, should be a question not only with regard to the

[6]However, the audience positively accepted the changes in the media sector and this is indicated by the fact that one of the first private channels, Mega Channel, has attracted 36% of the audience in contrast to ET-1 with 26% and ET-2 with 11% in the first week of its broadcasting (Doulkeri and Terzis, 1997: 124). The first wave of private TV stations (e.g. Mega Channel, Ant1, Skai) earned 77%–79% of the market share, while at the same time all the three TV stations (ET-1, ET-2, and ET-3) of the Hellenic Broadcasting Corporation, which belonged to the public sector, could not claim more than 7%–9% (Petrakis, 1999). In 1996, private television claimed 95% of the audience and 95% of the advertising revenue (Doulkeri and Terzakis, 1997, p. 124) indicating the necessity for structural changes in public television.

[7]Sims, analysing the development of radio, explains that the media market could accommodate only a certain number of radio stations, and similarly, newspapers, TV stations or magazines, and the creation of such an overcrowded market was not translated into pluralism, nor did it allow for the development of pluralism either (Sims, 2003, p. 213).

development of the media in Greece but, additionally, in relation to the contemporary media sector as well.

After the deregulation of media and the development of an ill-planned sector, the Greek government had several attempts at regulating the sector; in 2001, the Greek government decided to close 70 radio stations in Athens, due to the opening of the new airport in Athens[8]; in 2013, it closed ERT, and in 2016, it organised a licence auction too. Very often these attempts were also accompanied by or contributed to various political conflicts and goals. In most cases these bumbling attempts failed, highlighting the vulnerable relationship between the media and the state, as well as questions of corruption. After 2008, the development of the internet in juxtaposition to the outbreak of the Greek crisis dramatically affected the media sector. Similar to other countries, the development of the internet in Greece had a typical impact on the traditional mass media, shrinking the already existing market and creating a new one. This procedure was also influenced by the unique characteristics of the Greek mediascape as this was shaped by the relationship between investors, politicians and market characteristics.

In 2013, the financial and political crisis had already influenced every business sector and the market, while the internet had started demonstrating multiple usages that this medium could have within the Greek crisis context (e.g. independent media initiatives, etc.). At the same time, while the crisis was at its peak, the ND government was working on the development of a 'success story' narration (Enikos.gr, 2013). In this context, the closure of the Public Broadcast Corporation (ERT) was announced as a brave political decision against corruption or, according to the spokesman and deputy-minister responsible for the media, against a 'typical example of a unique lack of transparency' and a 'heaven of waste' (Iosifidis, 2013). The sudden and violent closure of ERT was primarily a political decision having a strong symbolism, which illustrated the impact of austerity in the country (Simcox, 2013) as well as the potentiality and multiple uses of digital media in the Greek crisis context.

Civil society and political groups responded to ERT's shutdown spontaneously and filled the gap immediately after the announcement of the closure, both

---

[8]In 2001, approximately 100 radio stations were broadcasting in Athens, many of which were operating without licences. Due to the opening of the new airport in Athens, the Greek government decided to shut down 70 radio stations, with special police teams and SWAT teams supporting the procedure (Sims, 2003, p. 202). Research suggest that this occasion could have been a starting point for the reorganisation of the chaotic media market but, in contrast, the outcome of this procedure was to emerge from a new game, with a new balance in the relationship between politicians and media investors (Sims, 2003: 203). Additionally, while the issue of pluralism has been constantly debated in Greek media history, the closure of more than half the radio stations in Athens, was a shock both for pluralism and freedom of expression; 'pluralism is not something that comes from God; it is something that one has to earn and work at to create and preserve' (Kalafti interview; Sims, 2003, p. 203).

online and offline. Solidarity networks at national and international level supported the organisation of events at the ERT courtyard, while independent media initiatives as well as the mainstream institutions, such as EBU, continued broadcasting online months after the closure (Clarke, Huliaras, & Sotiropoulos, 2016). ND founded NERIT, replacing ERT (Iosifidis & Boucas, 2015), which broadcasted parallel to the ex-ERT employees who occupied the headquarters and continued to broadcast online with the support of EBU and different alternative Greek online media initiatives (e.g. websites, news-portals, etc) until they were evicted by riot police months after the closure of ERT (Nikolaidis, 2017). Later, ERT kept broadcasting from a different location, adapting social movement practices (Iosifidis & Boucas, 2015). During that period SYRIZA, which was then the political opposition, did not recognise NERIT and strongly supported the ERT ex-employees' initiative (Iosifidis & Boucas, 2015). Months after coming to power, in April 2015, SYRIZA reopened ERT, merging it with NERIT (Iosifidis & Boucas, 2015).

The ERT shutdown was seen as having a significant impact on media pluralism, and as a result in 2015 Greece was among the two lowest EU ranked countries in World Press Freedom. During the crisis Greece fell by lost 56 places in the rankings (Nikolaidis, 2017). The ERT shutdown had a significant impact on the transition to Digital Terrestrial Television, which after the ERT closure was organised via Digea involving a few large private media organisations, raising concerns about media pluralism and democracy (Iosifidis, 2016). Indicative of the crisis impact on the Greek media sector is a survey from the Pew Research Center which found the Greek media to be the most inaccurate among the 38 countries that were examined (Mitchell, Simmons, Matsa, & Silver, 2018).

In 2016, the SYRIZA–AN.EL. coalition government tried to regulate the broadcasting sector concentrating on the legal/regulatory framework under which the TV licences should be formally be distributed. After a long discussion regarding the number of licences that would viable to be distributed, the government launched a broadcast licence auction for four licences (Sweney, 2016). The proposed media law proposed transparency of the media sector and ownership, which was dominated by shipowners and a construction mogul and delivered profits of over £210 m (Sweney, 2016.). Among the various stages through which this auction was completed was the review of media conglomerates and their association with public and private interests, including sports, as well as a detailed review of the loans received by banks before and during the crisis. However, this was considered to be a very controversial procedure, which was later deemed unconstitutional, with the highest court blocking the proposed media law (Financial Times, 2016). In January 2018, SYRIZA continued its attempt to regulate the broadcasting sector and the National Council for Radio and Television (NCRT) accepted applications from six media groups (Reuters, 2018).

The crisis strongly affected the media sector by bringing to the spotlight vulnerabilities and limitations which existed for decades but now resulted in a crisis of the media sector. The transition of the mainstream/traditional mediascape to the digital media environment indicated new opportunities for communication and the opportunity for the re-identification of the relationship between media, society and the state. Thus, it is important to examine the way that new/online media appeared and were associated with the sociopolitical structures in Greece, especially as these were shaped after 2008 and the development of digital communications.

The Development of New and Online Media: 2002–2015

The vulnerabilities and limitations of the Greek mediascape, including power relations between media, big business and politics weakened trust in traditional media (Mitchell et al., 2018). During the crisis, the Greek media sector shrank, the reliability of the traditional media was further disputed while at the same time the growth of digital media communication completely remapped the media environment. In 2017, Greece was the country with the highest rates of trust in social media for news, and also, the country with the lowest trust in traditional media (Newman, Fletcher, Kalogeropoulos, Levy, & Kleis Nielsen, 2017).

The evolution of Greek digital communication followed the EU example, which was diversified by the special characteristics and the limitations of the Greek context. Since the early days of growth of digital media communications in Greece, their association to the political and social turmoil was significant. One of the first examples arose in 2007, when political blogging and SMS (Short Message Service) started being used for the organisation of mobilisations (Mylona, 2008) while later social media was used as new 'political weapons' by both mainstream and non-mainstream political actors and organisations (Mylonas, 2014). Digital communications supported traditional forms of activism (Mowbray, 2010; Vatikiotis, 2011) and contributed to the emergence of contemporary manifestations of activism such as cyber-activism (Karamichas, 2009; Tsaliki, 2010). The wave of protest and social movements which emerged during the global recession pointed out the significant contribution of digital media within the development of contemporary social movements on a global scale. The case of Greece is examined in this context of global recession and the wave of contemporary movements and protest (e.g. M15, Occupy Movement) as this developed after 2008 (Manolopoulos, 2011).

The National Statistical Service of Greece (EL.STAT.) and the Observatory for Digital Greece (ODG) extensively researched the growth of the internet in Greece and compared the Greek case to digital communications in Europe. Looking at the period 2002–2015, the growth of the internet and the use of computers rapidly increased, especially after 2006–2007 when there is an increase in the use of internet and computer access for the population aged 16–74 (EL.STAT., 2014, p. 3) (Table 3.2).

According to EL.STAT., the population aged 16–74 who used a computer rose from 24.1% in 2002 to 66.6% in 2015, while at the same time Internet access rose from 14.7% in 2002 to 66.8% in 2015. The rapid growth of the Internet and computer access as observed after 2006–2008 is closely linked to the escalation

Table 3.2. Internet Access and Computer Usage in Greece 2002–2015.

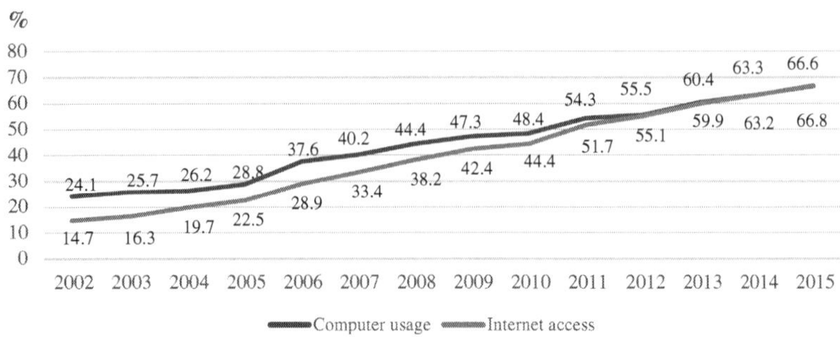

Source: Data by EL.STAT. – National Statistical Service of Greece – Hellenic Statistical Authority, 2014, p. 3.

Table 3.3. Household/Internet Access and Broadband Connections in Greece 2004–2012.

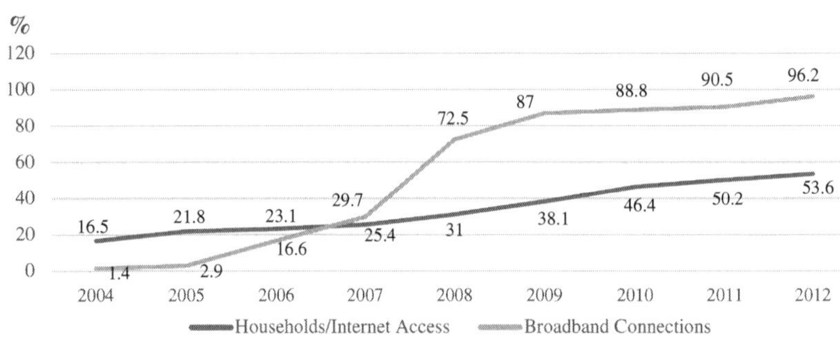

Source: Data by EL.STAT. – National Statistical Service of Greece – Hellenic Statistical Authority, 2014, p. 5.

of the digital media market in Greece, the growth of broadband services, as well as changes in cost, which until 2007 had been significantly high (Table 3.3).

Alongside the problems and limitations of traditional media, the rapid increase of broadband connections after 2007 contributed to the emergence of a new space for communication which had a significant impact on politics, on the formation of the public sphere and to an extent, on the organisation of protests and mobilisations. Some of the most significant examples in the Greek case arose with the so-called Wildfire protests in 2007 and, a year later, with the December riots of 2008. The impact of the growth of digital media on traditional media, communications and protests is not a Greek phenomenon, however, in the case of Greece, that the development of digital media was strongly influenced by the so-called crisis.

According to Maniadakis and Kountrias (2006), there are two major limitations on the evolution of digital media in Greece. The first one focuses on the users and the second on the broadband providers. Some of the main restrictions on the growth of broadband were both the high cost of broadband infrastructures and internet connections and also the limited access to broadband services and infrastructures (Maniadakis and Kountrias, 2006). On the other hand, similar to traditional media, the disadvantages, which were caused by the provider's limitations, were related to the insufficient regulatory framework, to the oligopolistic media market, the deficient support provided by the Hellenic Telecommunications Organisation (OTE), as well as the geographical characteristics of Greece (Maniadakis and Kountrias, 2006). Many of these disadvantages and limitations were overcome, contributing to the rapid evolution of broadband after 2008, while, at the same time, during 2002–2013 there were significant changes both in traditional media, the field of digital communications and the relationship between Greek society and technology. However, even if these changes followed the EU pattern, and despite the technological gap between the EU and Greece, the digital communications in Greece grew by replicating the concept and structure of the EU example (Table 3.4).

While these help us to understand how digital media developed in Greece in comparison to the rest of the EU, it is necessary to go a step further and look at users' profiles and characteristics, understanding how these shaped the use of the internet by different users and groups. During the period 2005–2008 the population accessing the internet was comprised 37% of female and 51% of male users. (Observatory for Digital Greece – ODG, 2010, p. 19). According to EL.STAT. (2010, 2013) the population aged 16–74, using the internet during the period 2008–2013 was comprised 56.4% of female and 63.5% of male users. Similar to the EU, there were no significant gender differences in the use of the internet in

Table 3.4. Percentage of Households with Internet Access at Home: EU – Greece.

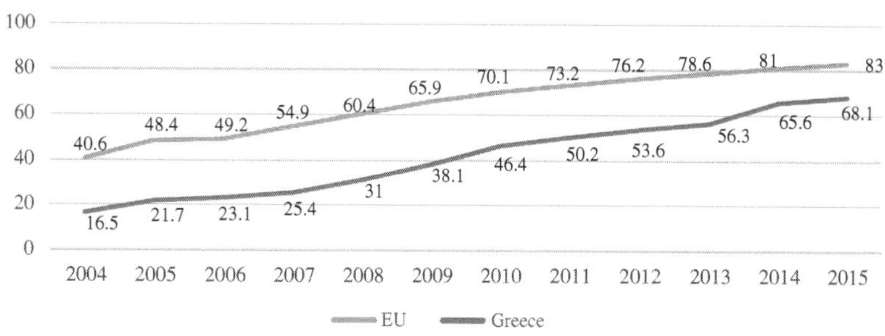

Source: Data by EU Commission, Digital Agenda for Europe, 2017; Eurostat, n.d..

Greece, although what is interesting is the increase in female users between 2008 and 2009, and the decrease in male users between 2009 and 2013. In 2008, the population aged 16–74, using the internet comprised by 38% of female users and 46.9% of male users whine a year later, in 2009 there were 57.8% female users and 49% male users (EL.STAT., 2010; 2015; ODG, 2010).

Age is another important factor regarding the use of the internet and social engagement. It is indicative that in 2015, more than 93% of the population aged 16–34 used the internet, while, similar, 88.3% of the population aged 35–44%. In contrast, 68.1% of the population aged 45–54 used the internet 40% of the population aged 55–64, and 12.5% of the population aged 64–74, 12.5% (EL. STAT., 2015). Alongside age, education is another important factor which contributes to the so-called 'e-exclusion' or the digital divide (EL.STAT., 2013; 2015, p. 5). It is indicative that 90.6% of the population who had a higher education was using the internet, in contrast to the 69.9% of the population which had an upper-secondary education and 24.8% with primary, lower, and secondary education. Most of the users, regardless of gender, age or education use the internet on a daily basis (EL.STAT., 2014, p. 4).

In 2013 more than three out of four users had low or average skills related to internet technology (EL.STAT., 2013, p. 8), while there was a balanced relationship between gender and internet skills. Other important factors that influence internet usage and the users' profiles include income rating and the employment sector. As regards the users' skills, almost all the users are able to search online for information (98%), while most can send emails and attach files (74.1%), participate in chat rooms and social media (61.1%), and use services such as Skype (53.8%) (EL.STAT., 2013). Fewer users choose to use peer-to-peer services for movies or music (18.3%), to create websites (11.8%), upload photographs, movies or music (38.6%), and to manage privacy settings on browsers (21.9%) (EL. STAT., 2013, pp. 7–8). Data from 2015 indicate that 85% of the users accessed the internet to read newspapers and magazines, while 80% of the users accessed the internet to search for information about products and services (EL.STAT., 2015, p. 9). The next most important reason why users go online is to access social media platforms (65.7%) and to send emails (77.1%) (EL.STAT., 2015, p. 9).

The technological advancements, such as the invention of smartphones, tablets and so on, provide further opportunities for internet access, highlighting the social aspects and the potential of internet features. Accordingly, users accessed the internet for communication reasons, using various methods and technological advantages[9] (EL.STAT., 2015, p. 6), while internet access using

[9]Search information for products and services: 80.4%; reading online news in websites, newspapers, magazines: 85.4%; email: 77.1%; social media (Facebook, Twitter, etc.): 65.7%; search information related to health issues, diseases, diet, etc.: 55.7%; online communication using webcam (Skype, etc.): 44%; usage of services related to travelling and hotels: 31.2%; searching or applying for job: 26.6%; downloading software (not including games): 22.2%; online banking: 20.8%; and sale products (e-bay, etc.): 5.1%.

Table 3.5. Social Media Platforms Use (2012–2013).

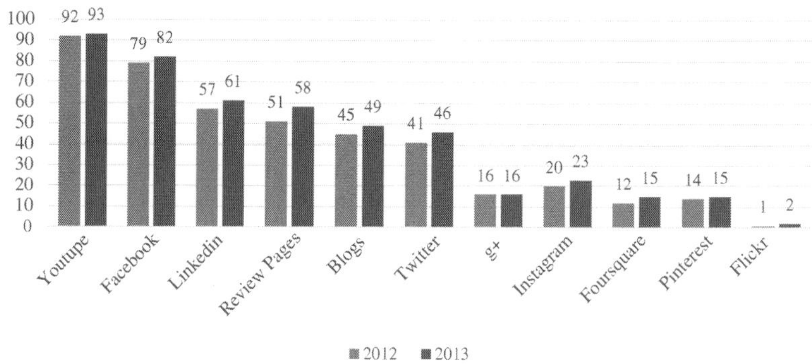

Source: ELTRUN (2014).

mobile devices during the period 2010–2015, rapidly increased (EL.STAT., 2015, p. 5). In 2010, 15.1% of the population using the internet was also accessing the internet from mobile devices, while in 2015 that increased to 66.4%.[10]

After the invention of the World Wide Web (WWW) in 1991, Web 2.0 was characterised by the evolution of social media platforms (Dijck, 2013, p. 5). In the late 1990s and early 2000s the first social media platforms were founded including Blogger in 1999 and Wikipedia in 2001 (Dijck, 2013, p. 7). Later, Myspace in 2003, Facebook in 2004, YouTube in 2005 and Twitter in 2006 shaped the social web and the ecosystem of connectivity as it is known today (Dijck, 2013, p. 7). While there is limited research relating to the popularity of social media platforms in Greece, research by EL.STAT. (2015) and the E-business Research Centre, Athens University of Economics and Research (ELTRUN, 2014; Fraidaki & Pramatari, 2013) indicate some interesting points regarding the popularity and characteristics of social media platforms, as shown in Table 3.5 for the period 2012–2013.

In 2012, the online population using Facebook is estimated to have been 77.29% or 3,898,360 unique users (Fraidaki & Pramatari, 2013), while the Twitter unique users are estimated to be 210,000, a year later rising to 503,975 (Fraidaki & Pramatari, 2013). Social media platforms were used mainly by people of younger ages, reflecting the issue of the digital divide and the adoption of technology by different age groups.[11] In 2015, almost 90% of the population

[10]Year: population accessing the internet through mobile devices; 2010: 15.1%; 2011: 26.4%; 2012: 40.9; 2013: 44.7%; 2014: 58.4; 2015: 66.4% (EL.STAT., 2015).

[11]Use of Social Media platforms by different ages groups (EL.STAT. 2015, p. 6). Age group: % General Public using social media platforms. 14–24: 87.5%; 25–34: 73.1%; 35–44: 51.8%; 45–54: 33.5%; 55–64: 16.8%; 65–74: 3.7% (EL.STAT., 2015).

aged 14–24 of the general public used social media platforms, while that falls to the 50% at the ages between 35–44 (EL.STAT, 2015). Following the internet usage trends, social media use was shaped according to the factors of age, gender, education and so on, which though, had a stronger impact on shaping the profile of the social media platforms users. In 2012, social media platforms were used mainly by users having higher education. YouTube and Facebook were the most popular social media platforms in Greece during June to December 2013, as 63.7% of the users had accessed at least once the YouTube and 51% had accessed at least once Facebook (FocusBari.gr., 2015). The next most popular social media platform is Twitter, with 7.5% of the users having access at least once the platform, while Blogs and LinkedIn are following with 3.5% and 3% (FocusBari.gr., 2015).

As regards the users' profiles, there is a fairly balanced relationship between participation in social media platforms and gender, with men being slightly more active. Users with higher education were double the number of users with only primary education. Age is an important characteristic, while the technological gap again being significant, with 96.4% of the social media platform users being between 13 and 24 years old and only 34.1% of the participants being between 45 and 70 years old. Social media platforms are more popular in the urban areas of Greece in contrast to rural areas. In more detail, in 2013, users' profiles can be illustrated as follows (Table 3.6).

At the same time, each social media platform attracted users with different characteristics. Starting with YouTube, users were equal males (52.7%) and females (47.3%), in the age range 25–44 (48.5%), living in Athens (48.1%). These characteristics are justified recognising that YouTube was among the first social media platforms to become popular in Greece, accessible via other social media platforms too. While the age group 13–24 became the most active group in the usage of social media platforms, the group 25–44 is very familiar with

Table 3.6. Users Profiles – Usage of at Least One Social Media Platforms in the Last Six Months (6–12/2013).

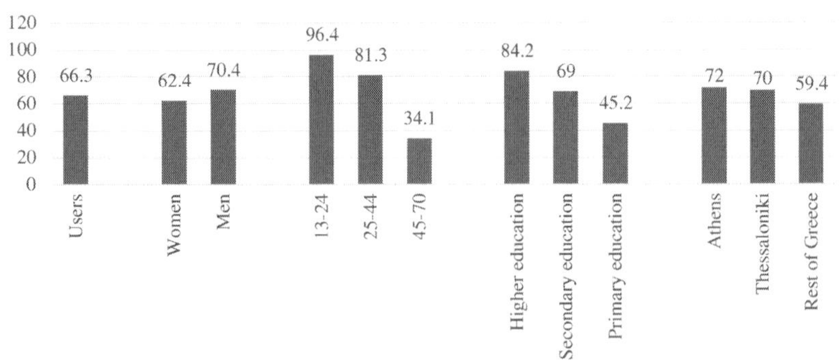

Source: FocusBari.gr. (2015).

YouTube, as it was one of the first social media platforms to become popular in Greece and this was the first generation of users that used social media. An interesting point of consideration is the geographical characteristics and differences between usage in Athens and other urban centres.

The average Facebook user was male (52.2%) or female (47.8%), in the age group 25–44 (48.6%), with secondary (33.8%) or higher (41.2%) education, living in Athens (48.3%). Once again, the low usage of the platform in other urban centres is interesting, and it reflected the YouTube example as well as global trends regarding Facebook usage. The average user of Twitter was male (69.6%), in the age range 13–24 (40.4%) or 25–44 (37.3%), with higher education (55.7%) and living in Athens (61.4%). An interesting point here is that this platform indicated a more balanced usage by different age groups (Table 3.7).

Blogs were among the first media platforms that became popular in Greece. The multiple usages of blogs for professional, personal or educational purposes explains the relationship between age groups and blog usage, while this relationship is also explained by the linkage between other social media platforms and the usage of blogs too. LinkedIn is a social media platform, which is used mainly for professional or business purposes. Therefore, it is not surprising that the users are mainly between 25 and 44 (67.1%), with higher education (87.4%) and living in Athens (75.7%) (Table 3.8).

Digital communications in Greece evolved later than those in the rest of the EU; however, Greece adopted digital media communication in a very similar way, indicating common characteristics in terms of the online participation and the users' profiles. These characteristics should be understood both in comparison to the EU as well as situated in the Greek social and political context and the broader Greek media environment.

After reviewing the basic characteristics of the evolution of digital media in Greece, an important point here is to understand the way that digital media is associated with the Greek political environment and the emergence of contemporary social movements.

Table 3.7. YouTube, Facebook and Twitter – 2013 Greek Users' Profiles.

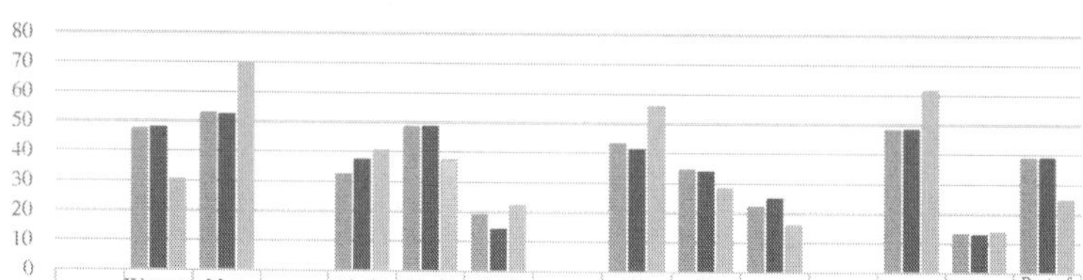

	Women	Men	13–24	25–44	45–70	HE	SE	PE	Athens	Thes.	Rest of Greece
YouTube	47.3	52.7	32.5	48.5	19	43.3	34.5	22.2	48.1	13.4	38.8
Facebook	47.8	52.2	37.3	48.6	14.1	41.2	33.8	24.9	48.3	12.9	38.8
Twitter	30.4	69.6	40.4	37.3	22.3	55.7	28.2	16	61.4	13.8	24.8

YouTube Facebook Twitter

Source: FocusBari.gr. (2015).

Table 3.8. Blogs and LinkedIn – 2013, Greek Users' profiles.

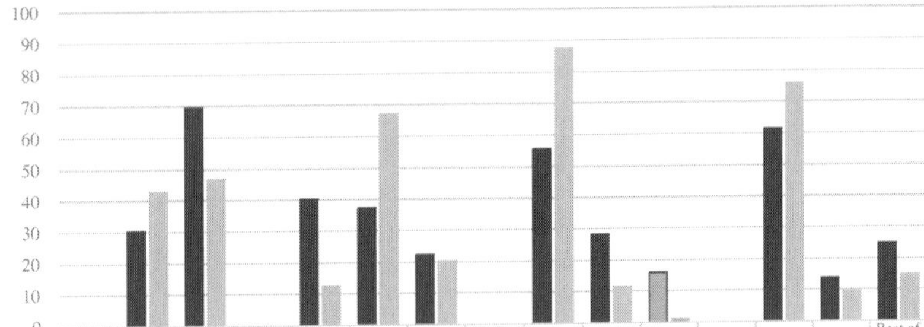

	Women	Men	13–24	25–44	45–70	HE	SE	PE	Athens	Thes.	Rest of Greece
Blogs	30.4	69.6	40.4	37.3	22.3	55.7	28.2	16	61.4	13.8	24.8
LinkedIn	43.1	46.9	12.6	67.1	20.3	87.4	11.4	1.2	75.7	9.5	14.8

Source: FocusBari.gr. (2015).

Digital Communications, Digital Activism and Greek Political Environment: The 2007 Mobilisations

The growth of digital media provided a new tool for political communication, supporting direct and interactive communication at a minimum cost (Mylona, 2008, p. 284). In Greece, parties of the left were among the first to use this new tool. SYNASPISMOS, later transformed into SYRIZA, started running a website in 1997, while PASOK followed in 1999. ND was one of the first political parties in Greece supported by professionals for both the creation and updating of its website and other online communication (Mylona, 2008). Until the 2000 elections, only 16 out of the 35 participating political parties operated websites, while most of the politicians participating in the elections were not familiar with internet technology (Mylona, 2008).

In 2004, political parties extensively used the Short Messages Service (SMS) technology, promoting their political campaigns for the European Parliament Elections (Mylona, 2008, p. 292). Mylona (2008) explains that while internet technology and the use of websites provide an opportunity for interaction, SMS provided only one-direction communication and didn't support the creation of dialogue and, therefore, political parties were more sceptical about using it. While the issues of participation and interaction are important, the digital divide is also very relevant especially taking into consideration the profile of the Greek users during the early 2000s and, most importantly, the profile of the voters. In contrast, the use of online media by different age groups and its use for different political purposes indicated the potential of the medium on the emergence of contemporary social movements and collective action in the Greek context. Digital communications in Greece provided an important alternative for political engagement, overcoming the limitations having arisen due to the characteristics of the politics and mediascape in Greece.

One of the first examples which indicated the potential of digital media in Greece was the 2007 mobilisations following the wildfires in Parnitha and across Greece. As Tsaliki noted, this was the first time in Greece that parallel to the formal political culture, an informal one emerged and was expressed online (2010, p. 154). During that period, the media environment was characterised by a 'low standard of political dialogue' (Tsaliki, 2010, p. 153), which resulted in limited programmes having political content and the rapid increase of the so-called 'celebrity culture' and shows (Tsaliki, 2010, p. 153). The 2007 mobilisations, which emerged due to environmental issues (Karamichas, 2009), highlighted that online media was indeed able to provide a parallel space of political engagement which also had a strong impact on the formation of the public sphere, online and offline. In these circumstances[12], the mobilisations of 2007 had a significant importance concentrating both on online media as well as on the reconsideration of the concept of environmentalism and its linkage to society and politics. In Karamichas' words, during that period, 'a new societal approach to the environmental issue' (2007, p. 525) emerged.

Already, before the 2007 wildfire mobilisations, some of the first protests with an environmental interest had taken place earlier in the same year when local authorities and citizens mobilised against business operations in the coastal zone of Athens (Helliniko and Moschato) demanding free access to the area (Karamichas, 2007, p. 526). Mainstream media covered the issue presenting a public debate with environmental and socio-political characteristics, and also when, months later, a fire broke out on mount Parnitha, a national park in Athens, on 26th of June. The catastrophe of Parnitha was described as 'one of the worst environmental national disasters' (BBC News, 2007). Parnitha lost 80% of its fauna and flora (Tsaliki, 2010, p. 155), which included 10,500 acres of forest land (Karamichas, 2007, p. 528). A few days later (2–3/6/2007) an SMS started to circulate among citizens of Athens and soon transferred to the web and the online community, through blogs, emails and social media (Tsaliki, 2010, p. 155): 'On Sunday 8 July, let's all gather outside the Parliament and demand the immediate reforestation of Parnitha. No more charred land. Do not stay "uninvolved".'

The way that this 'mobile protest' began is unclear. According to the press, an anonymous 25-year-old started it off by sending an SMS to his friends (Tsaliki, 2010), while, for others, the protest was called by a post on some blogs and continued to be circulated through SMS and emails (Karamichas, 2007, p. 528). The mobilisations began with a preparatory meeting, which was organised by bloggers, in Syntagma Square discussing how the SMS created a

[12]Focusing on citizens' participation in NGOs, Karamichas (2007, p. 524) emphasises the singularity of the Greek case, explaining that the quantitative indicators (e.g. membership of NGO or civic associations) do not effectively reflect the informal civic society, which is constituted by spontaneous and radical actions in times of crisis. At the same time, the political representation of environmentalism is not intensive and in most cases, it has a minor position on political agendas.

'snowball effect' both online and offline (Tsaliki, 2010, pp. 154–155). This was a new phenomenon and the first case in which the new and online technology was significant, resulting in the organisation of two street protests in the city centre of Athens. In the first protest, there were between 5,000 and 10,000 protestors (Karamichas 2007, p. 528) gathered in Syntagma Square who peacefully protested for a common interest, 'regardless of age, social class, or political orientation' (Tsaliki, 2010, p. 155). After Parnitha, wildfires broke out across several rural areas of Greece, including the Peloponnese, Euboea and others, destroying 'more than 1 million hectares of forests and arable land, along with thousands of buildings leaving some 77-people dead' and thousands homeless (Michaletos, n.d.). The wildfire of 2007 resulted in a national disaster which dramatically damaged the 'social, economic and environmental life of the country for years to come' (Tsaliki, 2010, p. 156).

Similarly to the Parnitha protests, a new message started circulating among citizens through new and online technology: 'You let Greece burn to the ground, why?' (Tsaliki, 2010, p. 156). The blog 'anadasosi', which was intensively active and supported the 2007 mobilisations, created a post/message calling for a new protest (Tsaliki, 2010, p. 156). An online poster encouraged the online community to forward the message through SMS, blogs, emails, via website banners or even offline, by printing and passing it around. The participation in this protest is estimated to have approached 10,000 people (Tsaliki, 2010).

The aftermath of these protests was that the potential of new and online technology had been illustrated, highlighting the opportunity for participation and autonomous public engagement, while at the same time, the mainstream media vulnerabilities were pointed out too. The protests of 2007 were organised independently and not by political parties and the only common characteristic of the protestors was their interest in the environmental disaster. The incidents following the protests of 2007 could not be considered as being straightforwardly related to each other in terms of causes, motivation or general context. However, the usage of new/online media and their features, as well as the different ways they were used each time, create an insight into the potential of the medium per se and its influence on the ideology, organisation, mobilisation, political opportunity structure, media representation and evolution of online conflict.

After providing an in-depth understanding of the historical political context and the political economy of media and communications in Greece, the study proceeds to analyse the key platforms for Greek mobilisations during the period 2008–2015. Although this might seem an excessive and long chapter, without it, it would have been impossible for me, or readers not familiar with the Greek context, to be able to grapple with the historical and political continuities evident in the polarised hybrid (digital and offline) environment of this period.

Chapter 4

Digital Research Methods, Techniques and Sampling

This chapter offers a rationale for the research design, the sampling rationale, in terms of timeline and empirical cases, as well as the analytical and computational tools based on which the examination of the selected online platforms and events, developed. A more detailed discussion of the research methods and techniques used for each of the examined platforms is provided at the beginning of each chapter of the examined case. Finally, a timeline of the evolution of the crisis and social media in Greece is provided.

The study of the Greek digital media begins with a review of the sociopolitical and historical background of Greece. Then, the study concentrates on the identification of sociopolitical and ethnoreligious cyberconflict/turmoil as observed online and then, linking back to the historical background, in association with the offline world. The identification and the analysis of cyberconflict developed via the collection and the analysis of online data from various digital and social media platforms (Indymedia, YouTube, Facebook, Twitter), comprising the empirical part of the study. The different characteristics of the online data collected from different platforms (Indymedia, YouTube, Facebook, Twitter) didn't allow the use of one tool of data collection and only one analytical approach. Instead, the research formulated and exploited a complex research design. The collection and the analysis of the online data were conducted using different analytical tools and a number of open-source software and apps.

The study of digital media on the Greek crisis-era conducted through the analysis of major cycles of protests and mobilisations as emerged in the crisis context. The study starts by looking at 2008, a year that was significant both in terms of the evolution of social movements and the expansion of digital media in Greece, signifying the beginning of the global recession. Therefore, the study concentrated on the early phase of the crisis 2008–2012, which was characterised by street politics and the mobilisations, and then it focused on the period between 2012 and 2015, which was characterised by the restructuring of the political system, the rise of the Golden Dawn and the SYRIZA era (referendum, double elections of 2015), leading, chronologically, to the refugee crisis that emerged and shaped by the already existing sociopolitical debates. These phases studied by the collection and the analysis of online material concentrating on the so-called December Riots and on the anti-austerity mobilisations (radical politics, austerity and street politics), which were straightforwardly related to solidarity networks and initiatives, and the referendum era.

The empirical analysis of cyberconflict concentrated on the examination of networks and discourse. The study conducted with the use of open-source software and tools (Netvizz, NodeXL, Gephi, NCapture) as well as packages such as NVivo, for both the collection, the analysis and the visualisation of online data, developing an insight into the examined platforms. The collection of the data began with the examination of Indymedia and YouTube, while later developing a focus both on Facebook and Twitter, the two most popular social media platforms in Greece. The examination of Indymedia and YouTube provided the base for an understanding of the already existing sociopolitical debates before the rapid growth of the crisis. Then, online networks (Facebook, Twitter) and discourse (Twitter) indicated social relations and structures, online coalitions, dominant actors/sets of actors and meanings, as well as additional relationships, which link the online conflict to the offline.

Thematic (Indymedia, YouTube) and Semantic (Twitter) analysis supported the examination of meaning and discourse, while Social Network Analysis (SNA) (Facebook, Twitter) is suggested as an efficient approach for the analysis and the investigation of 'kinship patterns, community structure, interlocking directorships and so forth' (Scott, 2000, p. 2). SNA provides a 'precise way to define important social concepts, a theoretical alternative to the assumption of independent social actors, and a framework for testing theories about structured social relationships' (Wasserman & Faust, 1994, p. 17). While Facebook suggests a more organised procedure in terms of organisation and communication, Twitter develops an insight into the way that discourse bursts forth in a more spontaneous way, moulding more open networks, and its examination is completed through an understanding of the evolution of networks, hashtags and meanings (Gerbaudo, 2012). The understanding of networks and online relations, as well as the content of these networks in terms of discourse, supported the mapping of cyberconflict (sociopolitical, ethnoreligious) as it developed in the Greek crisis context. After the analysis of the corpus, the Internet as a medium was then evaluated, focusing both on its significant characteristics and its contribution to the examined events, completing the cyberconflict study of the case of Greece and elaborating the theoretical framework of cyberconflict.

The research aimed only to apply an already existing theoretical framework, carrying through an analysis of the Greek case, but instead, this project developed as an evaluation of how digital research methods might be possible, and, also might contribute to the application of the theoretical framework of cyberconflict. The project developed based on the idea of discourse and networks, as these can be identified and discussed focusing on different platforms. While this project does not provide the opportunity to include an extensive discussion of every possible usage of online data for identification of networks and discourse, examining all the existing digital media platforms, it still manages to provide schemes of research, which can be used for the development of more specialised projects. Cyberconflict in this project is not understood through the users' perspectives or primarily by focusing on literature, but instead, is identified and analysed through focus on the actual online material produced by users. As will be discussed at the end of this project, this was not only among the most important virtues of the project, but at the same time, it was also among its limitations.

Digital Research Methods

With the growth of Internet, digital research methods became a very popular tool for social science researchers, building upon the established modes of social science research. At the same time, digital research methods provided multiple options on researching the Internet, concentrating, among others, on media, culture and politics. Web-surveys, online interviews and focus groups or ethnographic approaches, were only some of the most dominant methods that illustrated the potentiality of digital research methods, in the early days of Internet (Snee, Hine, Morey, Roberts, & Watson, 2016). The development of social media revolutionised communication and pointed out the use and impact of Internet in the everyday life. At the same time, social media provided the opportunity for users to produce content and interact in a direct, real-time, way. At this stage, digital research methods appeared to be promising in terms of researching these new and very complex online communication systems, and the multi-platforms embedded in the Internet and everyday practices. That created new trends on research, and research methods, which now should be able to map the relation between the online and offline space by analysing various and new forms of data (Snee et al., 2016, p. 3).

Concentrating on the method discussed earlier, the adaptation of digital research methods on this research was a very innovative and challenging procedure. Looking back on the literature, there were many researches that discussed the Greek digital media and online media platforms in Greece (Afouxenidis, 2014; Karamichas, 2007; Kyriakopoulos, 2010; Milioni, 2009; Mylona, 2008; Papagiannidis, Coursaris, & Bourlakis, 2012; Theocharis, 2011), but only lately, researches started to use digital research methods approaches looking on networks' dynamics and discourse (Siapera & Veikou, 2016; Smyrnaios, 2015; Theocharis, Lowe, & Van Deth, 2014; Tsaliki, 2012; Vatikiotis, 2011). Therefore, for this study, the use of digital research methods is explored as another approach to investigating and understanding the Greek digital media. In this venture, digital research methods are used for all the examined platforms and periods, looking on networks and discourse, mapping the linkage between the online and offline space. As Rogers (2009) pointed out, mapping space is not only a way to understand cyberspace, but at the same time, is also a way to understand the various ways through which politics are reflected online.

However, digital research methods do not only provide endless options as regards the technical or practical adaptation and application, but at the same time, also indicate important limitations and dangers as regards the study and analysis of online data, which should not be understood as being objective or accurate, but instead, misleading (Boyd & Crawford, 2012). At the same time, there is a constant debate on the way that digital research methods can be combined with traditional methods, as well as an on-going discussion on software and applications that can support the study of different online material and social media platforms. This study developed taking into consideration these limitations and concerns. Following previous studies that employed the Cyberconflict theory, this study originally intended to be developed by conducting interviews and CDA, focusing on the non-fixed relation between digital and traditional research methods and the way that these two could fit and support the examination of cyberconflict through the study of networks and discourse. However, the specialisation and training required for digital research methods, as well as the various tools required for the study of different platforms did not allow the development of an even more complex methodology that would combine both traditional and digital research methods. After conducting and analszing some semi-structured interviews, as originally proposed for the study of cyberconflict, it was clear that the project should focus either on interviews and CDA or on social networks and discourse.

Taking into consideration that digital research methods have never been used for the examination of Cyberconflict and accepting that online data is not the answer to all the contemporary questions regarding digital media, still the experimentation with new research methods and the opportunity to explore the intersection of social networks and discourse was a very motivating procedure. Large-scale data-driven researches that concentrate on social media platforms might be driven by various questions on the impact of such platforms in communication; however, a response to such questions can be given by investigating short-term events 'within and beyond the social media platform itself' (Snee et al., 2016, p. 18). Therefore, this study is developed by the examination of short-term events, looking at three periods, and on various social media platforms. The study worked on the combination of digital research methods and the study of cyberconflict, aiming to develop an example for future researches. At the same time, taking this research as an example, a combination of traditional and digital research methods would be an interesting mix of methods for the study of cyberconflict in bigger and more extended research projects.

The use of digital research methods raised various theoretical and practical challenges, starting from methodological concerns, matters regading the use of computational and analytical tools, and ending up to concerns on the nature and the type of the analysed data, the visualisation and presentation of such data, as well as the combination of the different tools. In other words, digital research methods might suggest an innovative research approach; however, at the same time, there are many concerns and flows on how each of the different stages of adapting digital methods might influence knowledge and findings. Within this procedure there are two major implications, with the first one concentrating on the effects of digital research methods on social sciences and humanities, and, secondly, in a micro-level, concentrating on the methodological flaws, which might arise by the choice and application of different methodological tools (Rieder & Röhle, 2012).

The first difficulty on adapting digital research methods is the epistemological dilemmas regarding the online phenomena that will be studied, questioning what these 'actually represent in social science terms and what assumption we may make when adopting new tools and new research practices' (Snee et al., 2016, p. 6). Then, the next big concern is related to practical challenges and difficulties on how to effectively use digital research methods. Each technological development, each examined platform, according to its significant characteristics and features and the analysed material, requires different techniques and tools for the collection, the analysis and the visualisation of data. Here, one of the biggest limitations was the cost of tools and the cost of accessing archive material and data, while the ephemerality of data in the examined platforms results to the research often be overtaken by events of the medium (Rogers, 2009). In this study, this was quite obvious with Netvizz when changes on Facebook influenced the data that was possible to be collected using the app, while, secondly that was also noticeable on NodeXL, when it stopped providing free access to all its features. While, luckily, in this research, these changes didn't influence the project dramatically, while such limitations and weaknesses should be taken into consideration when adapting digital research methods.

Another important contemplation on the adaptation of digital research methods can be found on the issue objectivity and, then, on visualisations techniques and the power of visual evidence (Rieder & Röhle, 2012). Starting with the issue of objectivity and the digital research methods, what is suggested here is that digital research methods borrow elements from natural sciences, and therefore, up to a point, perceived as promising a high level of objectivity. However, this is also the main point that raises strong critiques regarding the power of data and algorithms. Rieder and Röhle (2012) expand on that by discussing the notion of *mathesis universalis*, or in other words, 'the possibility to specify a set of rules of transformation that "automatically" generate new knowledge' (Rieder & Röhle, 2012, p. 78). This concept dominated the Western thought as regards the universality of the mathematic science and its implications in other sciences, while up to a point, also influenced the digital research methods. While computers and numbers might be able to overcome some limitations and flaws in traditional research methods, still questions of subjectivity and bias, which according to Rieder and Röhle (2012) might arise 'from modes of formalisation, the choice of algorithmic procedures and means of presenting results' (Rieder & Röhle, 2012, p. 73) should be carefully assessed. For such reasons, the use of digital research methods could not be understood separately from the critical discussion on 'mechanical objectivity' (Rieder & Röhle, 2012, p. 72). In this study, all the points mentioned earlier are taken into consideration, recognising that digital research methods are neither neutral nor unbiased.

The next important risk, when using digital research methods, is raised by the issue of visualisation and the power of visual evidence (Rieder & Röhle, 2012). Visualisations can have a great impact on the understanding of findings, while at the same time these possess powerful argumentative tools due to the argumentative power of images (Rieder & Röhle, 2012, p. 73). Visualisations and graphs, often supporting the findings of studies using research methods, tend to be perceived as representing something, rather than laboratory artefacts, which can be controlled and edited according to different variables and interpretations. Instead, visualisations of data and findings should be understood as tools or instruments employed for the investigation and presentation of data and findings and presenting data and findings (Rieder & Röhle, 2012, p. 74). Under this rationale, Rieder and Röhle explain that numbers and visualisations should be perceived as evidence and then, textual rhetoric serves as argumentation (Rieder & Röhle, 2012). Again, under this rationale, all the graphs and visual material provided are critically discussed, and at the same time, it is acceptable that other interpretations, supported by strong arguments, could also be valid.

While the adaptation of digital research methods raised long discussions and debates, as regards every stage and application, the points mentioned earlier developed an insight into some of the strongest debates on digital research methods as these are employed in this research. To understand more on the rationale regarding the way that the study overlapped some of the aforementioned limitations, what comes next is sampling of data, platforms and events, a presentation of the analytical tools and computational tools used for the collection, analysis and visualisation of data.

General Sampling of Timeline and Platforms: Evolution of Digital Media Platforms and the Crisis – How the Project Developed

This scheme supported the investigation of the evolution of Greek digital media during the Greek crisis, by looking on different social media platforms and events of sociopolitical turmoil. The research provided a longitudinal empirical examination of the social and political conflict and debates as shaped during the period 2008–2015, while it provided a latitudinal understanding of the usage of various digital media in the Greek crisis context, as well as its association with transnational examples. Starting from 2008 and taking into consideration the digital media environment in Greece and the literature on social movements in the globalised era, the study began with the study of YouTube and Indymedia, and the case of the December riots. During the early days of digital communication in Greece, YouTube was among the most popular online media platforms in Greece, while Indymedia has a significant role and contribution to the first examined case study. Therefore, looking at these two, the examination of the December Riots revealed the context in which the social and political turmoil or the so-called outbreak of the crisis that occurred during 2008–2009.

The second event on which the study concentrated was the case of the Greek Indignados, which emerged in 2011, and the study of Facebook. Until 2011, Facebook had already become one of the most popular social media platforms worldwide, and one of the most popular social media platforms in Greece. The case of the Greek Indignados was selected for both its importance on a national level and its association with global cycles of protest, which emerged during the same period (e.g. M15, OWS). On a national level, this cycle of protest is understood as a milestone for both the evolution of the anti-austerity movement as well as for the reconstruction of the mainstream political scene. On a transnational level, this was an indicative example of the Greek adaptation of the anti-austerity movement and the global cycles of protest of that period. Nonetheless, as noted by the literature review, the anti-austerity protests and mobilisations should be understood as 'networks' of mobilisations organised by different organisations and focusing on sub-themes as raised by the crisis context. Then, the project concentrated on the Greferendum, as an event with a significant impact on the new political environment in Greece and its association with the EU political context. That includes the study of Twitter, as a social media platform, which developed slightly later than Facebook, and lately also became popular in Greece.

Following the evolution of the crisis, the research study included three of the most popular social media platforms globally (Castells, 2015), YouTube, Facebook and Twitter, and, also, included an examination of Indymedia, as a supplementary case of an examination of a digital media platform during the examined period. Indymedia preceded the others and indicated the potentiality of digital media on social and political turmoil before the social media era. Later, in 2015 Greeks spent more than 80 minutes per day on social media platforms, with more than half of the population registered with at least one social media platform (Kassimi, 2015). Facebook became the most popular platform for Greek users and increased by 1.1 million new accounts in August 2015, reaching 6.7 million accounts in total, more than half of the Greek population (Kassimi, 2015). Twitter, which is the next most popular social media platform, increased by 509,448 new Greek accounts, a 49 per cent increase in comparison to 2014, while YouTube also had rapid growth too, indicating a 79 per cent increase in the number of accounts for Greek users in 2014–2015 (Kassimi, 2015)

For all these platforms, and the events, data were collected, concentrating both on the significant features of the platforms and the examined events. Looking on the examined platforms, the impact of digital media on the growth and the evolution of protests and mobilisations events (December Riots, Greek Indignados/Aganaktismenoi), on the rise of non-mainstream political parties and radicalisation (SYRIZA, Golden Dawn), as well as the formation of alternative structures of initiatives and networks are some of the points based on which this study developed. Concentrating on these social media platforms and the evolution of the crisis as discussed in the literature, the collection of the data was completed based on the following timeline:

Starting with YouTube and Indymedia, the collection of the data was conducted using the Indymedia archive, looking at material relating to the examined case, as well as the collection of YouTube comments. Similarly, the SYRIZA online diaspora data collected by targeting fan pages on Facebook, nationally and transnationally. In the case of Twitter, real-time data collection was required and therefore, keywords and trending hashtags were collected throughout the Greferendum period, building a rich data set, which was narrowed down and analysed concentrating on specific debates in that period. Based on the significant characteristics of each of the examined online platforms and the collected data, there are three analytical approaches and different computational research tools, which were used throughout the study. In the following section, both the analytical and computational tools are discussed, while for every platform and in each chapter, a more detailed description of sampling and analysis is provided accordingly.

Analytical Tools

Thematic Analysis (Indymedia and YouTube)

Thematic Analysis (TA) is a foundational method for qualitative analysis, which appeared in the 1970s (Merton, 1975), providing a theoretically-flexible approach to the analysis of qualitative data (Braun & Clarke, 2006). TA is situated in different epistemological and ontological positions, while different versions of TA are used in several disciplines and theoretical frameworks (Braun & Clarke, 2006). Following Clarkes and Braun's approach (2013), in this project, TA is used as an analytical method, rather than a methodology, and can therefore be applied in various theoretical frameworks, including the one used in this project.

This analytical method supports the study of a range of research questions associated with people's experiences and the 'representation and construction of particular phenomena in particular contexts' (Clarke & Braun, 2013, p. 121), while it is also used for the study of various types of data, including online data, media scripts and so on. According to Smith, '*thematic* connotes the analysis of story like verbal material, and the use of relatively comprehensive units of analysis', and as Smith further explains, that might include themas, themes or combination of different elements and categories (Smith, Atkinson, McClelland, & Veroff, 1992, p 4). At the same time, this method is used both for the analysis of large and small data sets, while according to Clarke and Braun, this method produces both data-driven or theory-driven studies (2013, p. 121). Thus, in this study, the method is appropriate for the analysis of YouTube and Indymedia material, with the analysis conducted based on cyberconflict theory.

TA focuses on the identification of 'thematising meanings' (Braun & Clarke, 2006, p. 78), as well as themes or patterns (Clarke & Braun, 2013). This method is used for the identification of themes in a selected set of data, while these themes were associated with the study of research questions (Evripidou & Drury, 2013) and theoretical framework. This was one of the most appropriate methods for the examination of the two examined platforms; as it not only did not raise any technical limitations for the examination (e.g. working with archive material and categorising various data), but at the same time, this method also managed to bring together the analysis of these two very different platforms and data forms, indicating the main themes/debates, which already comprise the sociopolitical debates, before the outbreak of the crisis, and the study of the next two examined platforms and periods. At this stage, what was important to be achieved was the identification of the main themes/debates of conflict and not to do a more detailed analysis on content and discourse. The TA was applied by coding the collected material according to Braun and Clarke (2006) through six phases of analysis as follows: (1) familiarisation with the data, (2) generating initial codes, (3) searching for themes, (4) reviewing themes, (5) defining and naming themes and (6) writing up (Braun & Clarke, 2006, pp. 86–93).

The selection of the themes does not reflect (only) the dominant patterns in the analysed data set but instead these are shaped according to the researchers' interest and questions in this occasion, the examination of cyberconflict (Braun & Clarke, 2006, pp. 86–93). Therefore, the themes identified focusing on cyberconflict theory and the four basic parameters of the framework (historical/sociopolitical background, sociopolitical conflict, ethnoreligious conflict, Internet as a medium).

TA was used for the analysis of Indymedia and YouTube material. Indymedia was one of the first online platforms indicating the potentiality of digital media in the Greek context, but it was already examined as a factor in anti-globalisation protests in a transnational context (Karatzogianni, 2006; Pickerill, 2006). Indymedia is broadly associated with activism and movements, while in the case of Greece, this platform was extensively used throughout the unfolding of the so-called 'December Riots', supporting both the organisation and coordination of protests and actions across Greece (Milioni, 2012; Schwarz & Sagris, 2010; Vatikiotis, 2011). However, taking into consideration the significant characteristics of the platform, among the major limitations at this point is that Indymedia tends to attract only a very specific profile of users and does not provide a broad understanding of digital media usage. YouTube was among the most popular social media platforms of those days, and at the same time, had a significant contribution on the emerge of the December Riots, when an amateur video that captured the shooting scene, was uploaded on the platform, before being presented by the mainstream media. While there are many different approaches for the examination of YouTube, focusing on comments (Thelwall, Sud, & Vis, 2011), on content (Madden, Ruthven, & McMenemy, 2013) or even detection of sentiment (Choudhury & Breslin, 2010) and others, the goal of this analysis of YouTube was the identification of the main themes, which were discussed during the so-called December Riots, supplementary to the study of Indymedia. Thus, focusing on this post, YouTube alongside Indymedia provided a sufficient data set for the examination of digital media in the December Riots and the application of TA pointing out the social and political conflicts and tensions, as these existed exactly before the occurrence of the global recession and, later, in the Greek crisis.

The step-by-step coding and analysis process is presented at the beginning of the relevant chapter. To sum up, the study of the two examined platforms developed bases on the detection of themes, following the six-phase coding/analysis (Braun & Clarke, 2006, pp. 86–93) and the four parameters of cyberconflict theory. Braun and Clarke explain that in the analysed data set, the detection of themes or patterns can be completed, following an inductive approach, a 'bottom-up' method, which is data-driven, and themes are linked to the data themselves (Braun & Clarke, 2006, pp. 83–84). Following this approach, the TA was completed under the theoretical framework of cyberconflict theory, indicating the themes/points of consideration discussed during the riots and later, their evolution or potential relevance to the crisis context debates.

Social Network Analysis (Facebook and Twitter)

Social networks have always been the key components of human life and this is reflected in the online world through the rise of virtual social networks, like the offline social networks. While social networks have always been shaped according to space and time limitations, the evolution of the Internet limited some of these barriers (Abraham, Hassanien, & Snasel, 2012). A network is a means through which power is exercised (Castells, 2011), while network science examines patterns of connection in both social and physical phenomena (Hansen, Shneiderman, & Smith, 2011). Networks and network science have a long tradition and have been used for the investigation of various topics and phenomena. Hansen et al. (2011) review the growth of the interest and the use of networks, starting from the nineteenth century and Kelvin's work on 'collective action, collaboration, and productive communities' (Hansen et al., 2011, p. 4). Since 2005, the references to 'social networks' in academia have rapidly increased, spanning all across the social sciences (Borgatti & Halgin, 2011). While there are many different theoretical elements, which support the analysis of networks, focusing on ties and structure (Granovetter, 1983), on power (Knoke, 1994), and so on, still, in many cases networks are suggested as a methodology rather than as theory (Borgatti & Halgin, 2011). Social network analysis (SNA) is understood as being part of the broader field of network science, which supports the examination of human relationships (Hansen et al., 2011). Scott (2000) points to three main traditions of SNA, which describe the lineage of SNA before it became a mainstream research tool. The first tradition of SNA is the sociometric approach, which focuses mainly on the examination of small groups using graph theory (Scott, 2000, pp. 8–9), while the second tradition developed during the 1930s when Harvard researchers explored patterns of interpersonal relationships and the formation of 'cliques' (Scott, 2000, pp. 8–9). The third tradition was developed by anthropologists in Manchester, who combined the first two traditions, and explored structures and relationships within communities. Later, during the 1960s and 1970s, again at Harvard, contemporary SNA was formulated (Scott, 2000, pp. 8–9).

During the 1980s, the development of technology made networks even more popular, and during the same period, Castells theorised the networked society, 'a society whose social structure is made up of networks powered by microelectronics-based information and communications technologies' (Castells, 2004a, p. 3). Castells (2011) discussed networks focusing on the notion of power, which is exercised and distributed throughout networks. Knoke (1994) concentrated on power as mode, and effect and interaction; 'Power is an aspect of the actual or potential interaction between two or more social actors' (Knoke, 1994, p. 1). Power is a dynamic and unstable relation, while power relationships are 'asymmetrical actual or potential interactions' between actors, which have a strong impact on behaviours and perceptions (Knoke, 1994, pp. 1–3). Especially in political relations, influence and domination are suggested as some of the most important types of relationships (Knoke, 1994, pp. 1–3). Influence is understood through the transition of information and communication between actors, while, domination refers to the control of behaviour between actors (Knoke, 1994). Going back to Castells' Networking Power,[1] Network Power,[2] Networked Power[3] and Network-making Power[4] are the main distinctive types of power, which are able to describe how power is produced and distributed in networks. Here, Castells describes the way that human activity not only develops networks, but also the way that networks exercise their power and influence on human mind (Castells, 2011, p. 785). Then, these multidimensional and complicated systems of networks construct their power around state and politics (Castells, 2011, p. 785). Thus, in these systems of networks, communication and power are understood in terms of domination and influence. Networks provide an additional experience of space and time, while at the same time they denote a homogeneity of practice across a global communication matrix, which, however, also indicates the dynamic transformation of the multi-scaled 'common global network culture' (Terranova, 2004, p. 72).

In this context, the examination of Facebook and Twitter material focused on the identification of cyberconflict, concentrating both on networks and discourse. The study of the two previous platforms indicated the main themes/debates that existed before the outbreak of the crisis, linking, according to the cyberconflict theory, the environment of online conflict – or in this case debate, to the two most conflicted and debatable examined periods since decades. These two periods are studies through Facebook and Twitter. Based on the significant characteristics of these two platforms, the technical limitations (e.g. access on archive material, real-time collection of data, and available computational tools) as well as the aim of studying these two platforms, different analytical tools were used. Facebook suggested an insight on networks and online (political/social) coalitions among national/transnational movements, while twitter concentrated mainly on the two-antagonistic campaign and conflicted discourses.

The selection of the examined platforms developed concentrating on when each platform emerged and became popular, as well as on the evolution of the events, and the association between the two – the platforms and the events. Facebook examination focused on the case of the Greek Indignados, which was the strongest cycle of anti-austerity protest in Greece and at the same time, was

[1]Networking Power: the power of the actors and organisations included in the networks that constitute the core of the global network society over human collectives and individuals who are not included in these global networks. (Castells, 2011, p. 774)

[2]Network Power: the power resulting from the standards required to coordinate social interaction in the networks. In this case, power is exercised not by exclusion from the networks but by the imposition of the rules of inclusion. (Castells, 2011, p. 774)

[3]Networked Power: the power of social actors over other social actors in the network. The forms and processes of networked power are specific to each network. (Castells, 2011, p. 774)

[4]Network-making Power: the power to program specific networks according to the interests and values of the programmers, and the power to switch different networks following the strategic alliances between the dominant actors of various networks. (Castells, 2011, p. 774)

also associated with the global wave of protest of that period. The study of Twitter concentrated on the so-called Greferendum, giving an insight into the national and EU sociopolitical conflict, as regards the austerity politics. While the collection of the analysis included material from different moments in the development of the crisis, during the period 2008–2016, these two events and periods of time were selected as indicative of the digital media use during the crisis, efficiently answering the research questions. What is examined at this phase of the research is the notion of the network as this is discussed and understood in terms of collective action, connective action and social movements (Bennett & Segerberg, 2012). Focusing on this point, the study concentrated on the analysis of online conflict as this can be observed in and among networks. There were points for which the study of Facebook and Twitter data analysis targets included the evolution of the themes/debates and sociopolitical turmoil as well as online/offline polarisation.

NodeXL, Netvizz and Gephi were used for the collection, analysis and visualisation of networks. Then, the findings were analysed and interpreted using Social Network Analysis (SNA), which is understood as the investigation of patterns of relationship between social actors, analysed on different levels (e.g. groups and individuals) (Brieger, 2004). Wasserman and Faust (1994) explain that SNA 'provides a precise way to define important social concepts, a theoretical alternative to the assumption of independent social actors, and a framework for testing theories about structured social relationships. As explained earlier, SNA is appropriate for the analysis and the investigation of 'kinship patterns, community structure, interlocking directorships and so forth' (Scott, 2000, p. 2). Golbeck (2013, p. 151) highlighted, that social networks 'allow all types of things to spread from person to person, from diseases and viral videos to rumours, different types of information all propagate from one actor to the other, throughout networks'.

However, Brieger (2004) explains that SNA investigates patterns of relationships on different levels, focusing on individuals, groups and so on. SNA supports the examination of different social entities or social units, including the individual, collective or even corporate social units. SNA provided an insight into the relational ties between actors and their relations, and then, an insight into the social network per se. The examination of groups and subgroups indicates additional points of consideration relating to the way that different actors are related to each other (Wasserman & Faust, 1994, pp. 16–21). Social networks can use both quantitative or qualitative, or mixed methods of analysis, although, social network analysis itself should not be conceived as being quantitative or qualitative, or a combination of the two, but instead is structural (Carrinhgton, 2014). SNA analysis supports not only the interpretation of networks, pointing out questions relating to the notion of structure, but also indicated points (e.g. actors, coalitions, nodes and pages) which it would be of interest to examine further, focusing on content and discourse.

Semantic Analysis (Twitter)

Twitter is a microblogging social media platform which, originally and at the time that the research was conducted, allowed users to communicate information of up to 140 characters on a one-to-one or even global basis, by sharing news and updates on real-time events (Williams, Terras, & Warwick, 2013). In this study, Twitter material was collected and analysed focusing on SNA and dominant actors, and then focusing on discourse, the usage of language and the production of meaning and semantics. Similar to social networks, semantic networks consist of nodes that represent concepts or clauses linked by various binary relationships (Krippendorff, 2004). The analysis of such networks is to respond to questions which are, or are not, clearly included in body texts (Krippendorff, 2004, p. 294):

> The idea of semantic networks probably originated in cultural-anthropological efforts to represent cognitive structures or mental models as relational graphs (D'Andrade, 1991, 1995; Quillian, 1968; Wallace, 1961 in Krippendorff, 2004, p. 294). It has been facilitated by the psycho-logical theorizing of Abelson and Rosenberg (1958), by Schank and Abelson's (1977) inquiries into actionable knowledge structures, by causal inference modelling (Blalock, 1964; Simon, 1957), by graph theory (Harary, Norman, & Cartwright, 1966; Maruyama, 1963), by evaluative assertion analysis (Osgood, Saporta, & Nunnally, 1956), by studies of communication networks (Rice & Richards, 1985; Richards & Rice, 1981) and social networks (Wellman & Berkowitz, 1988), and by theories of communication networks (Rogers & Kincaid, 1981).
>
> (Krippendorff, 2004, p. 294)

Semantic networks are used as a research approach for studying natural language (Krippendorff, 2004), and as in all the content analysis methods, semantic analysis has some limitations relating, up to a point, to the use of online data and computational tools. In this study, the study of language was conducted in combination with social network analysis, aiming to develop an insight into meanings and the information transmitted through networks. Therefore, after understanding the main themes and debates as shaped in the pre-crisis era, then the study developed an insight on how Facebook used and supported the development of networks and online political coalitions in national and transnational level. Then the research focused on semantics and discourse providing an insight on how networks contributed to the emerge of discourse as regards to the two antagonistic campaigns. At the same time, looking at the finding of all the examined periods and platforms, it is possible to observe the discursive transfusion/evolution of the debates in the crisis context.

Using NodeXL, the study concentrated on the detection of the most used/mentioned words, or co-occurances of words, and then, based on the frequency, the visualisation by graphical means forming semantic networks

(Friemel, 2008). This process is associated with the theoretical framework of cyberconflict, as it supports the detection of different or conflicting frames, while at the same time suggesting considerations relating to the historical, political continuity of collective actions and sociopolitical turmoil arising during the crisis, by drawing back to the themes of the YouTube and Indymedia analysis.

Explanation of Software Tools: Netvizz, NodeXL, Gephi and NVivo

After the selection of the analytical approach based on which the online data study was completed, it was necessary to review the research tools, the computational tools, which were used for the collection, the analysis and the visualisation of the data. One of the challenging tasks at this stage was to efficiently select the appropriate tools and software, which would be used for the collection and analysis of the empirical data. While digital methods is a trending research approach with various innovative developments, the study concentrated on 'small-data', using open-access apps and software, that is possible to be used even with no skills on programming and coding, but still though are able to efficiently support the in depth study of the examined platforms and events. Then, another important challenge as regards the selection of the computational tools, arose by the examination of different online and social media platforms, each of which could be studied with the use of different software and apps. Therefore, it was very important to conclude to a combination of computational tools, which ideally would support the study of more than one online platform. Based on these considerations and difficulties, I concluded to the selection of the following computational tools.

NodeXL is an add-in to the Microsoft Excel Spreadsheet software, which supports the identification of social and semantic networks based on analytical and visualisation features. NodeXL is relatively easy to use as it is designed for non-programmers but still, it is able to provide rich visual representations and analytics (Hansen et al., 2011, p. 47). Smith explains (Smith et al., 2009) that NodeXL features enable users to import online data and to develop network statistics as well as to develop network visualisation (sorting, filtering and clustering), while it can also be used for the analysis of data from different social networking platforms and services, such as Facebook, Twitter and YouTube. There are more sophisticated methods available to collect, analyse and visualise online material, while for this study, NodeXL was able to efficiently support the research objectives of the study, without getting into more complicated statistical and analytical schemes (e.g. use of Python, R, UCINet and Pajek). Another reason for the selection of NodeXL was its extremely user-friendly interface based on my previous experience and knowledge on working in the Microsoft Excel environment. Due to these characteristics, NodeXL was used for the collection, analysis and visualisation of Twitter material, supporting both the social network and semantic analysis of the data. NodeXL was of free access at the time that this research started, while it was also compatible with all the PCs used for this research. Some of the practical difficulties that rose was that not all the used PCs efficiently supported the visualisation of the data, and therefore, to avoid the risk of losing or destroying any of the collected material, the limit for crawling Twitter data each time was set to the 10,000 tweets and relations, instead of the 18,000, which is the NodeXL limit.

Secondly, Netvizz is described by Rieder (2013) as a data collection and extraction application tool, which allows users to export data in file formats from different sections of the Facebook social networking service. Again, Netvizz was selected among other similar apps (e.g. GetNet, API) due to its user-friendly interface and also, as an easy app which, still though was able to efficiently support the collection of empirical data. Netvizz enables the user to focus on friendship networks, on public groups, pages and profiles (Rieder, 2013). The output of Netvizz was visualised, when needed, using Gephi. Gephi is an open-source network graph and analysis tool (Cherven, 2015, p. 7). Netvizz was used to collect data with regard to Facebook fan pages, and then, Gephi supported a more efficient analysis and visualisation of these data.

To sum up, an in-depth understanding of digital media in the Greek crisis context could include many different online media platforms and could be supported by different research and analytical tools. However, as it would not be possible to examine every platform and service, the Facebook study indicated the formation of online networks and coalitions, indicating dominant actors and structural characteristics. On the other hand, Twitter described the evolution of discourses and real-time reactions to a variety of different events and processes (e.g. campaigns, coordination of events, public sphere and social response). Facebook and Twitter were among the most dominant social media platforms, during the examined period, while, as is also suggested by the literature, they support different processes and types of communication and tend to influence, in different ways and at different stages, the occurrence and expansion of collective actions, mobilisations and movements.

The chosen material from both platforms was identified and collected based on the examination of the crisis context and incident as described earlier. Researching digital media provides many options as regards the collected material, as well as the computational and analytical tools. Facebook and Twitter, constitute a rich source of material that could be analysed focusing on different elements and answering different research questions. While Facebook is more accessible on archive material, still there is an issue of temporality regarding the study of discourse and information that published months or years before the time of data collection (e.g. links, posts, or comments), therefore, this study cocentrated on the study of networks instead. On the other hand, Twitter provided the opportunity for developing insights into both social networks and discourse, although the issue of temporality is even more significant at the study of this platform, therefore the collection of data conducted on a real-time base. Facebook raised more limitations and difficulties on accessing and collecting data from the platform, while, in comparison, Twitter was more accessible.

As regards the analysis of Indymedia and YouTube, NVivo and NCapture were used for the collection and the analysis of the data from both of these two platforms. NVivo is one of the most indicative tools available to support the complexity of qualitative research (Richards, 1999). At the same time, NVivo helps in handling of rich data records and information about them, supporting coding visually or by categories, while it also provides a range of tools for coding and analysis of online content (Richards, 1999, pp. 1–9). Finally, it supports both the construction and testing of answers to research questions, which is the goal of this research (Richards, 1999, pp. 1–9). NCapture is a web browser extension, which supports NVivo to collect web pages' content either in a PDF form or concentrating on the collection of posts and comments (YouTube and Indymedia). Threads and comments from both YouTube and Indymedia were downloaded in Excel format, and then the data were imported and coded in NVivo.

This concludes a general explanation on how the theoretical frame informs the research design, the chronological and case sampling as well as the research techniques and software tools used for the analysis. In each empirical chapter, more detail is provided explaining how each tool was applied, and how it was directly relevant to each case was also examined. The following chapter offers a historical background of the Greek socio-political context, as the cyberconflict environment under examination, as a preparatory platform from which the thesis can launch the empirical analysis.

Chapter 5

The First Period: December Riots – Indymedia and YouTube

After the review of the theoretical framework of the research, this study concentrated on the understanding of the historical and sociopolitical background of the Greek case, following the basic steps of cyberconflict theory. After the cultivation of the research design, the project developed through empirical research on the topic, examining different online media platforms and their association with significant moments of the crisis. Chapter 5 is the first empirical chapter that focuses on the December Riots and the impact of online media on the event. Then, following Chapter 4, the research methods and techniques that were used for the examination of these platforms are discussed in detail. Finally, the examination of Indymedia and YouTube are completed through the analysis of online data.

December Riots 2008: Sociopolitical and Historical Characteristics

After the Wildfire mobilisations in 2007, the so-called December Riots is the next significant example, which pointed out the importance and the potential of online media in the development of mobilisations and protests in Greece. On 6 December 2008, Alexandros Grigoropoulos, a 15-year-old student was shot in the chest by a police officer in Exarcheia, an area of the city centre of Athens. Two hours after the fatal shooting, using mobile phones and the internet, the first demonstrations had already been organised in the city centre of Athens (Milioni, 2012, p. 10), resulting in a series of protests (Theocharis, 2011, pp. 203–223), which became known as the 'December Riots' and lasted for three weeks (Milioni, 2012, p. 1), costing an estimated 1.5 billion Euros (Sotiris, 2010, p. 203).

After the Parnitha wildfires protests, which had already indicated the use and impact of digital on organisation of mobilisations, the December Riots was the first incidence, which demonstrated the impact of digital communication on spontaneous organised collective actions in the Greek context. As Milioni puts it, this was the first case that online and social media were extensively used as 'coordinating and organisational tools', contributing to the creation of a collective identity (Milioni, 2012, p. 7). At the same time, the December Riots was one of the first digital media-enabled protests, and they paralleled the rapid growth of the digital communication sector in Greece, expanding the year before, in 2007 (EL.STAT., 2013, 2014). Although online media played an enabling role in the December Riots, participation and online access are important points, especially taking into consideration that young people, who had a high level of education and lived in urban areas, comprised the core profile of online users with daily access online during that period.

At the same time, December Riots could be considered a milestone in the development of the phenomenon of digital media usage in the organisation of collective action in Greece, while at the same time, 'a turning point in social movements against neoliberalism and capitalist restriction' (Sotiris, 2010, p. 203). At the same time, the December Riots was a significant point in contemporary Greek history as they denoted the limitations and vulnerabilities of the social and political structures, highlighting the disputed relationship between society and the state, which already existed before the outbreak of the crisis. Kyriakopoulos pointed out that both the Greek and the international media strongly compared the December Riots with other historical events such as the Parisian May of '68 (Sotiris, 2010, p. 242). At the same time, this was one of the first cases after the fall of the dictatorship, in 1974, that mobilisations were characterised by this extent of violence. Thus, the discussion about social unrest reoccurred, destroying the elusive image of a prospering Greece as shaped after 1980, which reached its zenith with the 2004 Olympics held in Athens. Civilians demonstrated for days and the violence both from the demonstrators and the state was intense, while there were many solidarity actions organised across the EU.

The December Riots is signified the end of an era, and the transition to the crisis and austerity context, while it also enabled the study of online and social media evolution in Greece. During the last decade the academic study of December Riots event was intensive and focused on a variety of different arguments and topics about the event, from civil society and institutions, contemporary and street politics to collective actions and social movements (Karamichas, 2009; Monastiriotis, 2009; Sotiris, 2010; Vradis & Dalakoglou, 2011). Here, the study of the December Riots was conducted concentrating on the sociopolitical and historical background of the environment in which the event occurred, focusing both on the national context of Greece and the EU context, taking into consideration that the December Riots occurred after the Paris Riots (2005), before the UK student protests (2010–2011), which was followed by the wave of anti-austerity and anti-capitalist protests of 2010. Therefore, the way that different cycles of protest emerged, overlapping each other, is an interesting point of exploration. At the same time, December Riots indicated the potentiality of digital media in the Greek context and situated the case of Greece in the pre-crisis and crisis collective actions, as emerged in an EU context.

Critically, the December Riots is often theorised as a milestone in terms of pre-/after-crisis discourse and structures (Vradis & Dalakoglou, 2011), and has been placed in the history of modern social movements (2010), proceeding with social discontent and the global recession, as it became apparent through the crisis later on. According to Karamichas (2009, p. 292), sectors of the European Left addressed the December Riots as a prelude to other similar incidents provoked by the global recession. However, an in-depth analysis of such incidents, or more specifically, an analysis of 'acts of resistance' should be carried out and linked to the 'individual cultural and national context' (Karamichas, 2009, p. 292), part of which is discussed in Chapter 3. In terms of scholarship, Anastasakis (2009, p. 7) and Psimitis (2011, p. 114) feel compelled to explain to an international audience that Greece is a country in which protests and riots are not a rare phenomenon. Greek society is familiar, or according to Karamichas (2009, p. 290) is 'not averse', to street politics and most of the citizens have participated 'at some point, in some sort of protest activity' (Karamichas, 2009, p. 290.). Demonstrations here should be understood as a cultural element and in linkage to collective actions of previous decades, starting from the 1960s and 1970s (Anastasakis, 2009). Psimitis (2011) describes the December Riots as a Greek Youth Movement, which could be perceived as being in linkage with other acts or mobilisations related to the student movement (Psimitis, 2011, p. 113).

For instance, Karamichas emphasises that along with student mobilisations, both anti-war and anti-globalisation protest campaigns, which traditionally have high levels of student participation, were some of the most indicative and recent examples of massive mobilisations before the December Riots (2009, p. 290). In a national context, the ground for the emergence of a collective identity had already been laid by the 2007 protests, and the defence of 'Article 16 of the Hellenic Constitution that provides for the public and free from tuition character of universities in Greece and against the government's Higher Education Bill' (Psimitis, 2011, p. 114). An interesting point here is that mobilisation in Greece occurred in the national context but was connected also to the transnational order of dissents (Karatzogianni, 2016). Therefore, December Riots were read not only as a spontaneous event related to the actual events but also as an expression of social disaffection against the evident social inequalities, which arose due to the dominance of neo-liberal ideologies and policies that has been in place since 1980 (Mouzelis, 2009, p. 1) both in the national and EU context (Anastasakis, 2009). The sociopolitical characteristics of the period of time that the December Riots emerged were decisive and could explain the phenomenon, which is understood as a prelude to the crisis that was about to follow in Greece (Karamichas, 2009; Vradis & Dalakoglou, 2011). The substantial causes of the riots and, later the debt crisis, could be perceived as being similar, concentrating on political and social problems, including corruption, unemployment, problems in education, industrial relations and others. Therefore, the way that all these issues were prominent in 2008, both at the national and European level, and then the way that these shaped the repertoire of mobilisation in the crisis and post-crisis era is an interesting point to note.

One of the most indicative examples is youth unemployment, which in 2009, in EU-27 reached up to 16.7% while the average in Greece was 22.3% (Sotiris, 2010, p. 204), rapidly increasing from an average of 19.1% in 2005 (Karamesini, 2005, p. 30). The paradox of a well-educated generation with limited employment prospects and poor or flexible working conditions, in combination with a weak Greek civic society and a corrupted state (Mouzelis, 2009, p. 2), created the conditions in which the December Riots emerged. Hence, social relations and structures produced and maintained inequalities between social actors (Psimitis, 2011, p. 114) and, later, in turn, resistance to these structures produced radical collective movements. What is presumed at this point is that the involved actors, the 'victims', will move to a more active participation against their social opponents. The neoliberal and capitalist policies that affected young people, including students, workers or employees (Sotiris, 2010, p. 204), contributed to the creation of a wider collective identity, which encompassed the special characteristics of each group/actor participating in the mobilisations (Sotiris, 2010, p. 113).

December Riots represented a generation which, for the first time after the fall of the dictatorship in Greece, was about to 'face worse economic prospects than its predecessors' (Featherstone, 2009, p. 2). In the case of Grigoropoulos, the stereotype of the middle-class family was a significant point, and debate with regard to the outbreak of the incident (Featherstone, 2009, p. 2.), especially focused on issues of participation and identity. Indeed, the origins of the December Riots can be found in former collective actions and movements, in terms of the historical background of Greece or even in linkage with the contemporary European social and political turmoil. However, while the social indignation about the sociopolitical structures and conditions was, up to a point, expressed throughout the emergence of the riots, the devastating issue that shaped the nature and the extent of the protest, was the fear of losing privileges, even in social groups, which traditionally tend to be protected or less affected during political and financial turmoil (e.g. well-educated and middle-class). Therefore, social groups whose privileges were threatened were the pillar of the riots, while marginalised groups (e.g. migrants) defined the broad spectrum of the mobilisations.

A major limitation of the December Riots was that, while there was a strong opposition to the disintegration of existing rights and privileges, still the mobilisations did not manage to make any kind of suggestion about future policies or structures. According to Argyrou (2013) though, this is the limitation of all revolutions or revolutionary acts, which tend to struggle for change, focusing on the past (lost privileges, etc.), rather than on the future. This results in the creation of a teleological cycle and continuously leads back to the point of 'departure' (Argyrou, 2013, p. 79). Another significant limitation of the December Riots was that this movement did not clearly identify its demands. Participants did not try to prevent a specific policy or ask for a specific change, but rather they just expressed dissatisfaction about the social and political breakdown through violence (Featherstone, 2009).

Methods, Sampling, and Analysis

Digital Media, and especially Indymedia and YouTube, had a significant contribution on the progress and development of the December Riots (Milioni, 2012; Vatikiotis, 2011; Vradis & Dalakoglou, 2011, pp. 133–150). Looking on these two platforms, the study questions the contribution of such platforms on collective identity and movement formation. At the same time, the study situates the Greek mobilisations within the wider theoretical problematic and debate on the role of digital media and the linkage to society and politics.

In order to offer an insight into the online media contribution to the incident, the collection of data was targeted first, looking on the earliest posts relating to the incident on Indymedia and secondly, on the amateur video, which captured the shooting scene and was uploaded on YouTube. Starting from the Indymedia posts, the collection and analysis of the data were conducted using NVivo and NCapture (see Chapter 4). Indymedia provides an extensive archive of old posts, which in the case of the December Riots, are organised in thematic sections. Therefore, data collection concentrated on Indymedia's thematic section 'December Riots 2008'.[1] This thematic section consists of 152 pages and 3025 posts, each of them linked to a thread/discussion (Dec 2008–Dec 2015). The analysis of all the posts could offer an insight into the way that the December Riot debates amplified during the period 2008–2015 and could also demonstrate the evolution of the mobilisations longitudinally as well as the differences in terms of goals, organisation and identity across time. However, this research focused specifically on the analysis of the first three posts and the threads/discussion after the shooting, in order to take a snapshot of the use of online media at that point in time. Therefore, the examination of Indymedia included the collection and the analysis of posts from three different threads. The first thread consisted of 52 posts/items (A) reporting and asking for confirmation about the incident.[2] The second thread consisted of 17 posts and concentrated on the confirmation of Grigoropoulos' death (B).[3] The third thread consisted of six posts and focused on the video of the shooting scene as this was broadcast by Mega Channel (C),[4] pointing out the differences between online and mainstream media. The sampling of Indymedia threads and posts consists of the following:

- The first analysed thread: 52 posts/items (A), posted between 06/08/2008, 21:18, and 10/12/2008, 12:39.
- The second analysed thread: 17 posts/items (B), posted between 06/12/2008, 22:02, and 07/12/2008, 13:07.
- The third analysed thread: 6 posts/items (C), posted between 08/12/2008, 15:16, and 08/12/2008, 16:26.

---

[1]https://athens.indymedia.org/topics/77/

[2]https://athens.indymedia.org/post/933042/, Emergency! Someone is heavily injured at Messologiou square, Exarchia ('Επείγον! Σοβαρός τραυματισμός στη Μεσολογγίου' (Εξάρχεια)) (52 posts) (Indymedia, 6/12/2008– 10/12/2008).

[3]https://athens.indymedia.org/post/933066/, The fifteen-years old boy is dead ('Ο 15χρονος είναι νεκρός') (17 posts) (Indymedia, 6–7/12/2008).

[4]https://athens.indymedia.org/post/935769/, MEGA cheat: they edit and add sound at the shooting video (Αλητεία του MEGA: πρόσθεσαν ήχους στο βίντεο της δολοφονίας) (6 posts) (Indymedia, 8/12/2008).

Using NCapture and Chrome, these threads and the posts were downloaded as PDFs and then were imported into NVivo. The coding of the material was accomplished based on Cyberconflict Theory and the theoretical framework as discussed in Chapter 2, as well as based on descriptive characteristics. Thus, the examined nodes concentrated on the historical background of the incident, on the mobilisations (organisation of actions, protests, etc.), on the mainstream media (representation and online media contrast, etc.) and on the incident per se (information and details). Focusing on these themes/nodes and on the descriptive characteristics of the posts, the categorisation was completed and analysed accordingly.

Then, at the next stage of the study, the examination of YouTube was conducted concentrating on the original amateur video, which captured the shooting scene and was posted online,[5] a day after the incident, on 7 December 2008. The video was posted on YouTube, after being posted on Indymedia, which, due to technical difficulties, was not broadly accessible. Following the links in Indymedia and using NCapture, 489 comments from the YouTube video were collected, downloaded and imported into NVivo. Again, a Cyberconflict analysis of the comments focused on the historical background, on mobilisations, the mainstream media and the incident per se. Due to the characteristics of this platform, three more nodes were included in the analysis, concentrating on the involved actors (police, state) and on comments that were irrelevant to the incident.

To sum up, following the suggestions in the literature, the examination of the December Riots focused on Indymedia and YouTube, as the most indicative platforms to illustrate the impact of online media on communicational and organisational processes. In 2008, before the rapid emergence and use of social media platforms such as Facebook and Twitter, YouTube and Indymedia provided a public space and alternative channels of communication. The extensive amount of online material produced then could support a more in-depth examination of the December Riots. However, the selected analysed material aims to efficiently support the review of the social and political debates, leading to an examination of digital media in the crisis context. Therefore, while the study of additional material would be possible, an important point that should be understood at this stage is how the online media contributed to the progress of the incident, rather than evaluating the influence of online media at every phase of the evolution of the incident. The selected analysed material provides an insight into the contribution of online media to the actual development of the incident, both in terms of representation and communication.

[5]https://www.YouTube.com/watch?v=b1wrDbw9KeQ

The Examined Platforms: Indymedia and YouTube

Indymedia in the December Riots

Indymedia, which was founded in Athens in 2001, is an indicative example of an online and alternative media platform, which supports communicational, organisational and representational processes, and contributed to the rise of collective action. Similarly, in the case of the December Riots, this was the first online media platform used for the organisation of the demonstrations, which emerged in late 2008 (Vradis & Dalakoglou, 2011, pp. 133–150). Indymedia's statistics of the page views show that one day before the incident, on the 5th of December, the website had approximately 600,000 hits, while two days after the incident, on the 7th of December (Vradis & Dalakoglou, 2011, pp. 133–150) there were more than 9,000,000 hits. Eight minutes after the shooting of Grigoropoulos, the incident was reported on Indymedia, while the mainstream media reacted approximately forty minutes later, by a 'breaking news' spot, on a private TV channel (Vradis & Dalakoglou, 2011, pp. 133–150).

The examination of Indymedia began with the collection of the first relevant post(s) at the Indymedia's thematic section 'December Riots 2008' and the selection of material based on the relevance of the threads to the incident, in turn was drawn from academic scholarship discussed earlier. As explained, using NCapture and NVivo, the posts were collected and analysed according to the Cyberconflict Theory, identifying the main themes and types of conflict, the political context and environment, social movement characteristics, the impact of online media use, as well as media dynamics, and conflict elements (Karatzogianni, 2006, p. 195). The coding of the posts was accomplished focusing on the following points/nodes (Chapter 2):

- Historical background and sociopolitical structures (references to the historical background and sociopolitical structures). This node illustrates how the environment of the conflict and the historical background is linked to the actual examined incident. At the same time, this node identifies the type of conflict (sociopolitical and ethnoreligious), in order to contextualise further analysis.
- Ideology, organisation and mobilisation structures This node provides an insight into the usage of online media within the conflict, and the contribution to the emergence of collective actions.
- Mainstream media (mainstream media representations, published information, censorship and control of information, identifying the actors dominating the political discourse). This node refers to the discussion of frames and the internet as a medium.
- Posts relating to the incident itself (what happened and how). This node mainly supports the analysis of the data, categorising information, which does not necessarily support any further understanding of conflict.

All the analysed posts were categorised into multiple nodes, according to their content. Using NVivo and the speed-coding bar, the data were manually coded based on a 'node coding system' (Richards, 1999, pp. 112–114). The aim of this system is to create and manage categories, providing an opportunity to view/review the material and to make distinctions between categories, dimensions or patterns of coding (Richards, 1999, p. 112).

The first analysed thread consists of 52 posts/items (A), while the first post, the seed of the data, posted on 06/12/2008, at 21:18, reports and asks for confirmation of the incident: 'I just received a phone call from a comrade who told me that there have been some clashes at Mesologiou Street and one kid has been injured by a rubber bullet of a cop and that he is in a critical condition. An ambulance has arrived and is transferring him to Euagelismos hospital... Those of you in Athens please confirm the information.' (in Greek).

The second analysed thread, consisted of 17 posts, with the first being posted on 6/12/2018, at 22:02, confirming that the 15-year-old boy was dead (B): 'The 15-year-old boy is dead, 06/12/2008, 22:02 pm. People are heading to the city centre. Let's all gather at Exarcheia square so not to let them shut down the area' (in Greek).

The third analysed thread focuses on comments on the video of the shooting scene as this was broadcast by Mega Channel (C) and consisted of 6 posts. However, in the thematic section of the December Riots, there is another discussion that concentrates on the video, which was not included in the sampling as it mainly focused on the technical characteristics of the video (Table 5.1).[6]

For the first examined node, concentrating on the historical background and the sociopolitical structures, there are seven different references, which drew a parallelism between the case of Grigoropoulos and the Kaltezas case, pointing out the police and state violence. Michalis Kaltezas was a fifteen-year-old who was shot dead by a police officer during a march to the American embassy on the November 1973 Polytechnic anniversary in 1985 (Kassimeris, 2013a, 2013b, p. 84); this resulted in violent protests and riots in Athens and other cities. At the same time, concerns regarding state corruption and injustice were strongly

Table 5.1. Nodes and References in the Three Threads/Posts.

	References				**Nodes**
Thread	**Total**	**A**	**B**	**C**	
	7	3	3	1	Historical background and socio-political structures
	35	25	10	–	Mobilisations
	9	2	1	6	Mainstream media
	33	25	7	1	Incident

[6]https://athens.indymedia.org/post/934020/, the video of shooting scene.

raised. In Kaltezas case, the police officer who shot the 15-year-old boy was sentenced and spent less than three years in prison, after which the court cleared him of all the charges.[7] In a comparative way, these two cases were discussed extensively focusing on the state's failures in terms of social justice and suppression policies, as well as state violence. Other issues raised from this node were relevant to conspiracy theories and the state, while the same consideration was later observed in the debt crisis discourse too (e.g. surveillance practices, discussion on historical incidents and police violence, how the incident outbroke). Finally, in this node the complicit relationship between state and capitalism are also debated.

The second examined node concentrated on mobilisation practices, communication, and organisation. This node is linked to 35 different references as observed in two out of the three analysed discussions. Even if the last discussion/thread (C) in relation to the shooting video did not have any references related to mobilisation, this was a major consideration in the other two examined discussions/threads (A, B). In this node, users discuss and exchange information on the real-time evolution of the incident after the shooting, as well as coordinating and organising future protests and collective actions. Therefore, organisational issues, strategies, and practices dominated the discussion at this point. This includes a review of police practices and opposition, advice related to the safety of protestors, while users used this platform for organisational reasons, settling and spreading information about meeting points.

As regards the privacy of online communication and the platform, users are aware of monitoring and surveillance practices of the state, warning other users not to reveal much information about mobilisation plans. Using this platform, users coordinated actions in different locations and cities across the country, while at the same time, a solidarity network emerged. While some of these points are already known from the literature, it is also confirmed here by the analysis of the relevant Indymedia posts/threads. Throughout the online discourse, a heavily debated issue is about the nature of problems and what type of actions should be organised. While there are examples of users encouraging participation in protests or calling for action against the police, on the other hand, there is much discussion and debate on what kind of actions should be avoided or not to be accepted (e.g. looting shops). Overall, strong critiques against the uprising, emerged in relation to acceptable protest action, with the debate concentrating on whether it is possible to recognise forms of resistance or struggle through destruction of property, vandalism and violence. This was debated by both participants and non-participants in the uprising.

The final thread concentrated on the video of the shooting scene. This was an amateur video, which was edited and broadcast by mainstream media presenting the shooting as a defence reaction, in contrast to the original video, which documented the real incident and was broadcast online (Vradis & Dalakoglou, 2011).

[7]http://www.tovima.gr/politics/article/?aid=245725

The post and the thread related to the video dominated the node of mainstream media, while some relevant references were observed in the other two examined discussions/threads (A, B). The dispute about the mainstream media was expressed focusing on different points (e.g. ownership), while the linkage between the state and the traditional media is also pointed out. At the same time, the contrast between the online and the offline incident's representation was highlighted and criticised throughout the discussion. Finally, there were 33 different references to the incident, discussing the conditions and the involved actors. Users exchanged information about the incident, in contrast to mainstream media information and representation. While the real-time information about the incident was important, at the same time, some of the online participants started organising actions and protests straight away.

Indymedia participants exchanged information about the victim's identity, the hospital he was transferred to, as well as the police officer's identity, confirming information and raising awareness of the incident. An interesting point here is that this is one of the first times in Greece when the online news agenda was transferred to the offline and mainstream media agenda (Vradis & Dalakoglou, 2011), raising debates about the impact of the digital media on the formation of the public sphere. Before continuing the analysis of the YouTube video post, it is worth mentioning that among the Indymedia posts there were some references to the first tweets about the incident as follows, highlighting Twitter's usage of the incident. The first tweet related to the incident informed that 'Someone got shot in Exarcheia' (Tsimitakis, 2009).

December Riots and YouTube: Video and Comments

As is also suggested by the relevant thread on Indymedia, the contrast between the mainstream and alternative media representation of the December Riots is clear in the case of the amateur video, which captured the shooting scene and the first reactions to the incident. Mainstream media edited and broadcast the video, presenting the shooting as a defence action to Molotov cocktails and attacks on police officers in the area. However, the original video was posted online raising strong criticism of the mainstream media, indicating the use of digital media as an alternative public space for the formation of public sphere, able to overlap limitations of mainstream media. Later, mainstream media presented the original video as well, blaming mistakes and problems in the editing process before screening for the misleading presentation of the incident (Vradis & Dalakoglou, 2011). Almost a month later, in mid-January, the Greek government tracked down Indymedia, making it part of the parliament agenda for days (2011, p. 143).

The examination of YouTube concentrated on the original video of the shooting scene as posted on the platform, in contrast to the mainstream media version. The analysis included 489 comments conducted under the node coding system as explained earlier. However, the final coding set was shaped according to YouTube's features and the rich corpus, which was provided by the collection of comments. In contrast to Indymedia, which is used mainly by users with specific political and ideological affiliation, YouTube caters to users affiliated with the wider political and ideological spectrum. Therefore, due to the length of the analysed material and the platform's features, a more detailed examination of the annotations and debates among users and about the actors involved in the incident is actually possible.

The analysis consists of the following nodes: (1) the incident, (2) the sociopolitical structures and the historical background, (3) mobilisation and the (4) mainstream media. Due to the rich corpus of data, three nodes were added to the data set focusing on the main actors involved in the incident (state, police), on the conflict as it occurred online (users' arguments and conflict) and on offline conflict (violence): (5) argument/conflict among users, (6) police, (7) state and finally (8) comments not related to the incident. The YouTube comment coding developed as follows (Nodes/Themes and Number of references):

- Incident: 90
- Social structures: 104
  –Historical background: 53
- Mobilisations: 13
- Mainstream media: 9
  –International attentions: 11
- Argument/Conflict among users: 95
  –Against riots: 13
- Police: 107
- State: 70
- Not related to the topic: 60.

Starting from the first examined node, there are 90 different comments/references relevant to the incident, with users discussing the conditions under which the incident emerged as well as the involved actors. Similarly, to Indymedia, discussion and information about the incident were expected to be among the most dominant themes of annotation, highlighting the way that different online media platforms provided alternative forms and channels of information, in contrast to the mainstream media and traditional journalism's practices. Users used online media platforms both to organise collective actions and mobilisations as well as to communicate real-time information about the incident, some of which transferred to the mainstream media. At the same time, themes and issues, which later constructed the crisis discourse are linked to this node and the examined incident. Some of the most indicative examples here are related to the domination of the mainstream media, the state and corruption (e.g. linkage between media and politics, ownership and historical background).

In this node, the incident is discussed focusing on the video content, as well as on characteristics of the shooting scene, including details regarding the number of shootings, the number of people involved and the type of argument (verbal, etc.). The next dominant discussed point concentrated on the involved actors. Here, the annotations are elaborated based on stereotypes, pointing out social structures and traditions, which arose within the historical context of the incident. Therefore, the state, the police, as well as the protestors and the people who did not support the mobilisations, were identified in stereotypical political debates and stereotypes (e.g. far-right – far-left, pro-/anti-government and the state).

Comments on the police officer who shot Grigoropoulos were mainly focused on his symbolic role as a member of the police and the state's power, while the critiques both on the police's practices and the state violence were also strong. In a similar rationale, the discussion around Grigoropoulos is elaborated based on the misconception of the anarchist teenager or the stereotype of the spoiled middle-class, fifteen-year-old boy. These stereotypes should not be understood separately to the period when the incident broke out, which was just before the beginning of the crisis – or in other words, as suggested, a prelude of what was about to follow (Vradis & Dalakoglou, 2011). In the Greek context, the clichéd perception of the violent and corrupted police officer, has its origins in the civil war and the dictatorship, while contemporary incidents, such as the Kaltezas case in 1985, reshaped this stereotype according to the contemporary Greek sociopolitical context. Based on these stereotypes, the discussion was further expanded focusing on an injustice framework expressing pre-existing historical political conflict continuities between actors.

The second node consisted of references to the main points of argument/conflict among users. This node consisted of 95 different references/comments, with the major argument among users being about whether violence and vandalism should be understood as appropriate actions and forms of resistance. Exarcheia, the location where the incident took place, is a student district of Athens, which is also characterised as the centre of radical political activism (Kretsos, 2012) and thereby, a strong critique on the motivation of the people and the teenagers visiting the area emerged. On this critique, Grigoropoulos' stereotypical characterisation as a middle-class spoiled teenager fulfilled this narration. On the other hand, the opposition to this approach pointed out the vulnerabilities of the state and the police, without straightforwardly linking the area to a specific political spectrum. A third approach to the issue pointed out that even if the incident justified the formation of collective actions and resistance, still violence and vandalism contribute to degrading protests (and the movement). On these cases, users accuse each other of fascist behaviour and ideology.

The next cluster of nodes included the node regarding police, state and the historical background. These nodes were analysed in groups, giving an insight into how the involved actors are framed, and at the same time, pointing out the public perception of the police as part of the state apparatus. These nodes are linked to the node of social structure and historical background, demonstrating the stereotypical and misconceived narration of the incident online. Starting with the police node, there are 107 relevant references/comments, which are not confined to the involved actors, but instead are focused on the institutional role of the police within the state apparatus. In this node, the examined incident is once again discussed in juxtaposition to previous cases, concentrating, though, on both the national and the international context, with references to the case of Kaltezas in Greece and Carlo Giuliani in Genova (2001). Police here is discussed as a part of the state's repression practices, while the youth is understood as a symbol of political opposition to the neoliberal capitalist system.

In this node, the examined incident is straightforwardly linked and presented as a result of the contemporary sociopolitical structure and the limitations of neoliberal democracy. Consequently, Greek society is to be blamed for the establishment and maintenance of the contemporary Greek political environment, which is characterised by injustice and corruption. Again, the issue of vandalism and violence is critically discussed, focusing on the destruction of the middle and lower-class properties as a strategy, which could impact on the policies and practices of the police and the state. Police and state corruption are among the main concerns in this node, while the association between the police and Golden Dawn is also pointed out. This is an early appearance of Golden Dawn, the neo-Nazi party, which came to prominence in the mainstream political scene only after the elections of 2012 (Bistis, 2013; Ellinas, 2010).

In the next node, there are 70 comments/references related to the state. This discussion is dominated by two sub-themes: corruption and power, which at this point is linked to state violence, justifying the incident and linking it to the historical background. Here, Grigoropoulos represents the youth, who is brutally offended by the state and therefore, there is a significant necessity for the youth to resist and reclaim its voice and position in society (rambokop1, 08/12/2008, comment 326). It is indicative that, during that period the discussion on the so-called 'G700' was intensive (Theodoropoulou, 2014, p. 183). 'G700' was a term with age, cultural and class characteristics and used to describe the younger generation (Theodoropoulou, 2014, pp. 183–190). This generation was the first, which was well-educated, with – mainly – a middle-class background, having low-paid jobs and part-time jobs, following the European trend, which increased around 2008, and eventually proved to be a prelude to the debt crisis. In contrast to this approach, instead of focusing on the younger generation, riots were described by opposing voices as having been organised by a minority, a specific small group of people, which traditionally tries to destroy the country through such behaviour and actions. Another point that is strongly highlighted in this node is that riots and violence were tools effectively used to draw attention from the profound meaning and concerns raised by the incident and managed to influence the media and political agenda (see previous and following comments).

The node of the historical background and sociopolitical structures is comprised of 53 and 104 references/comments. This node decodes the structures and stereotypes, which in all of the previous nodes results in argument and conflict, online and offline. At the same time, this process offers an in-depth understanding of the evolution of the incident per se. As regards the references focusing on the sociopolitical structures, unemployment, corruption and inequality, these emerge as the dominant issues of the online discussion. Another debate examines how and if there were specific practices and actions that could be related with fascism, while a discussion around racism and migration is also already raging away at this point. What is suggested once again is that contemporary democracy is unable to protect civil rights or protect lower and working-class rights. As regards the references to the historical background, Kaltezas and other similar cases are mentioned, with references to the complicity of police and state crimes during the dictatorship. Furthermore, migration, fascism and anarchism are discussed in linkage with historical examples and cases. There is clear attribution to neoliberal policies as well as to left- and right-wing parties and ideologies. Based on these points, state corruption is suggested as the surface issue of a multidimensional and historical political problem.

The strong linkages to the historical and sociopolitical background denote the emergence of a rich cyberconflict environment. The arguments and the conflicting ideas and ideologies are not only based on the contemporary difficulties of the time, but also additionally express traditional debates, which were expressed differently through history and time. This confirms the strong historical continuity, which up to a point explains the pre-crisis and the crisis era, while at the same time, the historical memory and the conflicting ideologies support the formation of contemporary social and political tensions. The ideological positions of the actors diversify when the case of Grigoropoulos is understood as an unfortunate momentary incident, rather than framing the Grigoropoulos murder as part of a historical political continuity of structural violence. In other words, the conflict arising online expressed offline is being understood as a sociopolitical conflict, whereby online platforms support the formation of mobilising structures (participation, recruitment, tactics, and goals), framing processes (strategy, identity and the Internet effect) and the political opportunity structure in which the Internet is considered as an important component (Karatzogianni, 2006).

The next node focused on the mainstream media, both as regards the national and the international interest that the incident attracted, as indicated by comments in different languages. The international interest resulted in the emergence of a solidarity network, which was strongly observed more in online media, rather than in the mainstream. A major point of consideration arises within the different narration and discourse as observed in comments in different languages. Users commenting in other languages expressed solidarity, while they also used online media to learn information regarding the way that the incident evolved. The dispute of mainstream media is strongly expressed, and the online platforms used to confirm or disapprove mainstream and offline media information.

The vulnerabilities and limitations of the Greek mainstream and offline media have already been discussed, while their impact on the public sphere is pointed out by the use of online media. The dispute about the mainstream media system is justified by the history of the Greek media environment, as well as by its linkage to political structures and the state (e.g. ownership, corruption, linkage to the state) (Doulkeri & Terzis 1997; Sims 2003; Smyrnaios, 2010; 2013; Tsimitakis, 2009). The gap raised by these limitations further amplifies the potentiality of online media, especially as regards the formation of the public sphere. As suggested by the analysis of online data, users reported the incident in real-time, thus influencing the narration of the mainstream media (e.g. YouTube video) and consequently, the discourses and debates in the public sphere.

The node on mobilisation is composed of a small number of references/comments, pointing out the necessity for the organisation of collective actions and mobilisations. That organisation was facilitated by the use of the two examined online platforms. In fact, participants adjusted to the characteristics and the features of each platform. In the case of YouTube, the features of the platform provided a space for debate and conflict, giving the opportunity for the discussion to be expanded continuously, but not in a chronological continuity and order, with users tending to respond to and criticise comments even years after the original post. In contrast, Indymedia's features supported the participation of a more specific demographic and ideological set of participants, who were highly involved in the organisation of collective actions. On both of these platforms, references to mobilisations and especially the participation of the organisational processes suggest that the online users were likely to participate in offline mobilisation. References to conflict or argument using swear words or references which were not related to the incident were grouped in one node. These references/comments did not contribute to the creation of online discussion and, therefore, were not included in the analysis.

Discussion and Concluding Remarks

The analysis of data was shaped according to the Cyberconflict framework. Therefore, the baseline of the analysis concentrated on the examination of the historical background of the incident, as indicated by the online material, and then, the findings were interlinked to the fourth chapter of the study and the review of the historical and sociopolitical background of the Greek political and media landscape. The next step of the analysis focused on the identification and the evolution of the major debates and conflict, starting from the examined incident up to the crisis era (e.g. state corruption, polarisation, far-right ideology). Participation has significant importance both in the online and offline environment. Users participated in the online discourse, organising mobilisations and initiatives, in an attempt to fulfil gaps raised by the already existing sociopolitical structures. At the same time, participation had a meaningful impact on the formation of the public sphere as well as on the representation of the incident.

The December Riots denoted a new era not only for communication but also for political participation, activism and protest organisation and coordination. Some of the initiatives founded during that period included the creation of online and alternative media projects, the occupation of social public spaces and squats, as well as neighbourhood assemblies. This created an appropriate *pre-existing environment of networked dissent, which at the crisis period supported the formation of alternative and solidarity structures and initiatives, which up to a point acted as a shadow* state, creating the foundation of the crisis movements and subsequent mobilisations.

The contrast between the representation of the December Riots in the online media and offline media indicated the way that the features of each media form influence the formation of the public sphere. At the same time, the analysis of the Indymedia and YouTube material pointed out the impact that the features of each platform have in terms of communication and participation in the online discourse. *Indymedia attracted users who shared a common understanding of the incident, common values and political ideology, in contrast to YouTube, which attracted users with characteristics from a wider social-political and ideological spectrum.* Thereby, YouTube supported the beginning of a complex discussion, as well as conflict at a more advanced level. Nevertheless, the areas of conflict and the discussed themes are identical on both platforms. Additionally, the features and the different opportunities provided by each media platform also had an impact on the organisational process of collective action. Indymedia was used for more in-depth and targeted discussion, including the organisation of protest, while YouTube was used mainly to raise awareness and recruit people, as well as a space for debate. Therefore, YouTube should be understood as a space for discussion and conflict, able to influence ideas and ideology, while, on the other hand, Indymedia is understood as a tool used for specific purposes, more strictly focusing on activism and supporting specific political orientation.

An interesting observation here is that the areas of conflict and the themes discussed online, in the case of the December Riots, were major considerations and issues, which dominated the crisis of sociopolitical changes and discourse, highlighting the gap between media, politics and society. Issues related to the state and politicians' corruption, violence, democracy's vulnerabilities in contemporary Greece and capitalism are some of the issues dominating the political discourse. *Online platforms were used to express and debate issues which, at that point in time, were not on the agenda or part of the discourse of mainstream media, pointing out, the weak inefficient linkage between media, society and politics.* At the same time, a strong bottom-up dynamic relationship between society and online media, which is a step forward in terms of expression, representation and understanding of the sociopolitical turmoil, is observed.

The December Riots were a 'monument to the glory of freedom of information and freedom of expression under capitalism' (Matsas, 2010b, p. 52), which challenged the 'monopoly of violence of the State and bourgeois power itself' (Matsas, 2010b, p. 52). At the same time, this was one of the first times in Greece that individuals participated in the construction of the public sphere, as it is shaped by the media, building the news agenda and finally, influencing the mainstream media representation of an incident (Tsimitakis, 2009). As is also highlighted by the literature, the mainstream media representation didn't manage to follow the online media discourse and content, which was updated in real-time, influencing the evolution of the incident per se. Although, later, the mainstream media reproduced news and information from the online media, a trend that still exists. Milioni discussed Owners and Palmer's opinion that traditionally, the radical social movements face a dilemma as regards media coverage and representation (cited in Milioni, 2012, p. 2). Mainstream media tend to ignore or misrepresent radical movements, while social movements are not able to control that representation. In contrast, while online and alternative media representations overlap such limitations, at the same time they do not provide the opportunity to communicate messages to a broader public (Milioni, 2012, p. 2).

In the case of the December Riots, *these resulted in a fragmented public sphere*. Nevertheless, while the concept of the public sphere should be studied in terms of public deliberation, dialogue or democracy, the Western establishments, including the contemporary type of democracy and the mainstream media structures, have already clearly indicated their vulnerabilities and limitations (Cammaerts & Carpentier, 2007, pp. 108–111; Dahlberg, 2001). In this context, online media offered an opportunity to overcome such limitations, providing a different representation of the riots different from the mainstream media representation. Although this creates ambiguity about the potentiality of online media, it still suggests a significant alternative to mainstream media limitations. At the same time, while at a later stage mainstream media adapted and transmitted information from the online media, still, the way that the information was adapted and presented by the mainstream media should be an issue of consideration. The example of the analysed YouTube video is one of the clearest examples of this procedure.

As Kyriakopoulos highlights, after the first week of demonstrations, the Greek and international mainstream media presented the situation as follows: 'the revolt of the spoiled: European youth are rising as they see the end of their privileges' (2010, p. 242). The representation of 'youth', of 'masked faces' or 'foreigners' participating in the riots (Kyriakopoulos, 2010, pp. 242–243) indicate references, which could be related to fear and terrorism. At the same time, media representation didn't extensively concentrate on Grigoropoulos' death but instead, focused on governmental practises and skills in handling the crisis, in contrast to the online media, thereby creating an interesting effect on the public sphere. Mainstream media were strongly criticised as regards journalistic practices and ethics, as well as the impact on public opinion. According to Fenton, 'the media, hungry for news fodder, routinely access and privilege elite definitions of reality and are claimed to serve ruling hegemonic interests, legitimise social inequality and thwart participatory democracy' (Fenton, 2008, p. 231). Thus, online media provided the opportunity for the formation of additional communicational processes and participation, having a strong impact on the evolution and structure of the incidents.

Consequently, the mainstream media's representation either had a weak influence on the public sphere or all together with online media contributed to the formation of a fragmented public sphere. The online media provided a public space for discussion and organisation of demonstrations in different cities across Greece and Europe, supporting the emergence of a network of actions as well as the creation of a new collective identity. Users participated in mobilisations both in local physical spaces and in online communities, reinforcing ideology and collective identity. Online media provided an autonomous and independent channel of communication, making explicit mainstream media vulnerabilities and their linkage to the state.

Traditionally, online media have always been more supportive of radical and social movements providing a more direct and effective method of representation and communication/organisation, in contrast to traditional media. For Atton (in Coyer, Dowmunt & Fountain, 2007, pp. 71–78), online and alternative media manage to reflect ideologies and support the creation of social movements and dissents, in contrast to mainstream media which tend to homogenise varieties of dissent, limiting the richness of ideologies and collective actions through simplified approaches and representations (Coyer et al., 2007). Indymedia, which is well known for its role in the anti-capitalist struggles of the 1990s, is an indicative example that points out the importance of online media in the case of the December Riots (Coyer et al., 2007). YouTube, on the other hand, illustrated how the different features and characteristics of the platform provide different communicational and organisational processes, supporting the formation of collective actions and social movements.

The case of the December Riots is a complicated and multi-dimensional example and it has been examined from a variety of different perspectives. In this analysis, what is examined is the main types of cyberconflict, which started with sociopolitical characteristics and was soon dominated by ethnoreligious debates (e.g. national identity, patriotism), indicating the grounds on which the crisis discourse was framed a few years later. At the same time, the December Riots represents the first case which situated the Greek context in the contemporary debate on the attributes of the internet and its effect on democracy – digital or not – highlighting the importance of online media in civil society and the contemporary social movements/protests.

Chapter 6

The Second Period: The Anti-austerity Movement – Facebook and Networks

The study of Facebook focused on the Aganaktismenoi mobilisations and the SYRIZA Online Diaspora, as two of the most indicative cases of the rise of the anti-austerity movement, and the restructuring of the Greek political environment during the crisis. This chapter provides, briefly, specific sampling and software techniques (for general explanation of the methodology see Chapter 4), the review of the overall statistics of the two cases and networks, and then proceeds to the analysis of the two cases (historical and sociopolitical background and analysis of data).

Sociopolitical and Historical Context: The Greek Indignados/Aganaktismenoi and SYRIZA Online Diaspora

The Greek Indignados/Aganaktismenoi: Sociopolitical and Historical Characteristics

The so-called Greek Indignados (Aganaktismenoi) can be understood close to the notion of waves of protest of contention (Tarrow, 2011), and constituted one of the first, and most significant, series of anti-austerity mobilisations in Greece. Therefore, there is a great number of different analyses and interpretations of this, focusing on social and political structures, on conflict and the crisis context (Douzinas, 2013; Mylonas, 2014; Psimitis, 2011a, 2011b; Theocharis, Lowe, & Van Deth, 2014). The analysis of the Greek Indignados became prominent as a consequence to the December Riots and in the context of the sociopolitical debates and conflict that is already suggested and observed by the December Riots. This view considers the historical continuity of events and collective actions, as well as the characteristics of the mobilisations, including discourse and participants. The examination of the Greek Indignados concentrated on the observation of online relationships, of patterns of connectivity and online coalitions. This process supported a supplementary understanding of the digital media use in the examined period, providing an identification of cyberconflict and its origins, as regards December Riots, as well as the detection of digital media's contribution to the development of online conflict, through networks and discourse.

Therefore, based on the main cases of cyberconflict, the examination of online relationships and coalitions, of patterns of connectivity, as well as the study of online discourse, an insight into digital media's contribution to the rise of collective actions, mobilisations and conflict can be proposed. A challenging consideration is whether and how the online conflict is linked or reflected in the offline conflict. At the same time, the study of the points mentioned earlier not only proposes an understanding of digital media in the Greek context but also situates the Greek case in the broader discussion in regard to the global wave of protest of that period, starting from the UK student movement and the OWS or the Indignados Movement, to the Arab Spring and Gezi Park and the contribution of digital media.

In January 2010, the IMF announced the 'Technical mission to Athens' (Crisis-scape.net, n.d., timeline, p. 6), while a few days later, in February 2010, the Greek government announced the first economic measures as well as the necessity of a rescue plan for the Greek Economy (Psimitis, 2011, p. 194). In April 2010, the Greek government announced the agreement on a stabilisation mechanism, which was created by the IMF and EU. At the same time, the first general strikes took place in February and parallel to the outburst of the crisis, which prevailed in all aspects of the sociopolitical spectrum, a series of anti-austerity mobilisations, demonstrations and protests emerged. During the period 2010–2011 the implementation of austerity politics according to the memorandum, and the 'rescue packages' based on IMF and EU requirements, resulted in a deconstruction of the sociopolitical structures in Greece. While for some, these policies rescued Greece from bankruptcy, the decay of social welfare, the degradation of key sectors such as public health, education or national insurance and pensions and raised taxes, together with the collapse of the two governing parties were only some of the counterpoints that deeply influenced social cohesion.

One of the first and largest mobilisations took place in Athens on 5 February 2010 and was organised against the first bailout agreement between the Greek government and the so-called 'Troika' (European Commission, Internationally Momentary Fund, European Central Bank). Despite the magnitude of fifth February protest, that was overshadowed by the death of three bank workers, among whom was a four-month pregnant woman. In the crowd, two or three people attacked the branch of Marfin Bank, which was located close to the Greek parliament, throwing two petrol bombs (Molotov cocktails) and setting the building on fire (McElroy & Anast, 2010). More than twenty employees escaped, but three of them were blocked as they tried to escape onto the roof and they were suffocated (BBC News, 2010). The case of Marfin Bank was a shocking incident, which should be considered within the broader context of historical police brutality and governmental repression policies of mobilisations (BBC News, 2010). Sotiris (2010) highlighted the 'tremendous amount of police violence against a huge demonstration' and the effect that such policies have on the escalation of violence in mobilisations. The CEO of Marfin and two other administrative members were later accused of negligence that resulted in bodily harm to the victims; they were also accused of their decision not to close the branch sooner. Add to that, the building's safety and security measures were considered to be inadequate. But at the same time, suspects for the bomb attacks were considered to be two anarchists. Although there was reduced participation in the austerity protests after the Marfin incident, mobilisations and strikes both in the private and public sectors continued. In 2010, the demonstrations in Greece were estimated at more than 580, of which 250 took place in Athens (Rudig & Karyotis, 2013, p. 12), while, in 2011, the mobilisations were estimated as being up to 445, including general strikes in the public–private sector (Katsoridas & Lampousaki, 2012, p. 90). Most of these strikes were organised as a response on the worsening of the labour conditions, consequently to the implementation of the austerity policies, as well as a response to the general outrage raised by a newly emerging sociopolitical reality.

At the same time, mobilisations such as the 'Indignados' in Spain, or even the 'Arab Spring' and the 'Occupy' movement, highlighted different perspectives of the crisis in the global recession as well as different forms of social expression. In the case of Spain, the financial and debt crisis indicated a 'moral' perspective of the crisis, influencing the sociopolitical spectrum and resulting in the emergence of the Indignados movement, which included a series of protests and occupations (Exadaktylos, 2011). On 15 May 2011, the so-called Indignados occupied the squares Puerta del Sol (Madrid) and Plaça de Catalunya (Barcelona) (Simiti, 2014, p. 5). The online media's contribution to the creation of the Indignados was significant (Hughes, 2011). Online and social media were used as an important 'networking and organising tool' able to 'express and coordinate discontent' against austerity measures, social injustice and so on, supporting resistance actions and mobilisation (Tsaliki, 2012, p. 5). The website 'Democracia real ya' (Hughes, 2011) had a significant role among other sources of online media, providing information and details of the concepts and the structures of demonstrations as well as the opportunity for participation and the launch of the concept of *Indignados*. The concept of Spanish demonstrations was supported and, in some cases, adopted by other countries. One of such cases was Greece and the square's occupations in 2011, which not only supported but also adopted the concept of Spanish demonstrations (Hughes, 2011).

The call for the occupation of Syntagma Square in Athens, and other central squares in different Greek cities appeared, following Greek media stories, which covered the Spanish protests in Plaza del Sol describing some of the protestors holding banners with the sarcastic slogan 'Silence or we will awaken the Greeks!' (Korizi & Vradis, 2012, p. 237); according to others, among the slogans heard in Puerta De Sol was a call to Greeks to 'Wake Up'[1] (Monastiriotis, 2011). Nonetheless, according to interviews with people who had a leading role

[1]According to blogs and in some cases TV, this was a message from Spain to Greece. Although, according to interviews with people who participated in Spanish demonstrations, this was never a slogan commonly known to demonstrators. Even if, indeed, this information was not documented, the way that it was presented via Greek media creates great interest. As an example see: http://www.washingtonpost.com/blogs/blogpost/post/spanish-revolution-thousands-gather-in-madrids-puerta-del-sol-square/2011/05/18/AFLzpZ6G_blog.html

in Spanish demonstrations, such slogans were never heard in Spain – at least on a massive level (Niaoti, 2011). In any case, the Greek mainstream and online media cultivated a discourse focusing on the Greek 'response' to the slogans at the Spanish demonstrations. The media representation of the incident created a strong social correspondence/effect, whether it was true or not.

The occupation of Syntagma Square on 25 May 2011 was one of the first mobilisations of the so-called Greek Indignados, or, as known in Greek, Aganaktismenoi (Αγανακτισμένοι) (Douzinas, 2013, p. 135). However, Simiti explains that the actual first attempt at Syntagma Square's occupation took place on 23 February 2011, but due to the limited participation of protestors and the forceful police actions, this attempt was not successful (Simiti, 2014, p. 5). After the February attempt, the online media mobilisation was intensive, calling people to participate in a peaceful protest disconnected to the traditional political ideologies, 'without holding any party flags or banners' (Simiti, 2014, p. 5). Social media was used both as an organisational tool, as well as a public space for promoting the formation of an online community with a shared collective identity. The online media provided a space in which motivations and ideas of the movement emerged, while they were also used as communicative channels through which users spread information about the movement, communicating its messages to a wider audience and influencing the news agendas of the mainstream media (Tsaliki, 2012).

On May 2011, people who characterised themselves indignantes occupied Syntagma Square. The point of reference for the Greek Indignados was the Spanish Indignados (M15), while a parallelism drawn with the Tahir Square movement is also discussed (Douzinas, 2013, p. 135). During the summer, Syntagma Square was the 'heart' of the movement, although the universal character of the movement was designated by the occupation of central squares in other Greek cities and the occupation of institutional buildings (e.g. hospitals and schools). Participation in the occupation was high, involving thousands of people (Douzinas, 2013, p. 135) and different events or rallies each day. However, the diversity of protestors in terms of ideology, class or age (Simiti, 2014, pp. 1–2, 8) did not allow the creation of a 'minimum collective identity', and therefore, the creation of a social movement, according to traditional characteristics was not possible. In contrast, Douzinas notes the importance of the high participation of people who shared a 'common political desire, which was the radical change of the political system' (2013, p. 135). From this perspective, the occupation of a public space such as Syntagma Square, which holds a large amount of symbolism in Greek political life (Douzinas, 2013; Simiti, 2014, p. 6), indicated an alternative structure of mobilisation, focusing on a 'debating, deciding and acting crowd' rather than on 'a manipulated and dictated crowd' (Douzinas, 2013, p. 135). Thus, even if the mobilisation formed a weak collective identity, the alternative structure of the mobilisation as well as the structural availability with regard to the opportunity for participation in the movement, were some of the main limitations and potentialities of the mobilisations (Olson, 1965).

In the case of the Greek Indignados, the characteristics of the physical and symbolic space strongly illustrated and, up to a point, supported the political tension that appeared during the first phase of the crisis. In contemporary Greek history, Syntagma Square, which literally means Constitution Square, where the Greek parliament is located (Simiti, 2014, p. 6), symbolised the struggle for democracy. This was already established from 1843 onwards, and there were mass mobilisations against King Otto, which resulted in the establishment of a Greek constitution (Madden & Vradis, 2012; Simiti, 2014, p. 6). On the other hand, Douzinas (2013) discusses the physical space of the mobilisation in parallel with the Athenian Agora, which is located a few hundred metres away. This parallelism denotes a linkage to contemporary civic society, which tries to redefine democratic processes, as well as the notion of citizenship and participation. Therefore, following the historical continuity of social struggles and the signified references of Syntagma Square, in the case of Greek Indignados, people demonstrated, creating a common body, or in Douzinas words, 'a political subjectivity' emerged, highlighting 'the right to resistance in post-industrial and post-democratic society' (Douzinas, 2013, p. 135).

Crucially, the spatial characteristics of the public space reflected and reproduced the – offline – political and ideological conflict, which did not enable the rise of a massive social movement against austerity. At this point, the dynamic relationship between the online and offline space with regard to the escalation of the political and ideological conflict is significant. Simiti explains that Syntagma Square is not a single, unified, physical space, but two different squares/levels connected by stairs that act as an invisible line to the physical space (2014, p. 8). This spatial division soon turned into an ideological one, revealing a tension between the upper and lower part of the square. Both the upper and lower part of the square expressed anger and indignation against the austerity measures and the political system. The 'upper' square formed a discourse concentrating on the crisis, which is understood as being a consequence of the corrupted political system, threatening the nation (Kaika & Karaliotas, 2014, p. 7), in contrast to the lower part of the square, which launched an anti-capitalist narration, situating the crisis on a global scale. The two parts of the square reflected two different ideological orders of dissent, national and transnational/global, as theorised in 'Surfing the Revolutionary Wave 2010–2012', mentioned in the theoretical framework in Chapter 2 (Karatzogianni & Schandorf, 2015, p. 46).

The upper square hosted everyone who lost their privileges (e.g. civil servants and pensioners), including professionals of all sorts as well as nationalists (Tsaliki, 2012, p. 3). Here, the demonstrators held Greek flags and presented both Greek and foreign political leaders as traitors, developing an anti-political populism (Simiti, 2014, p. 9). Groups such as '300 Greeks', 'The Greek Mothers' and others, formulated a xenophobic rhetoric, which transferred across the square's political spectrum (Kaika & Karaliotis, 2014, p. 8). An indicative example here is Kaika and Karaliotis' analysis of how the left-wing group 'Spitha' adapted some of the ideas of the upper square (Kaika & Karaliotis, 2014, p. 8). Even if it is not clear whether this xenophobic rhetoric was able to influence every participant in the upper square, the racist violence and the xenophobic incidents in Athens increased the tension between the upper and lower square's protests (Kaika & Karaliotis, 2014, pp. 8–9). While the discourse of the upper square was shaped according to a xenophobic and nationalistic ideology, there were not organised right-wing groups/parties participating in the process; however, left-wing activists tried to expel the extreme right groups of the upper square from the mobilisations (Simiti, 2014, p. 24). In the lower square, the rhetoric, the content of the rallies as well as the people who participated founded a different concept and frame of action.

The lower part of the square hosted more politicised and left-wing aligned people, comprising the 'hard-core' of the Greek Indignados (Tsaliki, 2012, p. 2). Here, professionals from various spheres participated, along with the 'marginalised, anti-established people' (Tsaliki, 2012, p. 2), representing the new generation of homeless people (Simiti, 2014, p. 5), as evolved after the 2011 austerity measures. Members of groups or political parties were allowed to participate in the occupation only as individuals (Simiti, 2014, p. 5); however, the left-wing SYRIZA and the extra-parliamentary left-wing Antarsya made a distinguished contribution to the movement (Simiti, 2014, p. 10). Activists who participated were considered to have a relevant experience of various movements and mobilisations, such as the global justice movement, the anti-war movement as well as the World Social Forum (Simiti, 2014, p. 10). An interesting point here is the way that the collective actions sculpted alternative organisational structures (Kaika & Karaliotis, 2014, p. 8), through the organisation of detailed labour divisions (Tsaliki, 2012, p. 2), such as a press office, a doctor's and nurses' office and others. At the same time, many artists contributed to the mobilisations, organising gigs, concerts, as well as dance and performance events (Tsaliki, 2012, p. 3). Simiti (2014, p. 10) highlights that protestors experimented with direct democracy by adopting horizontal decision-making, while protestors used cosmopolitanism's terminology indicating the international character of the occupation.

The spatial and ideological division of the Syntagma Square occupation reflected the fragmentation of the sociopolitical discourse of the mobilisations, which later contributed to the reconstruction of the political system (e.g. decomposition of the traditional political parties, the rise of Golden dawn, SYRIZA and so on). In terms of the participants' profile, Simiti (2014, pp. 16–17) utilising polls during the protest, concentrated on the following categories/characteristics of participants (Data from Chiotis 2011; Kollia 2012 cited in Simiti, 2014, pp. 16–17):

- Working Sector:
  - Private employees: 23.8%
  - Pensioners: 14.6%
  - Public servants: 13.7%
  - Unemployed: 13.7%
  - Self-employed: 13.2%
  - University students: 12.9%

- Age:
  - 25–44 years old: 25.3%
  - 35–49 years old: 27.4%
- Education:
  - Bachelor degree: 60%
  - Graduate degree: 8%
- Political background/affiliation:
  - Left-aligned citizens: 43%
  - Right-aligned citizens: 36%
  - No ideological background: 38%.

Parallel to the mobilisation processes and the organisational structures, another process that should be taken into consideration is the media representations of the movement. The contrast between mainstream and online media representation of the movement indicated the potentiality of digital media, not only in terms of representation, but communicational and organisational processes as well. However, digital media had a contradictory impact on the evolution and the success of the movement. These are the two issues we turn to next.

The mainstream corporate media, which produced the visualisation and the narration of the Greek Indignados events, (Tsaliki, 2012, p. 6) was influenced by digital media representations. Online media and especially platforms such as YouTube and Facebook crafted a 'carnivalesque' factor in terms of communication and representation (Tsaliki, 2012, pp. 5–6), and this was among the most significant reasons why the movement failed to overlap its 'carnivalesque' character, and from an urban feast to be turned into an act of 'revolutionising' the so-called 'democratic politics' (Kaika & Karaliotis, 2014, p. 10). However, the Greek Indignados supported the formation of an alternative 'political imaginary', very much as the Occupy Wall Street did at the same period (Castoriadis, 1987; Kaika & Karaliotis, 2014, p. 11), which resulted in the creation of a new generation of activist and radical politics. According to Dalakoglou (2012, p. 541), despite the limitations and the critiques, contemporary social movements, including the December riots, the Greek Indignados and movements with smaller dynamics, managed to construct a 'social infrastructure' based on which 'spontaneous (or not) revolutionary moments will not be just moments but a long-lasting situation', which, later on, will have the opportunity to deal more effectively with opposite political forces. Digital media contributed to the formation of a collective identity, which loosely arose through the different mobilisation throughout Greece. Also, digital media literally and metaphorically linked the movement to other international movements, developing an international solidarity network (Gould-Wartofsky, 2015, pp. 32–34). Digital media supported the creation of non-hierarchical, horizontal communicational and organisational processes (Karatzogianni, 2006), giving the opportunity for participation to individuals, groups or organisations, engaging them in a political/cultural conflict based on a shared collective identity but, according to Tsaliki (2014, p. 4), not necessarily sharing a common ideology.

Some of the most important mobilisations of the Syntagma Square occupation took place on 28–29/6/2011 parallel to the parliamentary discussion and vote on Greek austerity measures when the labour unions called for a 48-hour general strike (Sotirakopoulos & Sotiropoulos, 2013, p. 449). The mobilisations continued until the end of July when the municipal police intervened in the lower part of the square (30/7/2011) (Kaika & Karaliotis, 2014, p. 10). The non-violent character of the occupation was agreed and secured by the protestors, although the extreme police violence, as well as the ideological conflict between the 'left-spectrum' and the upper square was significant. The police attacked not only the demonstrators, but also journalists, passers-by, patients at the first-aid station in Syntagma Square (Simiti, 2014, p. 12), as well as volunteer Red-Cross doctors who treated the patients (Sotirakopoulos & Sotiropoulos, 2013, p. 449). Police brutality alarmed Amnesty International (Sotirakopoulos & Sotiropoulos, 2013, p. 449) and at the same time, limited participation to the mobilisations in Syntagma Square. Theocharis (2011) highlights that Greek citizens rank higher than any other European citizens in demonstration attendance and building occupations, comprising a tradition in relation to political expression, and, in a way, citizenship. In this occasion, more than two million people participated in the Greek Indignados' mobilisations accentuating the government's significant loss of political legitimacy (Sotirakopoulos & Sotiropoulos, 2013, p. 448).

The impact of digital media in the mobilisations should be examined focusing both on new practices and media usages, as well as the potential impact on political turmoil within the crisis context. The Greek Indignados demonstrated that digital media contributes significantly to the coordination, organisation and mobilisation of contentious movements and the obvious contrast between digital and mainstream media representations (Tsaliki, 2012). The extensive usage of digital media by groups with different ideological viewpoints (e.g. upper/lower square), who coordinated the digital media operations directly from the physical Syntagma Square occupation, depicted the polarisation, division and tension between the different online communities, and also internally in these communities (Simiti, 2014, p. 25), thereby linking the online division to offline political conflict in a way of hybrid continuation.

SYRIZA Online Diaspora: Sociopolitical and Historical Characteristics

SYRIZA stands for the coalition of the radical left (Ovenden & Mason, 2015) and it is composed of thirteen components (Moschonas, 2013), dominated by SYNASPISMOS (Rakopoulos, 2015, p. 180). The eleven of the groups participating in the coalition unified in 2004 and dissolved in 2013, when SYRIZA was finally founded as a unitary party. However, the origins of the party can be traced back in 1968 when the KKE was split into two groups (Moschonas, 2013). The pro-Soviet or orthodox communists remained as the KKE, while the Eurocommunists formed the KKE Interior (Moschonas, 2013). In 1989, SYNASPISMOS, Coalition of the Left and Progress (SYN–CLP), was founded as an electoral coalition between KKE and E.AR., which was part of the renamed KKE Interior and known as the E.AR–Greek Left. In the same period, the coalition of government between ND-SYNASPISMOS and later, in 1992 ND-Pasok-SYNASPISMOS, lead to further fragmentation of KKE, when the youth section of the party, KNE, formed the New Left Current also known as NAR (Ovenden & Mason, 2015, p. 21) and more recently part of Antarsya. In 1992, SYNASPISMOS represented the Eurocommunists and the critical/renewing communists, another group divided by KKE (Moschonas, 2013). In 1991, SYNASPISMOS (SYN–CLP) turned into a unitary party, while in 2004, smaller political parties of the left spectrum joined the party, creating the SYNASPISMOS – Coalition of the Left, of Movements and Ecology, based on which the Coalition of the Radical Left – SYRIZA was later formed.

During the 1980s and 1990s, KKE sacrificed its ideological purity in favour of electoral growth and at the end, governmental participation (Charalambous, 2012). At the same time, SYNASPISMOS, which was self-defined as a pluralist party, situated between the orthodox communist and the social democratic parties, and suggested a contemporary viewpoint on 'new issues' (Tsakatika & Eleftheriou, 2013). Both SYNASPISMOS and, later, SYRIZA strongly criticised and challenged the radical terrain of KKE, actively supporting the formation of social movements and contemporary initiatives. Nonetheless, the primary SYRIZA's aim was not only to guide but also to participate in the movements (Tsakatika & Eleftheriou, 2013), creating linkages to new social movements and the younger generation of activists. Therefore, it is indicative that SYRIZA created strong networks establishing the SYRIZA Youth Section and the SYRIZA Network of Trade Unionists (Tsakatika & Eleftheriou, 2013). Despite its poor electoral dynamics until 2012, SYRIZA had a strong impact on politics through its grassroots movements and social initiatives. After 2013, SYRIZA turned from a coalition of different components and tendencies to a unitary party, which though did not reinforce the cohesiveness of the party. In contrast, the ideological and political fermentations of the participated tendencies didn't manage to support the creation of a fresh programme able to suggest a realistic political alternative as regards the crisis' developments (Moschonas, 2013). After the 2015 elections and the referendum period, this proved to be a weakness that deeply influences the party's alliances with social movements, and their functionality as a political party, both internally and as having a leading role in the coalition government with An.El.

SYRIZA was the first political party in Greece, which took advantage of technology, creating and maintaining a website to support its pre-election political campaign in 1997 (Mylona, 2008). In 2012, SYRIZA's social media campaign was one of the most innovative online political campaigns in Greece, illustrating the potentiality of digital media adaptation in the Greek political context and communication. This campaign created increased interest in the communication strategies of the party, while this interest rises even further in the period between the 2012 and 2015 elections. Mainstream media concentrated on the online activity of the party and its communication strategies, claiming that an 'army' of employees or 'trolls' was working on the party's social media accounts, managing to establish or strengthen the linkages between the party, the younger generation of activist and the movements (Papadaki, 2012).

One of the first and the most characteristic examples here is Papadaki's reportage for the online news project on the 2012 elections (2012), published in the news portal Protagon, YouTube and Google (Protagon, YouTube, Google together again for June's elections – Elections 2012). This was among the first cases in which the mainstream media extensively focused on SYRIZA's online communication, presenting interviews with young activists and professionals who comprised the social media team of SYRIZA. In the reportage, politicised citizens and activist, working as volunteers explain how they organise their actions, pointing out the importance of working collectively and explaining that what they are doing, in terms of politics and digital media, has evolved since the Aganaktismenoi mobilisations. They describe how they created an (online) network across Greece, which concentrated on discussing current affairs, on answering questions, on organising mobilisations, as well as updating information on the events. Their role is not only bridging the party to the citizens, but also to support the formation of a transnational network, with citizens from different countries expressing solidarity and support. At the same time, the increase of the professional/or trolls' accounts and the way that this is reflected in the online conflict through organised online attacks is also among the topics extensively discussed. After the elections of 2015, when SYRIZA came to power, the social media team and the communicational strategy of the party were strongly criticised for different reasons, with three of the most indicative examples found in the participation of members of the social media team in government (AthensVoice, 2017), in using social media for blaming/threatening members of other parties (Ελεύθερος Τύπος/Eleftheros Typos, 2016), as well as reports about fake accounts used in the SYRIZA campaign (Dimokidis, 2016).

In the same period, in 2012, the antagonist party, ND, launched an equivalent campaign by establishing the 'Truth Team', reminiscent of the Orwellian Ministry of Truth (Samara, 2013) and having as an official mission everyday political analysis (Alevizopoulou & Zenakou, 2013). The Truth Team was created before the second elections of 2012, supporting the ND campaign, and then, stopped its operations. Later, and under D. Ptohos' supervision, the Truth Team reorganised and worked on the online communication of ND, which was at that point, in power (Samara, 2013). Opposite to the SYRIZA social media team, the Truth Team comprised experienced executives, mostly associated with A. Samaras, who served as prime minister between 2012 and 2015 and was a leader of New Democracy between 2009 and 2015. One of the most interesting examples here is the case of G. Mouroutis, who was the director of the Truth Team and Head of the Press Office of the General Secretariat of the Prime Minister, and the case of Th. Dravillas, who was associated with the Truth Team mainly before the elections and before being promoted to the position of Director General of the National Intelligence Service (EYP) (Samara, 2013). During the elections of 2012, the Truth Team campaign based its rhetoric on the 'Communist peril', making strong historical references to the Greek civil war and the Truman Doctrine (Manolopoulos, 2011, p. 67). This strategy cultivated a civil war atmosphere, supporting polarisation through the creation of the image of 'Us', the ND voters and 'Them' – anyone not supporting the party's policies as a potential 'communist threat' and supporters of SYRIZA (Alevizopoulou & Zenakou, 2013).

The political terrain of the period, 2012–2015, can be understood as a long-term pre-election period. Four rounds of national legislative elections and one European parliament election within four years radically transformed the Greek political environment. The elections of 2012 signalled the collapse of the Greek party system (Pappas, 2014). The election of May 2012 failed to produce a government and then, the elections of June 2012 were marked by the rise of SYRIZA, the entrance of neo-Nazi Golden Dawn (Chrysi Aygi) to the Greek parliament for the first time, as well as the pro-bailout ND victory. SYRIZA raised its votes from 4.6% and 13 seats in 2009, to 16% and 52 seats in May 2012, and 26.9% and 71 seats in June 2012 (Pappas, 2014.). Golden Dawn entered the Greek Parliament with 7% of the votes and 21 seats in May 2012, and 6.9% and 18 seats in June 2012 (Pappas, 2014.). ND was elected with 18.9% of the national vote and 108 seats in May 2012, and 29.7% of the vote and 129 seats in June 2012, forming a coalition government with Dimar and Pasok (Pappas, 2014.) (See Table 1).

In this context, SYRIZA's campaign, both on the 2012 in the 2015 elections launched an alternative political discourse which ended up dominating against the mainstream media and the antagonist parties. The campaign concentrated on creating a strong communication channel between the party and the users, who in turn co-created online political communities via social media networks to support the party. Until 2015 the SYRIZA campaign was linked to the slogan 'Hope is coming', which had a positive connotation emphasising on justice and dignity. In the referendum period, this slogan transformed into 'No', expressing the resistance to austerity policies. On the other hand, the antagonist party campaign and the ND's Truth Team created a campaign based on the division between Us and Them, a scheme which was reflected through the communist threat rhetoric and in the Greferendum slogans such as, 'We Stay in Europe', 'Resign'. In other words, what is observed here is the online manifestation of the politics of hope in opposition to the politics of the fear (Boukala & Dimitrakopoulou, 2016).

In a European context, Fuchs (2012) points out that the SYRIZA campaign of 2012, could be understood as an opposition to right-wing European mainstream media campaigns, which developed not only against SYRIZA but, also, in order to support the neoliberal discourse. It is indicative, that in this campaign, the crisis is discussed not focusing on capitalist interest, but instead focusing on racist stereotypes as regards the 'lazy Greeks' spending too much money (Boukala & Dimitrakopoulou, 2016). One of the most important things that happened after the elections of 2015, when SYRIZA came to power, is the way in which the discourse on crisis changed both in national and international mainstream media, through recognition of linkages between different manifestations of the crisis (financial, refugees, etc.) and neoliberalism.

Therefore, following the study of Facebook usage in the case of the Aganaktismenoi, and taking into consideration the ideological or political linkages between the social movements and initiatives during that period and the rise of SYRIZA, this study concentrates on the SYRIZA Online Diaspora. The study of SYRIZA Facebook is conducted through the detection and the analysis of a page-like network, giving an insight into the way that SYRIZA network evolved in the national and international context.

Methods, Sampling and Analysis

For the study of the use of Facebook, the online data were collected and analysed using Netvizz and Gephi (see Chapter 4). In both the examined cases, Aganaktismenoi and SYRIZA, a page-like network, was identified and discussed through a Social Network Analysis (SNA) approach. The selection of the FB pages was completed after searching on Facebook for the keywords/phrase 'Αγανακτισμένοι στο Σύνταγμα'/'Aganaktismenoi sto Syntagma', in the case of the Greek Indignados, and 'Σύριζα/SYRIZA', in the case of the SYRIZA Online Diaspora, using both Greek and Latin characters. Then, after the detection of the relevant pages and due to the high volume of detected pages, pages with more than one hundred likes/followers were included in the corpus. This was a factor that allowed the examination of pages, which were used to coordinate actions in different locations, or between actors and therefore, pages that were not active enough were excluded from the sample. The data extraction developed in three phases, starting from December 2014 to August 2015. Starting from December 2014 to January 2015, the data extraction concentrated on Aganaktismenoi network. At the same period, a second round of extraction concentrated on the SYRIZA online diaspora, focusing primarily and the transnational online SYRIZA Diaspora and secondarily on the SYRIZA online diaspora in national level (branches in Greece), from December 2014 to February 2015. Finally, a third round of extraction conducted from May to August 2015, fulfilling the national SYRIZA online diaspora (branches in Greece).

Then, based on this corpus, the page-like network included pages that were followed by other examined pages (depth 1), concentrating on the online coalitions, linkages and relationships between groups and pages. These Facebook pages acted more as websites in terms of why people read/follow and like them, rather than as typical examples of FB pages, in terms of individual use and social media features. Therefore, in this study, the examined pages are understood as nodes or actors, which represent different institutions and ideologies. The page-like network was examined through the detection of a cluster of pages (Gephi, Modularity Clustering), indicating main themes and linkages among them, online coalitions, etc. While the development of the page-like network indicated which pages each of the examined page likes/follows, it is indeed an important consideration whether these links/likes are a personal choice of the page's administration or indeed denote linkages between pages, groups, actors, identities and so on. However, even in the case that these links/likes are just personal/random choices of the page's administration, this is still a process which influences the production of online material as well as the communication process. Going back to the tools used in this study, Netvizz provides two different options as regards the depth of the collection of the online material. Starting from the examined page, the 'seed', Netvizz either retrieves all the pages that the pages liked (depth 1) or will continue trawling the links/likes between the liked pages and the pages that these pages like (depth 2). Thus, by trawling data at depth 1 it is possible to examine that page A likes page B and C, if this process continues at depth 2, then it is possible to examine which pages are then liked by pages B and C.

In the case of Aganaktismenoi, starting from the page[2] which was used for the organisation of the protests of 2011 in Syntagma Square, Athens, the page's network indicated linkages/relations to either pages with similar content, which supported the organisation and evolution of the anti-austerity protests in different cities, or pages vicariously related to the protest. The online network suggested an insight into the diaspora of the movement/mobilisations pointing out linkages to other (social) structures and initiatives. At the same time, the visualisation of the page-like network indicated additional points of considerations, focusing on dominant clusters, actors, positions, unexpected linkages between pages (e.g. far-right–far-left pages), as well as the linkage between the offline spatial division and online reproduction of online formations.

In the case of the SYRIZA Online Diaspora, starting from the official FB page of SYRIZA[3], the page's network indicated linkages/relations between FB pages of different SYRIZA branches, both national and international, while at the same time, providing an insight into the online relations between SYRIZA, EU politics and social movements. While some of these relations are already indicated by the origins of the party, its position in the national and EU political terrain and its association with social movements, still this analysis of the online network of SYRIZA offers a better understanding of these relationships and also a better understanding of the use of Facebook and SYRIZA's online communication strategy.

As noted earlier, the examination of online coalitions and the identification of online relationships and clusters, explains how different actors linked online and offline, pointing to strong or weak ties in group alliances and the interplay between online and offline conflict. Gephi was employed for the visualisation and analysis of the data collected. The development of a one-mode network (Wasserman & Faust, 1994), which refers to networks that measure a single set of actors (Wasserman & Faust, 1994, p. 36), provided an insight into the examined online networks, supporting the understanding of substantive connections (Wasserman & Faust, 1994, pp. 37–38) between communities and organisations as well as the transfer of non-material sources and movements in non-physical space (Wasserman & Faust, 1994, pp. 37–38). This is a very interesting procedure proposing an insight into online relationships, coalitions, the flow of information as well as the formation of online communities and networks. These

---

[2]https://www.facebook.com/AganaktismenoiStoSyntagma
[3]https://www.facebook.com/SYRIZAofficial/

relationships are understood by focusing both on cyberspace and the offline world, indicating a blurred complex of relationships; what is suggested here is that even if the online social units, the networks and the communities do not directly denote influences or interdependencies, the study of networks and communities still supports the understanding of actors and the way that these are situated in the examined environment.

For visualisation and clustering of both the examined networks in Gephi, the same parameters were used. Therefore, modularity, the community detection algorithm, run randomised, so as to produce better decomposition, using edge weight. On this occasion, concentrating on the qualitative characteristics of the network, it was important to look on more communities rather than on just the bigger ones, thus the resolution was set to one (1.0), so as to get more communities (lower than 1.0 would give fewer communities, but bigger ones). Visualisation of the networks developed based Eigenvector Centrality, which used to point out nodes that are highly connected to other nodes having a high level of influence (Cherven, 2015).

To sum up, the examination of the Greek Indignados and the SYRIZA Online Diaspora was conducted in three stages; firstly, the analysis concentrated on the examination of the environment of conflict; second, the study focused on the collection and the analysis of online material using Netvizz and Gephi, while the analysis was completed based on the theoretical framework of cyberconflict, using SNA and focusing on networks and discourse.

Aganaktismenoi Network and SYRIZA Online Diaspora: Overall Graphs Statistics:

The overall graph statistics of the two examined networks suggest some characteristics and attributes of the two networks and could be examined both through a comparative approach as well as individually. Here, the two networks are discussed individually, producing insights on the usage of Facebook in the case of Aganaktismenoi and SYRIZA Online Diaspora; however, in the future, a comparative approach could indicate some interesting points of consideration about the way that Aganaktismenoi might have influenced the formation of the SYRIZA network. At this stage, a quick review of the overall statistics of the two graphs, focusing on the statistical and numerical characteristics of the networks, led to the detailed analysis of their individual content and structural characteristics. Thus, after consideration of the overall graph of the two networks, the cases of Aganaktismenoi and SYRIZA are discussed individually focusing on the sociopolitical/historical background of each case followed by the analysis of the networks.

- Following the process described in the Methods, Sampling and Analysis, the corpus of the Aganaktismenoi page-like network consisted of data from 141 unique FB pages, while in the case of SYRIZA, the data set consisted of 391 FB pages, all trawled up to level one (depth 1). Then, the corpus of each case was imported into Gephi, which visualised a directed network. In the case of Aganaktismenoi, this consisted of 1,908 nodes and 21,247 edges, while in the case of the SYRIZA Online Diaspora, this included the 1,997 nodes and 15,404 edges. The nodes refer to any object in the network and in some cases, can be understood as an actor, while edges refer to linkages between nodes, also known as ties (Carrington and Wasserman, 2005). The network statistics were calculated as follows:

Overall graph statistics – Aganaktismenoi:

- Nodes: 1,908
- Edges: 21,247
- Network diameter[4]: 8
- Graph density[5]: 0.01
- Average path length[6]: 3.124
- Modularity[7]: 0.623
- Clustering coefficient[8]: 0.356
- Eigenvector centrality[9]: 0.139

---

[4]The network diameter refers to the maximum number of connections required to traverse the graph. Another way to look at it is to check how many steps it takes for the two most distant nodes in the network to reach one another (Cherven, 2015, p. 182).

[5]The graph density is a measure of the level of connected edges within a network relative to the total possible value and is returned as a decimal value between zero and one. Graphs with values closer to one are typically considered to be dense graphs, while those closer to zero are termed as sparse graphs [...] this is an important measure as explains how an individual network is structured and might help identify gaps or holes within the graph (Cherven, 2015, p. 183).

[6]The average path length provides a measure of communication efficiency for an entire network, by measuring the shortest possible path between all nodes in the network. An overall number is calculated for the entire network, with lower numbers giving an indication that the network is relatively more efficient, and with high average numbers signifying a relatively inefficient graph for information flow. This number will necessarily be less than the network diameter, as that value represents the maximum path length between nodes (Cherven, 2015, p. 183).

[7]One more approach to measure clustering in a network is through the application of the modularity statistic, which attempts to assess the number of distinct groupings within a network (Cherven, 2015, p. 189).

[8]With the Clustering coefficient, Gephi provides us the ability to measure the level at which the nodes are grouped together, as opposed to being equally or randomly connected across the network. Scores on this measure will have an inverse correlation with other statistics, including several of the centrality calculations, particularly when we are speaking at the global level (the entire graph). We can also measure this statistic at a local level, to understand the influence a single node within its own neighbourhood (Cherven, 2015, p. 189).

[9]Eigenvector Centrality explains the relation between nodes that are highly connected to other nodes with high levels of influence; this result to a high-level of Eigenvector centrality (Cherven, 2015).

- Overall graph statistics – Syriza
  - Nodes: 1,997
  - Edges: 15,404
  - Network diameter: 13
  - Graph density: 0.007
  - Average path length: 5.467
  - Modularity: 50.55
  - Clustering coefficient: 0.254
  - Eigenvector centrality: 0.095.

In the case of Aganaktismenoi and taking into consideration the 1,908 nodes and 21,247 edges, which make up this network, a network diameter rating 11 suggests an averagely linked network (Cherven, 2015, p. 182), while in the case of SYRIZA 1,997 nodes and 15,404 edges, and a network diameter rating of 13 suggests a strongly linked and tied network. For Aganaktismenoi, the rate of 0.01 graph density suggests a sparse graph (Cherven, 2015, p. 182), while the average path length rated at 3.1 suggests an average of information flow. For SYRIZA, the graph density was rated as 0.007 suggesting an even more spare graph, although this is justified after the visualisation of the network, and on this occasion, graph density does not efficiently reflect the characteristics of the network; as it is indicated by the visualisation this network is composed of two individual (sub)- networks, which are linked together with only a few nodes (See Figure 6.5). The average path length of the SYRIZA network was rated at 5.647 indicating an average to efficient graph of flow of information.

The modularity for the Aganaktismenoi network was 0.623, while for the SYRIZA network it was 0.55; according to Newman (2006), when modularity is >0.4, then it indicates that the partition produced by the modularity algorithm can be used to detect distinct communities within the network, highlighting that some nodes in the network are more densely connected with each other than with the rest of the network. The Clustering Coefficient for the Aganaktismenoi network is rated at 0.23 and for the SYRIZA network at 0.254, indicating the level at which the nodes are grouped together, as opposed to being equally or randomly connected across the network.

While the overall statistics suggests and gives an insight into the networks' characteristics, the calculation of the networks' metrics could describe in more detail the characteristics of the network. The first examined metrics calculated the Eigenvector Centrality. In the case of Aganaktismenoi, this was rated at 0.139, while in the case of SYRIZA it was rated at 0.095, indicating the importance of each node in the graph. Then, the calculation of the partition modularity measured the clustering in the networks, in an attempt to assess the number of distinct groupings within the networks. The group nodes formed are based on the strength of their relationships, while the nodes that are highly connected are likely to wind up in a common cluster.

Overall, the steps for the formation of the networks were as follows: visualisation of the network using Forced Atlas 3D. The Force Atlas 3D layout is

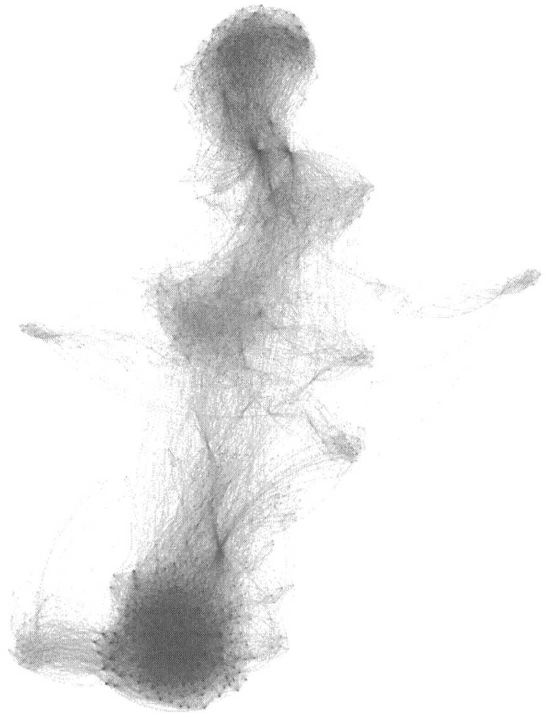

Figure 6.1. The Greek Indignados – Aganaktismenoi Network.[10]

identical to Force Atlas 2, with the additional option of setting the graph to 3D via a simple checkbox selection. As is noticed, though, the '3D graphs can lead to certain nodes being obscured from view (Chevren, 2015, p. 74). The differences between the two versions are often quite minimal, and mostly related to how the nodes are 'visually depicted' (Chevren, 2015, p. 74). The Force Atlas 2 layout is an algorithm, which is described as a good network analysis tool, which discovers and detects behaviour patterns (Chevren, 2015, p. 94). At the final stage, the calculation of the networks' statistics was completed; after this process, the networks were visualised by ranking the nodes according to the Eigenvector centrality and changing the colour and node size accordingly; the final step of the visualisation was completed using the Sigma.js template exporter. The Sigma.js exporter is based on the Sigma.js software, which facilitates the creation of interactive web-based network graphs using a template-driven approach (Chevren, 2015, pp. 294; 297–98). What the core characteristics description of these social networks means is examined in each case individually in the following sections.

[10]Group 1: 522 Members; G2: 2014M; G3: 417M; G5: 86M; G6: 400M; G7: 21M; G8: 50M; G9: 29M; G10: 3M; G11: 4M; G12: 16; G13: 5M; G14-34: 1M.

Greek Indignados/Aganaktismenoi Network Analysis (Page-like Network)

As explained earlier, after running metrics for eigenvector centrality and partition modularity (colours), the visualisation of the Aganaktismenoi network indicates five dominant groups, which encompass more than 100 nodes each (Group 1, 2, 3, 4, 6). Then the second category of groups consists of the groups encompassing between 20 to 100 nodes and the third category of groups encompassed 2 to 20 nodes. The fourth and final category of groups consists of isolated one-node groups. While each of these groups indicates a different level and type of connection/relationship, the first category of groups, which consists of Groups 1,2,3,4 and 6, encompassing more than 100 nodes, indicates the dominant communities in the network. Thus, instead of discussing the metrics and statistics of each of these groups/sub-networks, what is important here are the qualitative characteristics of each group, focusing on dominant actors and online coalitions, leading the discussion to the way that these can be understood in linkage with offline political turmoil (Figure 6.1).

The first group (Group 1[11]), is mainly composed of the online Greek Indignados' diaspora. In this group, there are strong linkages to the international equivalent movements/mobilisations (e.g. Occupy, M15, anti-austerity and anti-capitalist movements), suggesting an ideological kinship between movements as well as the origins of the anti-austerity movement. What is interesting here is not only the historical continuity and transformation of social movements, but also the way that anti-austerity and anti-capitalist movements were expressed in different contexts and countries. Therefore, while all the examined movements fall under the crisis context as this was shaped after 2008, the effects and the manifestation that the crisis had in each country can be identified through the unique features of the emerging movements. This draws the discussion from the local to the global and vice versa, pointing out the multi-dimensional character of the examined period.

Group 2[12] consists of FB pages against the 'New World Order', FB pages related to conspiracy theories (e.g. Against Masons, 9/11 attacks, and Paisios case), to the Greek Orthodox culture (Xristianos.gr, Church radio, etc.), as

[11]Group 1: 522 Members - Aganaktismenoi/Indignados in Greece and International mobilisations (Occupy, M15), Pages against parliament/Politicians, Corruption, Greeks united – pro-Greek and nationalist pages, Call for resistance or pages related to violence, Alternative structures and solidarity (media initiatives, neighbourhood assemblies & Squats), Drachma (National currency), APOEL (Cypriot football team) and Cyprus.

[12]Group 2: 214 Members – Pages against 'New World Order' (NWO), Greek Orthodox stereotype and culture, pages related to religion, Christians (Christians against NWO, Christians united, etc.,), Independent Greek/Anexartitoi Ellines (An. El.) – political party later member of the SYRIZA coalition government, Against globalisation, against digital surveillance and technology, 666, Paisios case, Church/god, home-country and religion.

well as pages related to the right-wing politics (e.g. Nigel Farage and United for the Nation) and the political party An.El. (Panos Kammenos, Anexartitoi Ellines/Independent Greeks, etc.). The ideological relevance between these pages and the formation of An.El., a new political party founded in 2012 (Ravanos, 2012), provide an example of social media's contribution to political polarisation and reflection online, suggesting a relevance to the eco-chamber argument. The later rise of An.El. confirmed the dynamic relationship between social media and politics; what is suggested in this case is that, indeed, like-minded people can be exposed to 'one-sided arguments that reinforce their initial predispositions' (Gainous & Wagner, 2014, p. 122) (e.g. Aganaktismenoi pages, pages with nationalistic content, anti-corruption, conspiracy theories, religious-related pages, and conservative/populists parties). An.El. which after the 2015 elections became a member of the SYRIZA coalition government, emerged as a populist right-wing party, having strong ideological relevance to the content of the examined group. On the other hand, focusing on the linkages between Group 1 and Group 2, what is interesting is the ideological differences between the two groups, as suggested by the actors comprising each group. While, concentrating on each group individually suggests the notion of polarisation, the opposite could also be noted, if the two groups studied together. However, while there are some linkages between the two groups, still these are not significant as to conclude to the aforementioned.

Group 3[13] includes pages against Illuminati and conspiracy theories and far-right related pages (e.g. Illuminati, Alex Jones and Infowars), creating a very heterogenous cluster of pages, which do not having a strong significance, but still suggest some relevance to both right-wing discourse and left-oriented activism, the antiglobalisation movement as well as contemporary social movements and collective action (Occupy Movement, Anonymous, Wikileaks, etc.). Group 4 is composed of humorous and entertainment pages (e.g. trance music, Mega Channel TV and Aganaktsimenoi in South Park). Finally, the last group in this category, Group 6, consists of pages of general interest; among the most dominant nodes in these groups is a page expressing opposition to the rise of the product prices in the supermarket (Aganaktismenoi with the supermarkets' prices, etc). In more detail, the first category of groups is shaped as follows (Figure 6.2).

The second category of groups consists of groups encompassing between 20 and 100 pages. The main group in this category is made up of Groups

[13]Group 3: 417 Members – Anti-Illuminati, against NWO, Zeitgeist, Alex jones, Rockefeller, Exposing the truth, awakening/awareness, Occupy Movement and related pages, Free Gaza, Free Palestine, Against Monsanto, Food Freedom, Demand safe water, Wikileaks, Google is evil, Anonymous and Anonymous Greece, ANTI-ACTA – against internet surveillance, Greek hacking scene, Anti-/Pro-Christ/religious pages, John Lennon, Greek Hip-Hop, Bob Marley and other entertainment related pages.

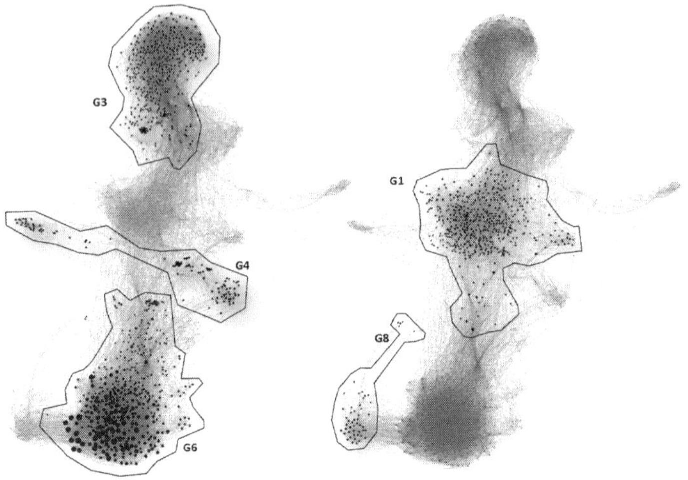

Figure 6.2. Aganaktismenoi Network – Group 3; 4; 6; 1; 8.

5[14], 7[15], 8[16] and 9[17]. Group 5 is characterised by university-related pages; Group 7 is related to SYRIZA, to the left as well as to anti-Nazi and anti-fascist pages; Group 8 is mainly composed of romantic exchanges and entertainment pages; Group 9 is composed of pages relating to the island of Crete and Olympiakos, a Greek football/sports club. Going back to the historical background of Greece, student unions always made an important contribution to the rise of social movements and to sociopolitical change. Group 7 and SYRIZA on the other hand, point to the increased impact of the movement and its rise in mainstream politics; both SYRIZA and An. El., have a strong presence in the network and this later materialised offline through the 2015 government coalition. At the same time, even if both parties were characterised as being populist, still there was not any political or ideological proximity between them. While An.El. emerged through the online environment, SYRIZA had an intense offline presence during the mobilisations. These mobilisations could be characterised as being a turning point in the rise of the SYRIZA party and its political and social impact.

[14]Group5: 86 Nodes – University related pages, Against University's occupation, Indignant students – Against Student/School Occupations, Elix-volunteering program, Tv Shows, Turkish soap operas, Greek Soap operas and series.

[15]Group 7: 21 Nodes – SYRIZA related pages, Alexis Tsipras, 105,5 Sto Kokkino portal, left.gr, H Avgi newspaper, Anti-Nazi and anti-fascist pages, against Golden Dawn, Against ND and Pasok coalition government, Aganaktismenoi, Anarchist, Communism.

[16]Group 8: 50 Nodes – Fan pages and entertainment, Romance.

[17]Group 9: 29 Nodes – Aganaktismenoi in Chania, Crete related pages, Olympiakos.

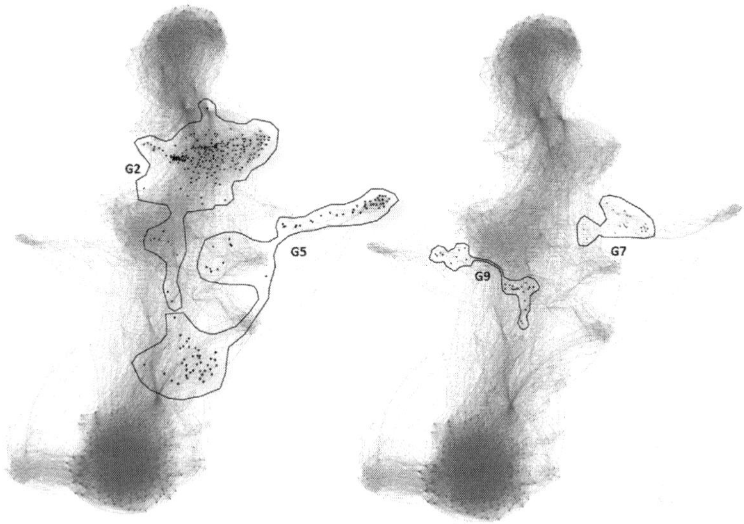

Figure 6.3. Aganaktismenoi Network – Group 2; 5; 9; 7.

For many, SYRIZA took advantage of the political turmoil of that period, because it was riding the wave of the movements starting from the December Riots onwards. This gave an opportunity to the people participating in contentious politics and collective action to be represented in the parliament, and at the same time, propelled SYRIZA to power after the 2015 elections (Figure 6.3).

The three most dominant themes in Figure 6.1, as indicated by the graph, are related to the cycle of protests as they broke out in Europe and in the US in 2011 (Occupy movement, Indignados), the conspiracy theories (Illuminati and new world order) and the stereotypical discussion of Greek Identity, which is very often, stereotypically linked to religious and the Greek-orthodox culture. The Greek Indignados appeared within the global wave of protests, which emerged after 2010, and were composed of anti-austerity movements in opposition to capitalism (OWS, Indignados, etc.), demanding the end of austerity, or even movements struggling for democratisation and regime change (i.e. the protests in the Middle East and North Africa, or the so-called 'Arab Spring revolutions'). Alongside similarities between the Greek Indignados and other movements, the online linkages of the examined network pointed out the position of the movement in the national and transnational context, as well as in different orders of dissent (Karatzogianni, 2012).

The first examined sub-network, Group 1, could be understood as being the backbone of the network, as it provides an insight into the Aganaktismenoi mobilisations, including online organisation and structure, as well as characteristics regarding identity and ideology. Aganaktismenoi emerged as a form of resistance against austerity politics, which in those days, were not discussed within a transnational context concentrating on contemporary capitalism, but instead, the discourse is much focused on the 'P.I.G.S.' narration, the Greek laziness and the division between the European north and south. In contrast, on a different point of view, Aganaktismenoi is understood as being a consequence of the 'unjust impoverishment of working Greeks, the loss of sovereignty that had turned the country into a neo-colonial fiefdom and the decline of parliamentary democracy into corruption, kleptocracy and clientelism' (Douzinas, 2013, p. 148). The difference between the mainstream and online media narration and framing of the crisis those days was intense, pointing out considerations of the formation of the public sphere, and focusing on the constructive process and the dynamic relationship between the offline and online public sphere.

As observed in the examined case, the contribution of social media at the time was significant, since it provided the opportunity and the space for the formation of an alternative political narration and ideology, able to fit in the new sociopolitical conditions, dealing with 'new enemies and new competitors' (Albertazzi & McDonnell, 2008, p. 222). The insufficient governmental and political response to the crisis, the social response in dealing with the 'new enemies and new competitors' materialised through the establishment of solidarity networks and initiatives, including examples of social economy and extra-parliamentary politics (Nasioulas, 2012). What is also described as 'creative resistance', included more than 550 active groups and collectivities during the period 2011–2012 in different sectors (Petropoulou, 2013, pp. 73–76), such as education, welfare, health, squats, neighbourhood assemblies and others. Digital media used throughout the different phases of these initiatives, supported the emergence, the maintenance and the further construction of hybrid (online and offline) resistance networks, while apart from social media, blogs and websites used to support these initiatives. In a similar way, blogs were very popular also for the Aganaktismenoi mobilisations, as these provided the opportunity to organisers of the protests to share information, manifestos, or polls and results regarding different activities (Pleios, 2013). This could be suggesting some sort of a hierarchical, top-down communication process between the most active members of the movement who had a leading role, and the participants; however, a more detailed study would be important, so as to understand the actual role and contribution of blogs.

In terms of their position in the network, Aganaktismenoi pages/nodes make a structural contribution, but at the same time, they were focal points for the social and political developments during the crisis. While media initiatives, house squatting, social kitchens and clinics were only some of the ways through which civil society recomposed its resistance, another significant point which is indicated by the first examined group concentrates on the issue of Greekness. Mylonas (2014) explains that in the case of Greece and the crisis, stereotypes were used as the prevailing truth, based on which the 'connection between (a rotten) Greekness and the economic crisis' was established (Mylonas, 2014, pp. 310–311). Therefore, the issue of Greekness is a point of contention and indicates polarisation terrain. Albertazzi and McDonnell (2008) explain that this is not a surprising phenomenon, because when the powers of the state shrink, control is taken by multinational corporations or organisations, while populist rhetoric attempts to reassure against fear and uncertainty by promising 'protection and security' vis-à-vis new enemies and new competitors and the 'rediscovery' of allegedly forgotten traditional cultures (Albertazzi & McDonnell, 2008, p. 222). Populist ideas and ideology, which are either left- or right-oriented, seem to be dominant in almost the whole of the network's spectrum. This type of process can be observed in more recent history with Brexit and the Trump-related mobilisations.

Aganaktismenoi was a wave of protests not directly or formally influenced by political parties and ideologies. This suggested an alternative in terms of political identities and ideology and it supported the appearance of populist influences and characteristics within the wider spectrum of the network, as well as the so-called politics of extreme. What was dominant in the mainstream media was an identification of the extreme politics of the far-right to the far-left in the Greek context, because of the bankruptcy of the politics of the neoliberal centre. More recently, in France Le Pen and Melenchon were seen as extreme parties and their ideologies were portrayed as such in a similar move, which saw Macron's party win the presidency (Smyrnaios, 2017). Gerbaudo extensively discussed the emergence of populism 2.0, which is described as a manifestation of the potentiality and threats of the contemporary 'global economic crisis, political innovation and fast diffusion of social network technologies' (Gerbaudo, 2015). However, what is critical here is that such linkages/tensions were already suggested online in the examined networks, before the 2015 elections propelled that coalition into power.

Groups 2 and 3 and the comparison between them indicate the way that populist ideas were adapted and reflected in both left- and right-wing groups. The major components of these two groups are pages relevant to 'New World Order' and other conspiracy theories (e.g. Illuminati), although, there are significant differences in the content of these group too. Group 2 is extensively related to the NWO and at the same time is strongly linked to pages that are related to Greekness and to religion (Christians against Illuminati, Paisios, Greek history, etc). The case of Paisios is a representative example of how religion is paradoxically and latently linked to the crisis and global politics. Paisios was a monk, venerated in Greece and Russia for miracles and prophecies (Eleytherotypia, 2014). The satire FB page Geron Pastitsios/Elder Pastitsios was a fanpage similar to the international Pastafarianism movement, which promotes irreligion, created by Philippos Loizos (Jauregul, 2012), playing with the name of the monk and a traditional Greek pasta food (Nevradakis, 2012). When the issue was raised at the Greek parliament, by Pappas, MP of the neo-Nazi Golden Dawn, the Greek cyber crime unit arrested Loizos, who was finally sentenced for malicious blasphemy and offending religion (21/09/2012) (Weisenthal, 2012). Loizos' case was one of the first cases, which at the time, due to the insufficient regulations relating to the Greek online environment, attracted national and international interest. In an act of solidarity and as a means of criticising the Greek authorities, the hashtag #FreeGeronPastitsios was trending for days on Greek Twitter. This case links to the sub-networks here because of the religious component and how that connects to prejudice and conspiracy theories, in turn feeding into far-right thinking and ideologies. The case of Paisios/Pastitsios indicates a conflict between two different ideologies, two different ways of understanding relationships between state apparatuses, such as the state and religion, digital governance and political-cultural hegemony in civil society. At the same time, this case straightforwardly illustrates the way that the debt crisis turned into a crisis of democracy and freedom (Nevradakis, 2012).

Therefore, indicative examples of the populist and far-right rhetoric of this group are pages related to Paisios, a Greek monk, to Greece and the 'beloved nation', as well as to pages related to Internet dystopia and technophobia. Such pages developed around inaccurate and bizarre perceptions and discussion on surveillance and globalisation. Here, technology and digital services are preset as the metaphysical 'evil', the abstract 'bad' and 'immoral'. Under this rationale, the nationalistic-oriented ideology and actions are suggested as the most indicative path for resistance. Nonetheless, these latent approaches should not be confused with the international global justice or anti-surveillance and transparency movements. This is closer to the New World Order conspiracy theory strands, where anti-globalisation rhetoric is developed under the thread of an abstract evil idea (NWO) and the threat of globalisation, which could destroy the notion of nation and national identity. This, however, is not discussed in academic debates and ideas, but rather is presented as a threat from the abstract 'superpower bad' whose true aim is to destroy the country, 'threatening our language, our culture', etc. In other words, due to the abstract 'superpower evil' and the existing conspiracy-related plans against the nation, etc., what should be protected is the idea of 'us' against the 'others' (Anderson, 2006; Billig, 1995).

Moving to the third group, while the issue of conspiracy theories still has a dominant position in the network, the way that this is detected here is slightly different in comparison to the previous one. The discussion here is related to the NWO and strongly linked to Illuminati, Rockefellers and other similar pages. Such pages as the ones in this group are also related to pages which call for 'exposing the truth', try to awake people or to raise awareness – about corrupted politicians, about the NWO and others. At the same time, another important theme in the network focuses on the pages that demand 'Free Gaza', 'Free Palestine' or express support for groups, which act against Monsanto, organisations supporting the right to free and safe water, etc. The next notable theme is related to technology and the digital world, which here is presented in a very detached way in comparison to the previous group. Links to Anonymous pages, to Wikileaks pages, as well as pages related to the Anti-ACTA campaign against Internet surveillance and the Greek hacking scene, suggest that indeed, a consideration of digital governance exists, although it is perceived through a less conservative and parochialist approach. Furthermore, this approach suggests a linkage with international movements and activism, which is expressed both online and offline. Other less prominent themes are related to this group concentrate on anti-/pro-Christ and religion pages and on entertainment-related fanpages. The next two groups, 4 and 6, could be described as less politicised or 'apolitical'. These groups consist of pages that are supportive of NGOs, vegan and environmental groups, of humorous

Aganaktismenoi versions of pages, making some connection with pop culture and entertainment (i.e. the Atenistas, a hipster-type pop culture phenomenon). Other notable themes in these groups are related to entertainment (music, TV Channels and Shows, etc.), to romantic exchange-related pages, as well as to pages of general interest.

The analysis of the second category of groups (Groups 5, 7, 8 and 9), points to a different perspective in terms of graph interpretation as well as the formation of small online communities. These groups concentrate more on themes limited to each group's boundaries. Group 5 focuses on an anti-occupation university community, supporting the New Democracy and other right-wing groups, which expressed opposition to the wave of university occupations at the time. In this last section of analysis, we are able to observe the dominant actors and their coalitions, in order to understand the fragmentations and emergence of network structures, which later dominate and transfer to Greek Twitter in the following chapter (Figure 6.4).

Focusing on the overall structure of the network, the most dominant group, Group 1 (Aganaktismenoi), could be characterised as the heart of the network, due to the content it carries. This group is linked to Group 2 (NWO, conspiracy theories/religion) while Group 4 develops by crossing with Group 1 and at the periphery of the network's main body. Group 4 consists of pages related to Greenpeace, to vegans as well as to entertainment pages. This group has no strong linkage to the other groups, although its position in the network could

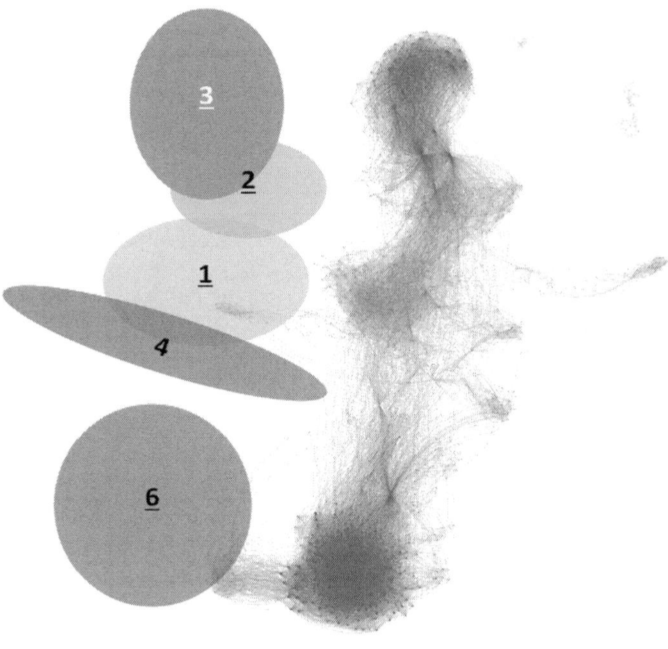

Figure 6.4. Structure of the Network and Sub-networks.

suggest an insertion to Group 6, which is composed of pages mainly relating to music and entertainment. Thus, the groups located below Group 1 are not straightforwardly related to politics or the crisis context. On the other hand, the groups located above Group 1 have more political-oriented content. Moreover, and this is significant, while Group 3 consists of pages related to contemporary social movements from different countries, focusing both on local and global politics, this group is not straightforwardly connected with Group 1, the Aganaktismenoi group. Instead, the connective group between Groups 1 and 3 is Group 2, which is related to pages linked to national and religious content as well as against the New World Order and conspiracy theories. While this is not supporting the bubble effect, as suggested earlier, another interpretation could also suggest that the Aganaktismenoi are essentially exposed to anti-globalisation movements and international discourse through conspiracy theorists and NWO groups.

Concluding Remarks and Discussion

The graph of the Aganaktismenoi network could be further analysed in a more advanced and in-depth approach, focusing on sub-networks and nodes, on dominant points and positions, and so on. However, the analysis of the network conducted was in order to track the emergence/evolution of the ideology and organisation through digital media starting from the previously examined cases/platforms (Indymedia, YouTube and December Riots) to the next examined case (Twitter greferendum) to explain the themes as raised by the December Riots, related to movements, corruption and resistance as well as solidity networks, move on to new themes such as the currency debate (Drachma/Euro) as well as to pro-Greek nationalists' pages. This is not impressive considering the historical continuity of the incidents as well as the evolution of the crisis and its effects on the whole range and structure of the social and political spectrum.

The networks of Aganaktismenoi pointed out issues of polarisation as well as the emergence of different ideologies. Starting from polarisation, the offline polarisation of the Aganaktismenoi mobilisations is reflected online through the development of groups and then, through the structural development/association of these groups to the main body of the network. The Aganaktismenoi pages (Group 1) are strongly linked to right-wing and populist pages (Group 2), which act as a bridge between the Aganaktismenoi pages and the pages related to national/transnational social movements (Group 3). In a different interpretation, Group 3 (Social Movements pages) acts as an ideological umbrella, based on which Group 2 (right-wing and populist pages) and Group 1 (Aganaktismenoi pages) developed. Apart from the ideological and structural opposition as observed by Group 1 and Group 2, opposition among smaller groups (Group 5 and 7) pointed out the contrast between left-wing and right-wing pages online. Going back to the case of the December Riots (Chapter 5) what is significant is the way that the indicated themes evolved and were expressed differently in the two cases. (December Riots and Aganaktismenoi). In December Riots, there are some linkages to transnational debates and movements; however, the debates of that example were related to national oriented issues and context. In contrast, the Aganaktismenoi are straightforwardly related to transnational debates, focusing both on the crisis and various ideological concerns/conflict on issues related to technology, politics and so on.

SYRIZA Online Diaspora (National – Transnational): A Page-like Network

The visualisation of the SYRIZA Online Diaspora network indicates four dominant groups, which encompass more than 100 nodes each (Groups 3, 2, 1, 4). Then, the second category of groups consists of groups encompassing between 10 and 50 (Groups 5, 6, 10, 20) nodes and the third category of groups encompassing 1-node groups and up to 3-node groups. The first category of groups, which consists of Groups 1, 2, 3 and 4, encompasses more than 100 nodes, suggesting the dominant communities in the network. Similar to the Aganaktismenoi analysis, the analysis focuses on the qualitative characteristics of each group, concentrating on dominant actors and online coalitions, in order to understand their relationships with the offline political culture in the years

Figure 6.5. SYRIZA Diaspora.

2012–2015 and their impact on the several elections taking place during that period (Figure 6.5).

In the first category of groups (up to 100 nodes), Group 3 is the heart of the network as it consists mainly of SYRIZA-related pages. Group 2 is comprised of pages related to AEK FC, a Greek association football club. Group 3 and Group 4 could be understood as two different networks as there are only five linkages between them, among which are entertainment pages, and youth SYRIZA branches and youth Football branch pages. Group 1 is associated with various pages, including media, politics, social movements and initiatives.

The second category of groups (less than 100 nodes) is comprised of Group 10, Group 6, Group 5 and Group 20[18]. Group 10[19] is composed of pages against austerity and pages related to nationally oriented debates (Macedonia, Cyprus, etc.) and anti-racist pages. Group 6 develops around the coalition of SYRIZA – An.El., and similar pages, as well as around pages about Exarcheia. Group 5 is composed of pages related to SYRIZA and Exarcheia, while Group 20 is related to SYRIZA pages and various left-oriented pages (e.g. Antifa and Youth section Ecologist-Green). Nevertheless, this category of groups is composed of small groups/sub-networks, which consists of a maximum of 40 members/nodes. Therefore, these groups were not perceived as having critically influenced the SYRIZA network and therefore, are not discussed in depth. A closer look at the first category of groups supported the in-depth understanding of how this platform contributed to the case of the SYRIZA Diaspora, and at the same time, indicates linkage between SYRIZA, movements and other coalitions. In more detail, the most dominant groups are shaped as follows (Figure 6.6).

Group 3[20] is the backbone of the SYRIZA Online Diaspora, consisting of the national and international SYRIZA pages as well as SYRIZA candidates' fanpages. Secondly, left-wing oriented pages, including media pages (left.gr, Aygi Newspaper, RednoteBook, Leftlab, etc.), communism/Eurocommunism and EU left-wing parties' pages (Die Linke, International Workers Left, European Left, L' Altra Europa con Tsipras), as well as Greek, left-wing groups (Antarsya) are also included in the group. This group is indicative as regards the national and transnational formation of the SYRIZA network, both online and offline, suggesting an insight into the party's coalitions. To a lesser extent, pages relating to historical and contemporary philosophical and political

[18]Group 6: 20 members; Group 5: 14 members; Group 20: 12 members.

[19]Group 10: 39 members, Pro-EU, anti-nationalist traditions, anti-fascism, anti-Golden Dawn.

[20]Group 3: 835 members – SYRIZA national/international pages, Communism – Eurocommunism pages, solidarity initiatives & networks (media initiatives, neighbourhood assemblies & Squats), ERT- ERTOpen, Indignados & Greek Indignados, Occupy, Anonymous, Free Palestine pages, Podemos, Socialist workers, international workers left, MP candidates & Academics pages, Marx, Lenin, Žižek, Castoriadis, etc., Die Linke, European Left, L' Altra Europa con Tsipras, Media organisations pages.

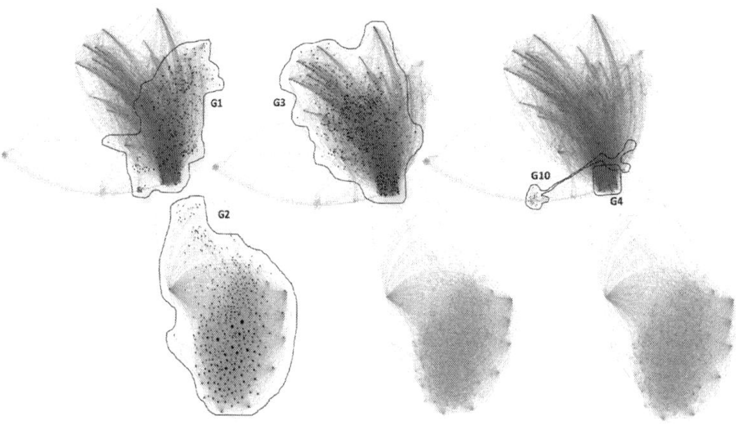

Figure 6.6. SYRIZA Network – Groups, 1; 2; 3; 4; 10.

figures (e.g. Luxemburg, Althusser, Marx Engels, Castoriadis and Žižek), pages related to contemporary national and international social movements (Anonymous, Wikileaks, Aganaktismenoi, OWS, Podemos, Cleaners-Ministry of Finance, Skouries, etc.) as well as pages of solidarity networks and initiatives (ERTOpen, Stand with Greece, Network for Solidarity and Change, Neighborhood assemblies and housing squats and Solidarity Community), are also part of this group. The historical and political references/links observed in the network reveal the way that SYRIZA reflected its ideological and identity characteristics online, situating itself in the online network of social movements and initiatives.

Group 2[21] is a sub-network with only a few links and is composed of pages related to AEK FC, football club. While this sub-network could have been excluded from the SYRIZA Online Diaspora, it is still a great opportunity to point out limitations of computational and software-assisted analysis, highlighting the importance of the efficient analysis of qualitative characteristics of each examined case as well as the contribution of the efficient understanding of the historical and sociopolitical background of each case.

The most dominant actors in Group 1 are pages related to SYRIZA national branches (SYRIZA Neapolis and SYRIZA Magnisias) as well as anti-fascist pages and anti-Golden Dawn pages (We say no to Golden Dawn, Antifa Paros, Antifa Magnisias, Action against Racism, Sunday Migrants' School, Anti-fascist action for Greece, etc.). This group is indicative of the online association between SYRIZA and social movements or collective actions, especially at a national level, including pages related to environmental mobilisations (e.g. Save Skouries and Save the Water) and autonomous initiatives (BIO.ME). Few nodes of international pages such as Solidarity Water Europe or EU citizens' initiative

[21]Group 2: 426 members – AEK FC.

point out clear alliance-building or, as Bennett would call it, 'connective action' (Bennett, Date) between national and international collective actions. Other nodes such as SYRIZA and left-wing University (EAAK, Antarsya, etc.) student associations' pages as well as left-wing youth organisations (e.g., Students Antifa-movement), suggest a linkage between the younger generation of activists and SYRIZA. Again, pages related to historical political figures (e.g. Evo Morales, Hugo Chavez, S. Allende, Che Guevara and Velouhiotis) as well as revolutionary pages pointed out the radical background of the party, while left-wing oriented media pages highlight once again the ideological association made in relation to and for the benefit of the party.

SYRIZA's pre-election campaigns of 2012 and 2015 emphasised the bottom-up structure of the party, which could almost be understood in terms of networks – a network composed of small networks and initiatives. Therefore, this group together with Group 3, demonstrates how the SYRIZA network spread among different political institutions and actors at the national and European level, which then jump-scaled to the international level. Finally, linkages to media institutions indicated the way that SYRIZA, during that period, was heavily supported by mainly non-mainstream and left-wing oriented media organisations.

Group 4[22] is comprised of the SYRIZA transnational diaspora, drawing from the Greek academic diaspora (e.g. University of Cambridge and European Left Summer University 2013) and the Greek diaspora (e.g. Berlin Greek Society), which was actively involved in EU politics (Communist Party – Cambridge Branch). University and media pages in English, French, German and Italian highlight the way that the SYRIZA network expanded in different countries, linking the party to the European and international mobilisation against austerity and neoliberalism (e.g. For a European Spring, Naomi Klein, Blockupy Europe, Assembly against austerity, Refugees Welcome, US Uncut and Podemos diaspora). Interestingly, in this sub-network there are not many linkages between SYRIZA international and the national diaspora, but instead the SYRIZA international diaspora is linked to social movements and solidarity networks and initiatives (US Uncut, Free Gaza, Coalition of Resistance: Can't pay won't pay, Social clinics – Rethimno, etc.).

In contrast with the Aganaktismenoi network, the SYRIZA network is having a strong coherence between the pages included in the network and the analysed groups. Therefore, the type and theme of pages in this network focus on the ideological terrain through which SYRIZA evolved, as well as on the linkages between SYRIZA and different institutions, organisations and social movements. Here, the Internet is not used as a weapon for attacking the

---

[22]Group 4: 197 members – International SYRIZA diaspora, University pages, Media pages (England, France, German, Italy), Left EU parties, SYRIZA international (Scotland, Sweden, etc.), EU parliament, US Uncut, Podemos diaspora (Berlin, etc.) For a European Spring, Naomi Klein, Blockupy Europe, Assembly against austerity, Refugees Welcome.

opposition in endless debates and trolling; instead, it is as much a tool for coordination, organisation and mobilisation of large national and international groups of the public for support building to connect the party to the masses. This led to the creation of the online SYRIZA identity, forming ideology produced and reproduced by hybrid (online/offline) coalitions (Figure 6.7).

Focusing on the structure of the SYRIZA network, the division of the network in two sub-networks (Group 2 and Groups 1, 3, 4) is pointed out. These sub-networks are formed due to the poor linkages between Group 2 and the upper part of the network (G1, G3, G4). While this group could have been excluded from the corpus, it highlights why an in-depth understanding of the historical and sociopolitical background of each examined case is equally important to the analysis of online data. Therefore, on this occasion and based on the context of the examined case, Group 2 is not directly associated with and relevant to SYRIZA and was only included in the network because of some weak linkages to the core network.

The upper part of the network is composed of G1, G3 and G4. G4, formed by transnational SYRIZA pages – G1 by SYRIZA national branch pages, while G3 is dominated by social movement pages. G4 has a strategic position in the network as it acts as a cross point for G1, G3, and G4. G1 (SYRIZA

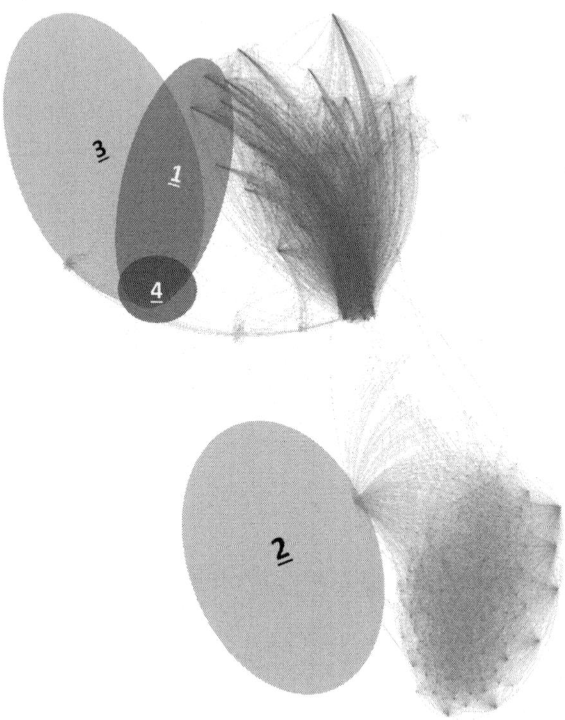

Figure 6.7. Structure of the Network and Sub-networks – SYRIZA Network.

national branch pages) is strongly connected to G3 (social movement pages), while G4 (transnational SYRIZA pages) has an important position in the network's structure, binding all the groups of the network together.

Discussion and Concluding Remarks

The SYRIZA Online Diaspora is composed of the national and transnational diaspora as well as the participation of civil society actors. This network demonstrates the strong association between SYRIZA and the movements, starting from the case of Aganaktismenoi and concluding with more contemporary examples. While there are some similarities between the Aganaktismenoi network and the SYRIZA network, SYRIZA appears to be more concentrated and has clear frameworks as regards themes and its political and ideological orientation. Still, however, references to historical and political figures, or references on social movements with origins in the anti-capitalist and anti-war movements, indicate the association of SYRIZA both with Aganaktismenoi and international social movements. At the same time, contemporary examples, such as environmental mobilisations (Skouries), solidarity initiatives (social clinics) and linkages to the anti-fascist movement also demonstrate the transformation of the crisis. Another interesting point suggested by the network is the way that SYRIZA took advantage of contemporary collective actions and social movements in order to build a political platform to represent these civil society actors by riding the mobilisation wave. This point was among the most significant points of criticism against SYRIZA, which might indeed have managed to gain the vote of people participating in social movements, although it did not manage to successfully represent them in the mainstream media arena.

The SYRIZA network highlighted the political debate as regards the evolution of the EU crisis. SYRIZA appeared to be strongly linked to the EU left political scene, which supports the necessity for change in Europe (Podemos, Die Linke, etc.). In this discussion, and in the network too, the role of Academia is important, while after the election of SYRIZA in 2015, many academics, become in charge of neuralgic positions in the government. SYRIZA's pre-election campaigns of 2012 and 2015 developed in contrast to the New Democracy rhetoric, which was based on the division between 'us' and 'them', focusing on the pro-/anti-austerity debate as it appeared both on a national and European level. Therefore, the linkages between SYRIZA and social movements, which emerged in the crisis context, as well as the linkages between SYRIZA and the European left, suggested the formation of a unitary political front with dynamics from 'below'. Grassroots mobilisation by SYRIZA formed an online network bringing together the social movements of the left and the debates on austerity, anti-austerity related pages, pro-refugees and anti-fascist pages, suggesting the transformation of the debt crisis of 2008 into the multilayered crisis after 2015, which was dominated by the refugee crisis and the rise of the far-right.

While the SYRIZA network strongly indicated the importance of the social movement dynamics both online and offline, this was a structure that collapsed after the election of SYRIZA and the 2015 elections. The (de)coalescence of the movement and its bureaucratisation, indicated the impact of social movements on the party and vice versa. Another consideration that might arise here is the impact of SYRIZA on the EU and national left-wing politics as well as its impact on anti-austerity politics. Within all these procedures, the online space is suggested as a basic component of political opportunity structure, influencing offline social and political formations. While the SYRIZA network suggests a revolutionary virtual world (Karatzogianni, 2012) of digital materialisation with inherent potentiality for social change, this revolutionary virtual world confined itself to an ineffective government unable to provide alternative governance structures of resistance to the EU. After the referendum period, these online diaspora activists were to conclude that the SYRIZA government mutated resistance into a great betrayal.

Chapter 7

The Third Period: The GReferendum – Twitter, Networks and Discourse

The study of Twitter fulfils the examination of the most dominant social media platforms used in Greece during the period 2008–2016 (FocusBari, 2015). The study of Twitter was completed through the analysis of trending and significant hashtags focusing on the period of the Greek referendum (June–July 2015) and the third memorandum era. This period and the examined events were selected looking on the development of the crisis, as these are considered to be significant examples illustrative of the contribution and linkage of digital media to the sociopolitical turmoil of that period. The study explains and contextualises the Greferendum case, and elaborates on the methods, sampling and research techniques. Lastly, it provides an analysis of the data collected, focusing on the two rival campaigns – the SNA and semantic evolution of the event.

Methods, Sampling and Analysis

The Greferendum debate started in a national context, but soon transformed into an EU one, which then jump-scaled further into a debate relating to the global recession. In a similar way, the crisis that started by focusing on the 'lazy-Greeks' narration (Fuchs, 2012; Žižek, 2012, p. 13), soon turned into a European crisis with critical sociopolitical and economic aspects and impact on the future of the EU, as well as symptomatic manifestations, such as the rise of populism (Stavrakakis, 2014) and the dysfunctional response to the refugee crisis in Greece and in Europe more generally (Dalakoglou, 2016; Ellinas, 2013; Voutyras, 2016).

The study of Twitter begins with the examination of the Greek Referendum, concentrating on the two antagonist campaigns (#oxi vs #menoumeevropi). The examination of the hashtags #syntagma and #17junegr, which were used in the mobilisations organised before the announcement of the referendum on 17 June 2015, offer an insight into the protest discourse and the tensions before the referendum. The analysis of the selected hashtags gave an insight into the patterns of communication and networks, noticing the origins of debates and conflicting ideologies already observed in the web sphere, before the announcement of the referendum (#syntagma, #17junegr). Then, the analysis focused on the comparative examination of #austerity – #antiausterity hashtags, looking on the first protests (18 June 2015), and on the #nai (yes) – #oxi (no) hashtags, looking on the day of the referendum (5 July 2015). The study of the two antagonist campaigns explored the evolution of #menoumeevropi (we stay in Europe) and #oxi (no) hashtags, focusing on three indicative dates (Bailout Expiration, 30 June 2015; Referendum Eve, 4 July 2015; Post-Referendum, 6 July 2015), analyzing both networks and discourse. The study also looked on the evolution of #greferendum, focusing on three different dates (Referendum announcement, 27 June 2015; Bailout expiration, 30 June 2015; Referendum, 5 July 2015). In the final stage, the examination of these hashtags provides an insight into the so-called politics of fear, concentrating on the main debates and criticisms arising from the announcement of the referendum and its output (Boukala & Dimitrakopoulou, 2016).

Here, the study of the aforementioned material included tweets, RTs and mentions. Retweets and mentions are suggesting slightly different structure and discourse in comparison to the study of Tweets (Conover et al., 2011), as users might have different reasons for mentioning other users or even retweeting posts. However, at this stage what is examined is the general characteristics of networks, dominant/influential actors and discourse, and that might include both Tweets, RTs and mentions. On a later stage, a follow-up study of this material would be interesting to be conducted, examining Tweets, RTs and mentions separately, even through a comparative approach, looking on the type/reason of domination and influence that actors are having in the examined networks.

The Twitter features raised two major methodological difficulties regarding the study. The first one lies in the well-known problem of the Twitter political economy, which only supports quick and real-time communication, without giving the opportunity to access archive material, unless purchased from the platform (Tornes, 2015). This is reflected in the collection of the data, which was conducted on a real-time basis during the period June 2015–March 2016, focusing on trending hashtags and keywords. While this has resulted in a rich corpus of material, a major limitation is that the days that the hashtags were collected were not always same with the days that these were trending on Twitter. However, this is not always a requirement, especially when it comes to the examination of different campaigns, where the analysis of keywords is more important. The next challenge raised the rich analytical and interpretational options for the online material. The analysis of hashtags concentrates both on the analysis of social and semantic networks, as well as on the evolution of networks. At the same time, a comparative examination of the evolution of networks provides the opportunity for a more in-depth examination of the analysed material, understanding the linkage between the evolution of the examined incidents and the evolution of the online network. Concentrating on the evolution of networks, the exponential random graph modelling (ERMS) could support an in-depth understanding of the patterns and the evolution of both social and semantic networks, giving an insight into the procedures of forming and maintaining a network-based social system (Lusher, Koskinen, & Robbins, 2012, p. 9). While this approach is able to support a longitudinal study of Twitter, it also requires a more statistically oriented study and the analysis of a bigger data set, or even big data. Therefore, for this study, a comparison of different snapshots of networks, taken at different times, still provides an efficient understanding of the emergence and rise of networks.

Here, I have used NodeXL, through which I collected 10,000 Tweets and relations, per hashtag/per day, including tweets, retweets and mentions. Based on how dense the usage of each of the examined hashtags was, hours or even days of material produced under an examined hashtag could be trawled. However, taking into consideration that NodeXL trawls up to a week of archive material, the collected Tweets, Retweets and mentions are sometimes less than the 10,000, in cases with little usage of the examined hashtags. After data collection and the calculation of the overall graph metrics, I grouped the data by cluster using the Clauset-Newman-Moore algorithm (Clauset, Newman, & Moore, 2004) and visualised them accordingly. This included all the tweets and relations (RTs and mentions) collected. The Clauset-Newman-Moore concentrated on modularity and 'takes into account the number of in-cluster edges and the expected number of such edges' (Djidjev & Onus, 2013). In other words, this algorithm creates groups that bring together nodes that are more connected or disconnected from other nodes.

Then, I detected and analysed the top items of the networks based on the most dominant, most repeated dyads of words, and I identified and analysed the semantic network focusing on meaning and discourse. For the detection, visualisation and analysis of meaning and discourse through semantic networks, occurrences or dyads of words, which appeared more than 50 times, were included in the sampled material. In most of the examined hashtags, dyads that appeared less than 50 times were the majority, without though having any significant difference or any important influence in the final network. That tended to create noise on the graphs without giving additional information. Therefore, setting the limit of 50 times as regards the dyads that appeared in each hashtag, it was possible to reduce the noise in the graphs and concentrate on the most influential and dominant meanings and discourse. This process supported both the examination of social and semantic networks and it was also repeated for each of the examined hashtags.

As regards the discussion and the analysis of each of the examined hashtag, this varied based on the aims of each analysis. Starting with the first study, the #syntagma and #17junegr hashtags, intended to develop a first insight, an introduction, on how the two conflicted campaigns and the discourse, developed online. Therefore, what is examined here is the structure of the networks, before looking into more details on the top items of the networks (i.e. domains, hashtags, words and pair of words). Then, the study of #austerity vs #antiausterity concentrated on the contrast between the two, looking on the top items of the networks, going a step further from the previous study, helping us to understand in more depth the online conflict or contrast between the two antagonistic campaigns. The study of the #nai vs #oxi hashtags goes even deeper looking not only on top items, but also on influential actors and hubs in the networks. These two hashtags were the most common in terms of describing the two campaigns, and where not directly associated with any political or party affiliations as other hashtags (e.g. menoumeevropi). Therefore, after looking on the structure of the networks and the contrast between the campaigns, then, it is also important to examine the most influential actors.

While, generally, such an in-depth discussion and analysis would be of interest in all the examined hashtags (i.e. discussion on structure, top items, dominant actors and hubs), still such a detailed presentation and discussion of all the data would not be appropriate to be presented in this book. The goal here is to understand how the two conflicted campaigns developed and employed twitter, rather than to look into the contrast and the differences among all the analysed hashtags. Therefore, such a detailed analysis and discussion would be beneficial neither for the research objectives nor for the reader, but instead would create a confusion and an overanalysis of the hashtags. Thus, the study of various hashtags supports the in-depth examination of the two campaigns and the online conflict or contrast, and while more discussion and in-depth analysis for each hashtag would be possible, this is not provided when it is not completely necessary for the study of the campaigns. Under the same rationale, the study of the #menoumeevropi vs #oxi, concentrated on the evolution of the two campaigns, while the study of the #greferendum looked on the evolution of the overall discussion on the Greek Referendum, including top items, actors and semantics.

Greferendum: #Menoumeevropi Versus #Oxi

On 27 June 2015, the Greek Prime Minister A. Tsipras announced a referendum on the bailout conditions and agreement proposed by the so-called troika (IMF, EC, ECB). This was the first referendum in Greece, after the collapse of Junta and the 1974 referendum, which supported the transition to democracy, abolishing the monarchy (Pappas, 2014).

The political turmoil of the summer of 2015 was already articulated with the mobilisations of 17th and 18th of June 2015. The mobilisation of the 17th of June 2015 was the first mobilisation against Greece's creditors and austerity politics since SYRIZA came to power after the January 2015 elections (Khan, 2015). This mobilisation took place 13 days before the bailout expiration, with many members of SYRIZA also participating. This was the first time that an anti-austerity mobilisation was also perceived as being a pro-government mobilisation. The 18th June 2015 mobilisation 'we stay in Europe' (#menoumeevropi) was organised in opposition to the 17th of June mobilisation, with the gathered crowds indicating their consent to the implementation of additional austerity measures (Maltezou & Koutantou, 2015). The political and ideological division between people participating in these mobilisations was strong, while polarisation intensified further after the announcement of the referendum. The mobilisations of 17th and 18th of June can be understood as the manifestation of the anti-/pro-austerity and later anti-/pro-EU debate, which, already since the 2012 elections and following the two-party system, had been represented in the mainstream political scene by ND and SYRIZA. Therefore, these two protests, which later transformed into the two antagonist campaigns of the referendum should be understood directly in relation to the 2012 and 2015 election campaigns of the two antagonist parties, SYRIZA and ND.

In contrast to ND's narration of the crisis, which was similar to the one of the mainstream media, both at the national and European level, SYRIZA, at that point was considered to provide an alternative political discourse, focusing on justice and dignity, coming up with a slogan 'Hope is coming'. During the referendum period, this transformed into the 'Oxi' campaign, expressing resistance to the austerity policies. On the other hand, the Menoume Evropi (We stay in Europe) campaign had strong ideological linkages to the ND's Truth Team, which already, since the 2012 and 2015 election, reinforced the division between Us and the Them, revitalising the stereotype of the 'communist peril' and the signified historical references. Therefore, following the ideological characteristics of the Truth Team, the Menoume Evropi campaign, and, later, the #Resign campaign, expressed opposition to any alternative political and ideological proposals, supporting the austerity politics. The origins of the Menoume Evropi[1] can be found back in 2011 when G. Papandreou requested a confidence vote in Parliament before stepping down and small-scale mobilisations, organised by G. Prokopakis, took place in Syntagma Square, Athens (Zoulas, 2016). G. Prokopakis, who later served as CEO of ND founded public broadcaster NERIT, the successor of ERT, repeated the attempt to successfully organise pro-EU mobilisations, representing the 'silent majority', which for the left comprised the bourgeoisie (Zoulas, 2016). This was the origin of what during the referendum era, can be described as politics of fear and hope (Boukala & Dimitrakopoulou, 2016).

During the referendum period, the two antagonist campaigns, and the two antagonist parties' rhetoric, created a scheme of conflict and disagreement, having strong historical references and 'synthesizing collective memories and the "affects" of fear and hope, simultaneously' (Boukala & Dimitrakopoulou, 2016, p. 52), further supporting the division between Us and the political Others/Them. What is suggested at this point is that Samaras' discourse supported the dichotomy between the Greek 'Patriots' against the utopian political vision of the 'communist peril' – SYRIZA, emphasising the traumatic past and a dramatic future (Boukala & Dimitrakopoulou, 2016). In contrast, Tsipras discourse focused on neoliberal European policymakers and the Greek political elite, and that discourse supported the unity of the nation, which though here is committing to the politics of the hope (Boukala & Dimitrakopoulou, 2016).

The two antagonist campaigns were supported by different political parties assembling two conflicting political and ideological poles, according to the #oxi and #menoumeevropi characteristics. The #menoumeevropi front was comprised of ND, PASOK, DIMAR and smaller conservative parties and parties of the centre, while the #oxi front was comprised of SYRIZA, AN.EL., Golden Dawn, Antarsya and smaller left-wing parties; KKE didn't support any of these

[1]https://menoumeevropi.com/, https://www.facebook.com/menoume.evropi/

options (Ministry of Interior, Hellenic Republic, 2015). While the imposition of capital controls had a significant impact on the vote, still, the results indicated that the vote had class and age characteristics, with the poorer and younger supporting the No campaign (Ntelis, 2015; Tsakiroglou, 2015). Following are some of the most significant social characteristics of the 'Oxi' (No) Vote (Public Issue, 2015):

- Employment:
  - Self employed 57.7%; public sector 70.9%; not currently in employment 71.3%; students 85.2%.
- Education:
  - Higher 55.7%; secondary 65.7%; primary 61.7%.
- Age group:
  - 65 plus: 44.9%; 55–64: 59.4%; 45–54: 69.2%; 34–44: 67.4%; 24–34: 72.3%; 18–24: 85%.
- Sex:
  - Women: 62.3%; men: 60.2%.
- Total vote: 61.3%.

After looking at the social characteristics of the No campaign voters, it is interesting to consider the correlation that this vote had to traditional politics, by looking on the party affiliation of the voters, the intention of voting as well as the way that they were self-placed in the political spectrum of the left and right, as follows (Public Issue, 2015):

- Party affiliation – %:
  - Syriza: 87.3; ND: 20.4; Golden Dawn: 77.3; Potami: 22.4; KKE: 77.3; ANEL: 78.5; Pasok: 19.6.
- Voting intention – %:
  - Syriza: 95.9; ND: 8.3; Golden Dawn: 84.3; Potami: 2.8; KKE: 83.8; ANEL: 91.6; Pasok: 12.5.
- Left-right self placement scale – %:
  - Left: 91; centre-left: 73.6; centre: 43.9; centre-right: 17.2; right: 31.9; N/A: 70.1.

The anti-austerity mobilisation of 17th of June 2015, was organised by a citizens' collective action 'Eurochange Europe – Το εξπρές της αξιοπρέπειας' (Dignity Express) (Euronews, 2015), calling people to protest against austerity and having as slogans 'Democracy cannot be blackmailed', 'Our lives do not belong to the lenders' (Sputniknews.com, 2015), 'We take the negotiation to our hands', 'We put an end to austerity' (Kathimerini.gr, 2015). The anti-austerity mobilisations of 17th of June, which took place in more than 25 cities in Greece (Sputniknews.com, 2015), had a significant value, as these were the first mobilisations during the Greek crisis, which were both against austerity and pro-governmental. In contrast, the mobilisations of Thursday, 18th June 2015, were organised as a response to the 17th June mobilisation (Kathimerini.gr, 2015). The 'Menoume Evropi' group, a small collectivity, called for citizens of Athens to gather at Syntagma Square and expressed their concerns and opposition regarding the government's negotiations with the lenders, coming up with slogans such as 'Greece belongs to Europe', 'Yes to the EU' (Kathimerini.gr, 2015). Again, in this mobilisation, MPs of the ND participated expressing both opposition to the government and their consent to the austerity policies.

Both the anti- and pro-austerity protest organisers used specific hashtags to coordinate the protests (Kathimerini.gr, 2015), #syntagma and #17junegr, in the first mobilisation and then in the second instance, through a comparative analysis of #austerity and #antiausterity. The rationale here is that instead of focusing on the organiser's hashtags (#change4all, #stopausterity, #mazi, #menoumeevropi), the analysis concentrated on keywords and hashtags, which were used by supporters of both the rival campaigns, developing an insight into how the conflicting ideologies and campaigns were reflected or shaped online, independently of the top-down organisers' discourse.

Social Network and Semantic Analysis of #syntagma and #17junegr

The hashtags #syntagma and #17junegr were sampled as the most dominant hashtags used for the anti-austerity mobilisation which took place in Syntagma Square, Athens and other cities of Greece on 17 June 2015 (Fraser, 2015; Waerden & Fletcher, 2015). These hashtags were extensively used for reporting the mobilisation, both in the press and Twitter (Fraser, 2015; Waerden & Fletcher, 2015). Even if these hashtags were not trending on the collection day, however, these were the keywords of the campaigns, heavily used by the mainstream media and the public. The data crawling was conducted on 18 June 2015, collecting the last 10,000 tweets and relations, for each of the examined hashtags. While the last 10,000 tweets and relations were based on the hashtag #syntagma, which evolved between 15 June 2015, 15:30:42 and 18 June 2015, 17:17:30, the evolution of 10,000 tweets and relations of #17junegr emerged between 16 June 2015, 11:04:46 and 18 June 2015, 16:18:22 (Figure 7.1).

The #syntagma network is composed of 1,145 vertices and 2,121 total edges, while the #17junegr network consists of 629 vertices and 1,108 edges, where edges are users and vertices are either users that other users interacted with (i.e. RTs and mentions), or tweets (i.e. same edge and vertex). The #syntagma network is bigger than the #17junegr network, indicating some differemces and similarities in terms of structure. The #syntagma network is composed of two large groups (G1: 217 vertices, 240 unique edges; G2:150V, 239UE), three medium groups (G3: 97V, 124UE; G4: 86V, 114UE; G5: 74V, 95UE), and then smaller groups (G6-8 having between 67-61V, 67-58UE; and from G9 to the isolated users), before reaching the isolated users. The #17junegr network is composed of two large groups G1 (176 vertices, 163 unique edges) and G2 (174V, 156U). Then, there are two medium groups G3 (97V, 161UE) and G4 (87V, 162UE), while the rest of the groups are becoming smaller before reaching the isolated users.

#syntagma[55]: 15/06/2015, 15:30:42 - 18/06/2015, 17:17:30	#17junegr[56]: 16/06/2015, 11:04:46 - 18/06/2015, 16:18:22

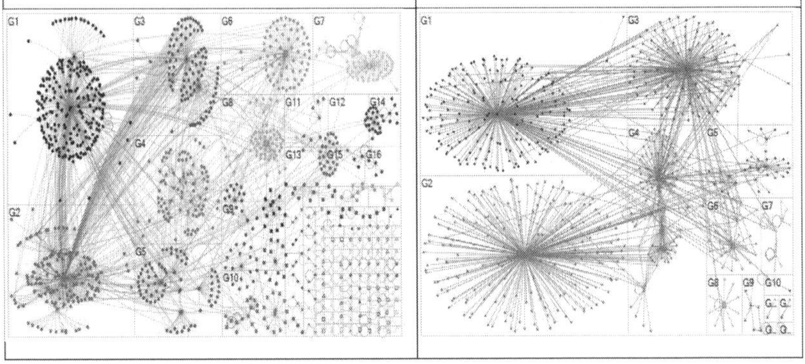

Figure 7.1. #Syntagma and #17junegr Social Networks.

Smith, Raine, Hemelboim, and Shneiderman (2014) suggest seven basic archetypes of networks, based on which we can develop a more-depth insight on polarised crowds and political conversations, studied with NodeXL. Looking into the two examined networks based on graph metrics, the #syntagma network is developed by the community cluster and the broadcast network, while the #17junegr can be identified close to the community cluster archetype (ibid).

Looking into the structure of the next #syntagma network, there are two large groups, with the first one slightly bigger and then, three medium groups. Next, the network consists of a few smaller groups, before reaching to a small number of isolated users. This network is having features of the broadcast network and according to Smith et al. (2014, p. 8), the broadcast network is developed around breaking news, focusing on which, users retweet and transfer information from media outlets and agenda setters, as also observed in the examined network. Here, most of the participants are not much connected to one another, and instead they are mainly connected to the hub, which is either media or agenda setters. On the other hand, the #17jungr has two bigger and two medium groups with moderate connections, and a few smaller groups, while it has only a few isolated users. These characteristics could be found in global media events, where groups develop around a few hubs having their own influencers and courses of information (Smith et al., 2014, p. 8), and this is indeed observed at the #17junegr. Such networks indicate the diversity in terms of discourse and opinion on social media topics (2014, p. 3), although in the examined case the topic of discussion is rather focused. Therefore, this network could also be understood focusing on some of the tight crowds' characteristics. While the examined network is not as tight as suggested by this archetype, still there is a discussion around similar topics, indicating how different communities' function, facilitating mutual support (2014, p. 2). In tight crowds, we usually have two to six medium groups, with many connections and few isolated actors, and this archetype is usually developed around topics, without having many outsiders (e.-g. conferences and professional topics).

In both the examined networks, there are some larger groups (G1, G2), although, on the other hand, the differences in the secondary groups' sizes are not always significant (#syntagma – G2, 3, 4, 5, 6; #17junegr – G2, G3). At the same time, the #syntagma network has many isolated users, as expected by the broadcast network, whereas the #17junegr network have fewer isolated users, as expected in the community cluster structure (Smith et al., 2014, p. 2). While these two archetypes suggest some characteristics of the networks' structures the identification of top items suggests a more in-depth understanding as regards the formation of communities, influential actors and discourse. The dominant domains, the dominant hashtags and words/pairs of words lead the analysis on the examination of semantic networks. The calculations of the top items indicate the following dominant domains.

Top domains in tweets in entire graph/entire graph count:

- #Syntagma
  - twitter.com: 73; rt.com: 73; naftemporiki.gr: 17; theguardian.com: 14; instagram.com: 10; mediasoup.gr: 10; storify.com: 8; publicpolicy.it: 5; co.uk: 4; ert.gr: 4.
- #17junegr
  - rt.com: 37; theguardian.com: 14; thepressproject.gr: 14; twitter.com: 12; telesurtv.net: 11; blogspot.com: 4; stokokkino.gr: 3; facebook.com: 2; zerohedge.com: 1.

The dominant domains of the #syntagma network were mainstream media domains (Guardian, Naftemporiki etc.), in contrast to the #17junegr network where both mainstream (RT, Guardian, Telesurtv) and independent media domains (Zerohedge, The press project, etc.) and URLs, dominated the network. Taking into consideration the differences in the size of the #17junegr network and the #syntagma network, it is interesting that the smaller network had a greater variety in terms of media content and hyperlinks than the bigger one. As expected though, the #syntagma network included domains from different countries (.it, .uk, .com, .gr), whereas #17junegr (.com, .gr, .net) included material mainly from Greek (.gr) and worldwide domains (.com). The top hashtags, words and pair of words of the examined networks are as follow:

- Top hashtags in tweet in entire graph/entire graph count:
  - #syntagma
    - Syntagma: 1,770; Greece: 647; Stopausterity: 424; change4all: 272; menoumeevropi: 227; 17junegr: 221; Europe: 208; Grexit: 166; Mazi: 115; Athens: 94.
  - #17june
    - 17junegr: 868; Greece: 363; Syntagma: 270; Stopausterity: 142; change4all: 73; mazi: 45; austerity: 26; athens: 25; grexit: 22; greek: 22.

- Top words in tweet in entire graph/entire graph count
  - #syntagma
    - Syntagma: 1,767; greece: 655; stopausterity: 424; austerity: 420; athens: 399.
  - #17june
    - 17junegr: 838; syntagma: 447; greece: 374; hibai_: 260; ronanburtenshaw: 221.
- Top word pairs in tweet in entire graph/entire graph count:
  - #syntagma
    - anti,austerity: 291; stopausterity,change4all: 248; syntagma,asking: 236; asking,stopausterity: 236; austerity,demo: 227; rally,syntagma: 216; nice, warm: 205; warm,night: 205; night,athens205; athens,people: 205.
  - #17june
    - syntagma,17junegr: 169; anti,austerity: 113; plaza,syntagma: 113; 17junegr,stopausterity: 110; venceremos,17junegr: 101; lives,belong: 100; hibai_,una: 99; una,pancartas: 99; pancartas,más: 99; más,grandes: 99.

The most used hashtags reveal the contrast between what was later discussed as the #yes and #no campaigns of the referendum. The issue of austerity and Grexit are discussed in both the examined hashtags and as I point out later, these were the main points around which the discourse of the two campaigns developed. At the same time, this reflects the pro-/anti-austerity and pro-/anti-EU debate as it evolved during the Greek crisis and politics. While there are many similarities in the sets of hashtags used in both the examined hashtags, there are clear differences shown by the study of the dominant pairs of words used in the tweets of the examined hashtags (Figure 7.2).

Based on the most mentioned dyads of words, a semantic network for the #syntagma developed, and then the dominant groups were detected. The first group, G1, developed around updates and information on the mobilisations (e.g. tonight, people, athens, gathering and syntagma). The G5 is composed of keywords related to the purpose of mobilisation, expressing opposition to austerity, both in the national and European context (e.g. mazi, europe, austerity and change4all). G5 is directly linked to G6 through the nodes Grexit and stopausterity and this is an interesting linkage highlighting the debate on austerity and the danger of Grexit. While G3 consists of keywords denoting opposition to austerity, Grexit is also linked to G4, which refers to the protest and the pro-/anti-governmental mobilisations at the time. The node grineuro acts as a bridge between G6 and G2, while G6 could also be understood as a bridge between G2 and G5. What is observed here is the linkage between these two debates, which later translated into two rival campaigns in the referendum context. The interesting point here is that while this debate is already observed through the crisis discourse, the tension between these two conflicting perceptions of the austerity policies is clearly reflected in the online discourse, exactly before the formal announcement of the referendum. G10 is not linked to the main network and is in Spanish, while all the other groups are in English, and only a few words

Figure 7.2. #Syntagma Semantic Network.

appear in Greek or the so-called Greeklish (Greek, written with Latin characters) (Figure 7.3).

In the #17junegr semantic network, there are seven groups. The first group, G1, consists of words both in Greek and Spanish, while words, such as venceremos, stopausterity or austeridad draw from the SYRIZA – Podemos coalition and the slogan, 'SYRIZA, Podemos, Venceremos' (Kassam, 2015). During the pre-election period of January 2015, after which SYRIZA finally came to power, the coalition of SYRIZA and Podemos suggested a South-European anti-austerity front of the countries once named PIGS. On 25 January 2015, Podemos leader, Iglesias, saluted SYRIZA's election with the phrase 'SYRIZA, Podemos, Venceremos' with the two leaders promising change in Europe, 'the name of change in Greece is SYRIZA, in Spain Podemos', 'people speak the same language when they fight, we will win' (Avgi.gr, 2015). While the relationship between these anti-austerity parties could extensively be analysed, each one of these was differently and deeply influenced by the Greek referendum and the so-called SYRIZA U-turn (Tadeo & Penty, 2015). More importantly, the discourse of these parties shifted the centre of the crisis discussion, and from a PIGS' crisis, or Greek debt crisis, the Spanish crisis and so on, they shifted to a discussion of the European crisis, and from there on to a global neoliberal recession.

Groups 5, 6 and 7 refer to the mobilisation (e.g. greek, parliament, tonight and picture), although G7 is not linked to the main network. In terms of meanings and discourse, G4 and G3 can be understood as peripheral to G1, consisting of both Spanish and Greek words, linked around the anti-austerity discussion. G2 indicated the turmoil between the Greek government and the EU, addressing the debate on surrender and rejection (e.g. Greece, creditors, surrender and rejection) and pointed out the conflict and tension between Greece and the EU. Focusing on the spatial formation of the networks, the nodes greece

Figure 7.3. #17junegr Semantic Network.

and creditors develop into two opposite horizontal axes derived from the examined hashtag 17junegr.

#austerity VS #antiausterity

The #austerity and #antiausterity hashtags collection was conducted on 18 June 2015, when one of the first, if not the first, pro-EU demonstrations took place in Athens, as a response to the anti-austerity mobilisation, which took place a day earlier. While the anti-austerity protests during the crisis era were not a rare phenomenon, after the election of SYRIZA January 2015, the context of such mobilisation changed and from anti-austerity and anti-governmental mobilisations, turned into pro-governmental, pro-SYRIZA mobilisations; however, opposition to austerity still remained. Therefore, after the anti-austerity protests, which took place on 17 June 2015, the first pro-EU protest took place on 18 June 2015, in #syntagma (Protothema, 18 June 2015). Using NodeXL, I crawled data on 18 June 2015, collecting the last 10,000 tweets and relations (RTs and mentions) of each of the examined hashtag while the output and the graphic metrics developed as follows (Figure 7.4).

The #antiausterity network is composed of 1,504 edges and 923 unique vertices, while the #austerity network is composed of 6,354 edges and 4,530 unique vertices, indicating a significant difference in the size of the two networks. After the calculation of the graph metrics, the data were grouped by cluster and resulted in the network structures as shown in Figure xx. The #austerity network consists of 1,159 groups and the #austerity and the #antiausterity network of 123 groups. The calculation of top items of both networks indicated some interesting considerations about the dominant domains, hashtags and word dyads. The dominant domains of the #austerity network are characterised mainly by mainstream media and actors (e.g. WSJ, RT and Guardian), while there are

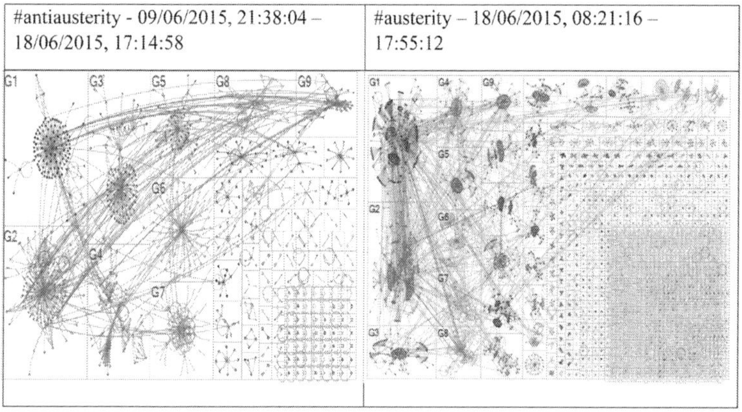

Figure 7.4. Anti-austerity vs Austerity.

only a few alternative/independent media and actors (e.g. Unite the Union). On the other hand, the #antiausterity network is dominated by social media (e.g. YouTube and FB) and many alternative or independent media and actors (e.g. The Peoples' Assembly and Openermedia). This is not impressive, though, considering that the #austerity network consists of many more actors and users, in contrast to #antiausterity network, which is not only smaller in terms of participation, but it also seems to be more concentrated in terms of audience, focusing on a specific ideological spectrum.

- Top domains in tweet in entire graph/entire graph count:
  - #antiausterity
    - youtube.com: 201; twitter.com: 99; news786.in: 84; co.uk: 65; facebook.com: 29; org.uk: 20; theguardian.com: 15; soundcloud.com: 14; indiegogo.com: 7; cityam.com: 6.
  - #austerity
    - theguardian.com: 556; co.uk: 419; wsj.com: 233; twitter.com: 222; org.uk: 161; youtube.com: 99; trib.al: 88; rt.com: 63; facebook.com: 60; cityam.com: 60.

The dominant hashtags of the #anti-austerity network concentrated mainly on the UK Labour Party and the leadership elections hustings period, which started one day before the collection of the data on 17 June 2015 (e.g. #jeremyo4leader and #labourleadership, #toriesoutnow), while few hashtags are directly associated with the Greek mobilisations (e.g. #greece and #tsipras). In both cases, though, hashtags such as #endausteritynow, #austerity, and #theleft, highlight the EU debate on austerity politics and the opposition to neoliberal policies. The #austerity network is more directly concentrated on the Greek case (e.g. #greece and #SYRIZA, #grexit) and the mobilisations (e.g. #mazi and #junedemo). Again, the EU dimension of the political debates of that period is expressed not only through the usage of hashtags related to the Labour elections (e.g. #labourdebate) but related to the #grexit and #eu debate as well (e.-g. #grexit, #eu, #endausterity, #imf and #austerity).

- Top hashtags in tweet in entire graph/entire graph count:
  - #antiausterity
    - Antiausterity: 1,101; jeremy4leader: 238; endausteritynow: 140; greece: 127; tsipras: 85; labourleadership: 74; jeremycorbyn: 72; theleft: 57; toriesoutnow: 52; austerity: 35.
  - #austerity
    - Austerity: 764; greece: 349; endausteritynow: 336; grexit: 137; eu: 106; syriza: 99; labourdebate: 91; imf: 85; junedemo: 75: mazi: 72.

The dominant words in the #antiausterity network are focused both on the UK and Greece (e.g. antiausterity, jeremy4leader, corbyn4leader and Greece), while the #austerity network is concentrated on the issue of austerity and the express of opposition, including the Greece-EU tension (e.g. austerity, Greece, anti, against and eu). What is interesting here is that #austerity and #antiausterity hashtags are used both in relation to the Greek mobilisations, the EU debate and the UK Labour leadership election. At the same time, the austerity debate has blurred boundaries in terms of discourses, even though austerity has a different context in the Greek, the UK and the EU context. The dominant word pairs both in the #antiausterity and #austerity networks suggest an insight into the networks' discourse, and this is extensively discussed later concentrating on the semantic networks that arise.

- Top words in tweet in entire graphEntire graph count/entire graph count:
  - #Antiausterity (total words: 16,453)
    - Antiausterity: 952; jeremy4leader: 232; corbyn4leader: 145; greece: 141; 2: 118.
  - #Austerity (total words: 83,245)
    - Austerity: 4,179; greece: 691; anti: 652; against: 468; eu: 390.
- Top word pairs in tweet in entire graph/entire graph count:
  - #Antiausterity
    - antiausterity,communists: 84; communists,occupy: 84; occupy,greece: 84; greece,finance: 84; finance,ministry: 84; ministry,tsipras: 84; tsipras, mulls: 84; mulls,walking: 84; walking,over: 84; over,Russia: 84.
  - #Austerity
    - anti,austerity: 585; against,austerity: 392; reason,accept: 316; accept,austerity: 283; austerity,defeated: 249; end,austerity: 247; seumas,milne: 189; defeated,Seumas: 167; austerity,now: 153; austerity,march: 140.

The semantic networks for each hashtag were completed through the selection of the word dyads, which appeared more than 50 times in tweets and relations/interactions in each network. The #antiausterity semantic network that developed was composed of 23 vertices and 31 edges, whereas it was grouped by cluster and indicates 6 different groups (Figure 7.5).

The #antiausterity semantic network indicates that the network was created focusing mainly on the UK Labour leadership election and the Greek mobilisations are referenced to the networks without making up a significant contribution, either in terms of actors or in terms of discourse.

The #austerity semantic network is composed of 88 vertices and 84 edges, grouped by cluster into 16 groups (Figure 7.6).

In both the examined semantic networks, it is interesting to note that even in the groups where the Greek mobilisations are dominant the Greek language is not used, but instead, the discussion developed in English. The #austerity semantic network indicates more discussed issues in contrast to the #antiausterity semantic network. Starting from G1, the network around austerity indicated the multidimensional content of austerity and the interrelationship between different dimensions. Additionally, a discussion on the pro-/anti-austerity and EU is observed around the node antiausterity. What is quite interesting here is that keywords from both the conflicted positions and narrations, as produced by pro-/anti-austerity discourses, appear (e.g. menoumeevropi, anti-austerity, defeated-austerity, measures, Grexit) G1 is linked to some of the groups of the network, (G4, G5, G7, G8, G9, G11 and G12) while there is also a big number of groups (G2, G3, G16, G13, G14, G10 and G15) which are isolated. The multiple approaches and discussion on austerity as developed in G1 are further associated with the linked groups, focusing on policy and debt control, on news, mainstream media and mobilisations.

The Social Network Analysis and Semantic Analysis #nai VS #oxi Campaign

The #nai (yes) and #oxi (no) hashtags data were collected on 5th of July, when the referendum took place. Again, using NodeXL, I collected 10,000 tweets and

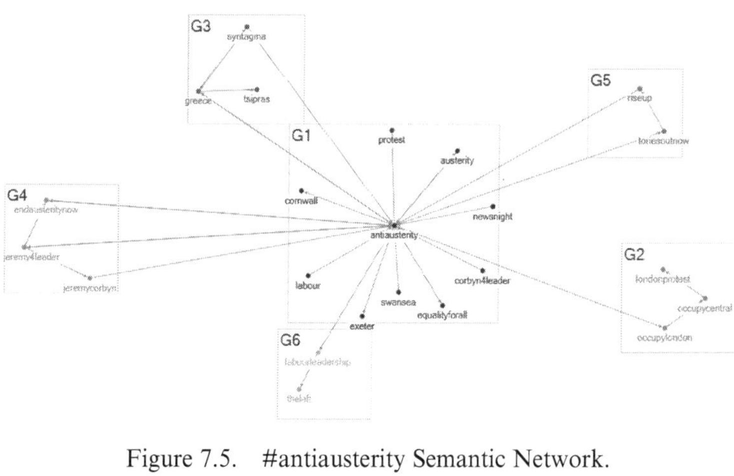

Figure 7.5. #antiausterity Semantic Network.

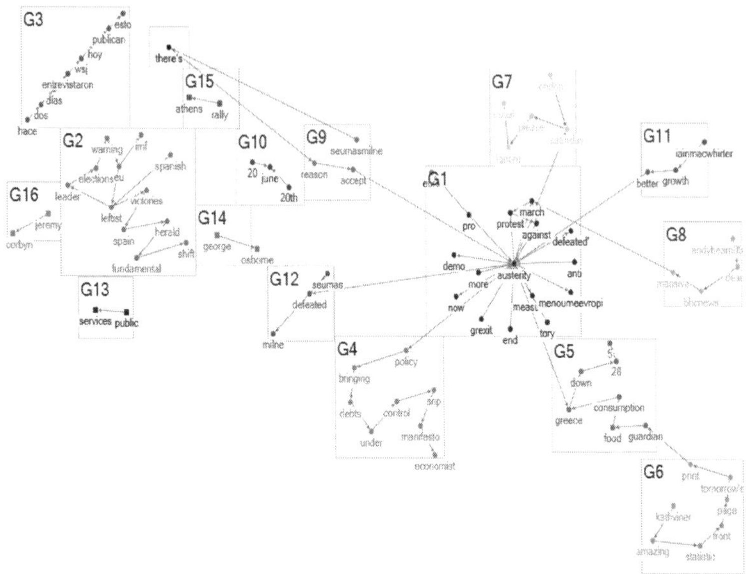

Figure 7.6. #austerity Semantic Network.

relations from each of the examined hashtags. The #nai network is composed of 8,609 vertices and 9,105 unique edges, while the collected material covers the period from 5 July 2015, 13:59:32 to 6 July 2015, 02:13:51. The #oxi network consists of 8,621 vertices and 10,552 unique edges and the collected material covers the period from 5 July 2015, 23:04:57 to 6 July 2015, 00:22:40. The 10,000 tweets and relations collected from each of the hashtags and the period that these cover suggest that the hashtag #oxi (no) was used more intensively in comparison to the #nai (yes) hashtag. After the calculation of the metrics, the visualisation developed in clusters as follows (Figure 7.7).

The comparison between the #nai and #oxi networks indicates that the structure of the #nai campaign is not as tight as the #oxi campaign. The G1 of the #nai campaign is loosely linked to the other groups, while it is the biggest in the network. This group was formed around the user @econcharlesread, a British journalist reporting on the referendum results. Groups 2, 4 and 7 have strong ties between them. Group 2 developed around users tweeting mainly in Greek, commenting on the results of the referendum, on politics as well as on the limitations of exit polls and traditional media to predict the results. The users who dominate this group are popular twitter users related to the media (e.g. a comedian, users who describe themselves as trolls and journalists), SYRIZA members and activists, and ND members (@geogkou10, @fraufotini, @giorgoskyritsis, @alexandrosfl350, @kmitsotakis). The most dominant users in this group refer directly or indirectly to corruption and the structures that support it (e.g. media and politics). G4 developed around the user @kallergisk, a Greek journalist, reporting on the resignation of A. Samaras, head of the ND party, which was

#Nai (yes): 05/07/2015, 13:59:32 – 06/07/2015, 02:13:51	#Oxi (no): 05/07/2015, 23:04:57 – 06/07/2015, 00:22:40

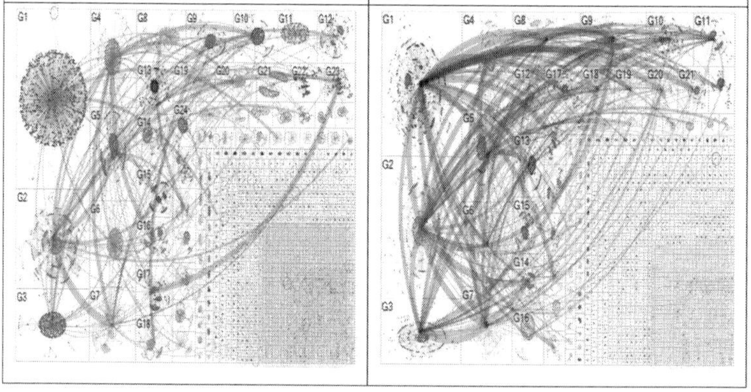

Figure 7.7. #nai[2] VS #oxi[3] Social Networks.

then the opposing party. G7 consists of users related to politics ((@topotami, @SYRIZAgr, @adonisgeorgiadi), to media ((@skaigr, activists ((@blockupy) as well as ordinary users, commenting on the results. Groups 9, 11, 19, and 20 consist of tweets in Spanish and French, while mostly there is a balanced relationship between groups posting in Greek and in English.

On the other hand, the network #oxi is characterised by a high density of groups and users, while in comparison to groups, there are many isolated users too. G1 is segmented and comprised of many smaller hubs and accounts/users, who are related to politics (e.g. @SYRIZAgr and @anothergreen), bloggers and media accounts (e.g. @FunnyR3tweets and @IvorCrotty), academics (e.g. @MarkSleboda1) and ordinary users commenting on the referendum. This group developed around tweets that expressed criticism against EU, Germany, banks as well as neoliberalism. In these tweets, pointed out by hubs, the referendum results are understood as a victory of the people against banks, 'not a victory of the Greek people but a victory of the whole world against the banks/banking system. There are strong criticisms of elites and austerity politics and at the same time, the division between society and politics in the EU is highlighted. This discussion sits alongside the consideration of democracy, while solidarity is expressed here as well. The linkage between Podemos and SYRIZA as an opposition pole to neoliberalism

[2]#Nai – G1: 946 vertices, 885 unique edges; G2: 521V, 603UE; G3: 386V, 380UE; G4: 332V, 337UE; G5: 317V, 308UE; G6: 295V, 291UE; G7: 255V, 304UE; G8: 184V, 175UE; G9: 180V, 280UE; G10: 167V, 188UE; G11: 148V, 152UE; G12: 143V, 154UE; G13: 138V, 160UE; G14: 137V, 162UE.

[3]#Oxi – G1: 806 vertices, 1,219 unique edges; G2: 792V, 884UE; G3, 366V, 498UE; G4: 341V, 399UE; G5: 322V, 374UE; G6: 295V, 389UE; G7: 273V, 323UE; G8: 252 V, 353UE; G9: 248 V, 486UE; G10: 179 V, 223UE; G11: 155 V, 167UE; G12: 145 V, 155UE; G13: 142 V, 152UE; G14: 124 V, 160UE.

and austerity politics is observed as well. Another interesting observation is that the results of the referendum are directly linked to the Grexit debate and the end, the dissolution of the EU, while there are also justifications of the results. The accounts participating in these groups are from different countries, the EU and international, and the discussion is conducted mainly in English.

The main hub of G2 develops around the user @rcabrero75, who describes himself on Twitter with the phrase 'The crisis has only served to save the French and German banks' 'We are governed by the Mafia. We can and must', in Spanish. Other hubs in this group formed around the users @tsipraseu, around Spanish media and bloggers accounts, while SYRIZA accounts participate too. G2, as well as the smaller groups in the examined network, are shaped focusing on the referendum's results, while in most cases the issue of capitalism is fiercely debated. Most of the discussion develops in English and Spanish, while there are fewer tweets in Greek and French. In the smaller groups of the network, @democraciareal there is a hub for one of the non-numbered groups, while US and international accounts are hubs in some of the small and the non-numbered groups. While dominant or influential actors were not discussed on any of the other examined hashtags, taking into consideration that the #nai and #oxi hashtags were some of the most significant and were used independently to political or party affiliation, clearly expressing the contrast between the two conflicted campaign; it was, at this stage, interesting to have a look on who dominated the network, or who were the most influential actors.

- Top domains in tweet in entire graph/entire graph count:
  - #Nai
    - economist.com: 1,106; rt.com: 435; twitter.com: 342; ypes.gr: 218; naftemporiki.gr: 135; electograph.com: 70; youtube.com: 41; ekathimerini.-com: 37; facebook.com: 35; prognosismedia.info: 27.
  - #Oxi
    - twitter.com: 401; youtube.com: 381; rt.com: 218; facebook.com: 64; theguardian.com: 59; economist.com: 51; ypes.gr: 46; instagram.com: 44; bbc.com: 38; org.uk: 34.

What is suggested by the dominant domains for both examined networks is that the mainstream media have a leading role as regards the material and information transferred or discussed in the networks (The Economist, RT). The #nai network includes more Greek domains than the #oxi network (Ypes, e-Kathimerini), while social media platform domains appear in both the examined networks.

- Top hashtags in tweet in entire graph/entire graph count:
  - #Nai
    - Nai: 10,121; oxi: 8,533; greferendum: 2,879; grefenderum: 2,206; greece: 1,707; greekreferendum: 973; dimopsifisma: 688; grexit: 423; greececrisis: 384; eurocrisis: 369.

- #Oxi
  - Oxi: 10,328; grefenderum: 2,456; greferendum: 1,589; greece: 1,528; greekreferendum: 1,290; syntagma: 496; oxi2015: 424; grecia: 357; grexit: 332; nai: 237.

The most dominant hashtags used in the #nai and the #oxi network have many similarities. Both refer to the referendum, although the #nai concentrates more on the issue of the crisis (e.g. eurocrisis and Greececrisis), while the #oxi dominant hashtags include hashtags, such as #syntagma, #grecia and #oxi2015, which are also used after the announcement of the results, supporting the celebrations that took place the same day in the Syntagma Square. The #grexit appears in both the examined hashtags, pointing out a major political and social debate that arose based on the threat of the so-called Grexit.

- Top words in tweet in entire graph/entire graph Count:
  - #Nai (total words: 180,360)
    - Nai: 9,774; oxi: 8,458; greferendum: 2,827; yes: 2,198; grefenderum: 2,031.
  - #Oxi (Total Words: 161137)
    - Oxi: 9,845; grefenderum: 2,354; greece: 2,165; greferendum: 1,474; greekreferendum: 1,260.
- Top word pairs in tweet in entire graph/entire graph count:
  - #Nai
    - oxi,nai: 1,806; nai,yes: 1,022; oxi,61: 985; counted,oxi: 899; nai,38: 845; votes,counted: 779; yes,nai: 747; nai,oxi: 742; yes,greferendum: 507; financial,chaos: 473.
  - #Oxi
    - grefenderum,oxi: 782; oxi,grefenderum: 744; oxi,oxi: 489; greekreferendum,oxi: 451; oxi,greece: 389; oxi,greferendum: 380; syntagma,square: 285; greece,oxi: 259; oxi,greekreferendum: 232; oxi,austerity: 223.

As well as in top hashtags, top words and dyads of words indicate many similarities relating to the two examined networks and the discourse. The dominant words and pairs of words in the #oxi hashtag appear to concentrate more on the results and the 'no' campaign, while the #nai hashtags and the top words and pair of words include keywords of the 'no' campaign as well. A comparison between the top pair of words of the two hashtags indicates that the #nai hashtag has been created around the antagonism between 'yes' and 'no' discourse and ideology (yes – no, financial – chaos, nai – yes), as well as focusing on the results (nai – 38, oxi – 61). In contrast, the meaning and the discourse established based on the 'no' campaign concentrates more on the results and the celebrations (syntagma – square, oxi – greferendum). Selecting the pairs of words, which are mentioned more than 50 times, as explained in detail earlier, according to each hashtag network item metrics, the following semantic networks were detected (Figure 7.8).

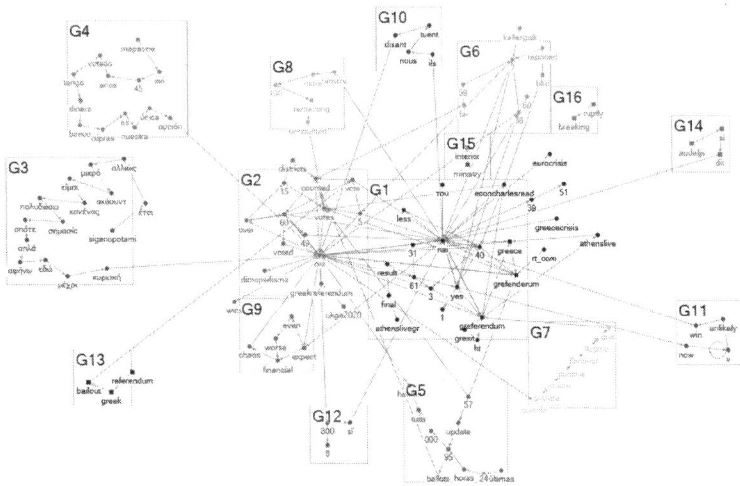

Figure 7.8. #Nai, Semantic Network.

The pair of words used as vertices and edges formed the aforementioned semantic network and detected 15 groups, using the Clause-Newman-Moore algorithm. Due to the high number of vertices, the visualisation of the network developed in different boxes for each group. Groups 1 and 2 are strongly linked and both refer to the referendum results, with yes (nai) and no (oxi) being at the centre of each group. Most of the other groups developed following the same rationale and in different languages (G4, G5, G8 and G11). G9 is linked to G2, while it has fewer linkages with G1. These groups concentrated on the financial chaos and uncertainty, which was about to follow the oxi campaign's win Figure 7.9).

Following the same process as described earlier, 11 groups were detected in the #oxi semantic network, which, even if they are fewer than for the #nai network, suggest a variety with regard to the discussed themes. G1 develops concentrating on the referendum results, G2 concentrates on the gathering of people at Syntagma Square, celebrating the win of the 'no' campaign (e.g. syntagma, athens, celebrating, thousands, captures and drone). G3 consists of words in Greek, although it refers to Spain and Barcelona's Mayor, who supported the Greek government (βρίσκομαι, στο, πλευρό, της, ελληνικής, κυβέρνησης). This leads to G4, which concentrates on the democratic will of the Greek people (κυβέρνηση, δημοκρατική, βούληση, του ελληνικού, λαού). G5 refers to a phrase regarding the heroism of Greece, which – as an urban myth – is supposed to have been said by Churchill during WWII. Groups 9, 11, 12 and 13 have loose or no ties to the network, while again after English and Greek, Spanish is also noticed in the network.

Evolution of Campaigns Discourse: #menoumeevropi and #oxi

After the examination of keywords and hashtags that supported the study of the two conflicted political and ideological approaches to the referendum debate,

Figure 7.9. #Oxi Semantic Network.

what is also important to examine is the evolution of hashtags and discourse, in juxtaposition to the evolution of events and incidents, both in the Greek and the EU context. This will support a more in-depth understanding of the usage of twitter, the online discourse and the linkage to the offline discourse and political polarisation.

The evolution of the two antagonistic campaigns is studied focusing on the hashtags #menoumeevropi (we stay in europe) and #oxi (no). The first examined hashtag #menoumeevropi was trending for several days during the referendum period, representing mainly the centre-right, the right-wing and mainstream angle on the referendum debate. The usage of this hashtag was so intense and straightforwardly linked to the right-wing oriented ideological and political view on the crisis debate, that a year after the referendum it is still used, denoting a specific cultural and ideological framework represented by right-wing and conservative parties. On the other hand, the hashtag #oxi (no) is an indicative example of the 'no' campaign, which was used to denote the opposition to austerity.

The study of the evolution of the hashtags was completed through the collection of data on three key dates. The analysis started with the collection of data on 30 June 2015, the day when, after the bailout expiration, Greece defaulted on its creditors failing to make its 1.5bm euro payment to the IMF (Allen, 2015). The second day to be examined concentrated on the day before the referendum and then the last day to be examined was the day after the referendum. While the actual day of the referendum has already been discussed earlier, what is suggested is that this date concentrates more on the actual process of voting and the results of the referendum, rather than on the political debate. Therefore, the examination of a day before and after the referendum supports the offline and online dynamic relationships and impact of the events.

Following the same process as in the previous examples, 10,000 tweets and relations were collected for the hashtag #menoumeevropi on the following dates: 30 June 2015 4 July 2015 and 6 July 2015. The bailout expiration network is composed of 4,918 vertices and 7,662 unique edges, from 24 June 2015, 20:46:49 to 30 June 2015, 20:58:38. The referendum eve network consists of 5,500 vertices and 8,248 unique edges, covering the period from 30 June 2015, 18:51:19 to 5 July 2015, 00:14:49. Finally, the post-referendum network is comprised of 5,524 vertices and 8,181 unique edges, covering the period from 30 June 2015, 20:33:41, 23:07:57 to 6 July 2015, 23:54:14.

What is interesting here is that the data and the period covered in each examined date in some cases overlap with each other, resulting in the phenomenon of having the same tweets/relations included both on the pre- and post-referendum dates. However, this does not influence the sample of the data, as the analysed data clearly indicates the changes, which occurred in the networks and discourse during the examined dates. In other words, what is already suggested here is that the changes in the examined dates are not radical, in terms of participation and discourse, while the examined dates are used as an axis, around which 10,000 tweets and relations collected each time. Therefore, as long as the concentration remains on these dates, the different attributes and features that these indicate, e.g. low evolution of data and repetition, are still points that should be analysed.

The data collection for the #oxi hashtag was conducted on the examined dates (30 June 2015, 4 July 2015, 6 July 2015) collecting the last 10,000 tweets and relations for each date. The #oxi bailout expiration is comprised of 6,404 vertices and 8,701 unique edges, giving an insight into the data produced between 30 June 2015, 12:09:01 and 30 June 2015, 23:37:18. The second #oxi network consists of 6,376 vertices and 9,754 unique edges, covering from 4 July 2015, 21:15:08 to 4 July 2015, 23:17:18. The last examined #oxi network is comprised of 9,158 vertices and 10,989 unique edges, for the period 6 July 2015, 17:59:40 to 7 July 2015, 01:04:54. The output of the data collection for all the examined dates and hashtags already suggests that the #oxi hashtag was intensively used during the examined dates in contrast to #menoumeevropi, which was sparsely used. After the calculation of the overall graph metrics, the data were grouped by cluster using the Clauset-Newman-Moore algorithm (Clauset, Newman, & Moore, 2004) and resulted in the following network structures (Figure 7.10).

On all the examined dates the #menoumeevropi and the #oxi hashtag developed close to the Community Clusters and the Broadcast Network archetype (Smith et al., 2014).

The Community Cluster emerges around global media topics and consists of many small and medium groups, developing moderate connections between them and having a few isolated participants. In this archetype, the importance of the smaller groups and hubs is highlighted, with each one having its own centre of activity, influencers and sources of information. In most of the cases, the multiple conversations illustrate the diversity of opinion and audiences, while this type of network appears based on global news stories (Smith et al., 2014). On the other hand, the Broadcast Network archetype too, which is composed of one large and

Bailout Expiration[59] 30/6/2015	Eve of the Referendum[60] 4/7/2015	Post-Referendum[61] 6/7/2015

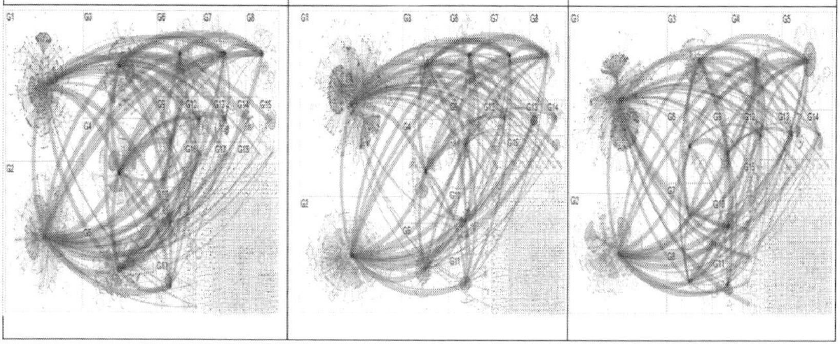

Figure 7.10. #Menoumeevropi Social Network (30 June 2015; 4 July 2015; 6 July 2015).

many secondary groups, having inbound connections between groups and moderated unconnected participants. The similarities of the top items on the network are many, as usually the words, URLs or hashtags used in the groups are raised by the dominant group and its characteristics. The broadcast archetype of the network is formed based on breaking news stories with many network members repeating 'prominent news and media organisations tweets' (2014, p. 3). In this type of network, power agenda setters and accounts with many followers have a strong impact on the networks' discourses; however, high numbers of disconnected participants remain, choosing to participate in the online discourse, without interacting with many people or their personal network.

In the first network, on 30 June, the #menoumeevropi consists of two large groups (G1 and G2) and then, few medium size groups, before the smaller groups lead to a moderate number of isolated users. The number and the size of the groups suggest some similarities to the community cluster; however, due to the high number of the inbound connections, this could also draw on the broadcast network. Next, the #menoumeevropi network, on 4 June, comprised one large group (G1), a secondary large one (G2) and a number of medium and smaller groups before reaching to the isolated users. Here, focusing on the significant difference between the size of the largest groups, on the inbound connections of the network and the isolated users, it would be possible to identify the structure of the network close to the Broadcast network archetype. Finally, looking at the last #menoumeevropi network, on 6 July, here the structure of the network is again similar to the broadcast network and the previously discussed network, as it had a large group (G1), a secondary one, a number of medium and small groups before reaching a moderate number of isolated users (Figure 7.11).

Similar to the evolution of the #menoumeevropi network, the #oxi network is also borrowing feature of the community cluster and the broadcast network

Bailout Expiration[62] 30/6/2015	Eve of the Referendum[63] 4/7/2015	Post-Referendum[64] 6/7/2015

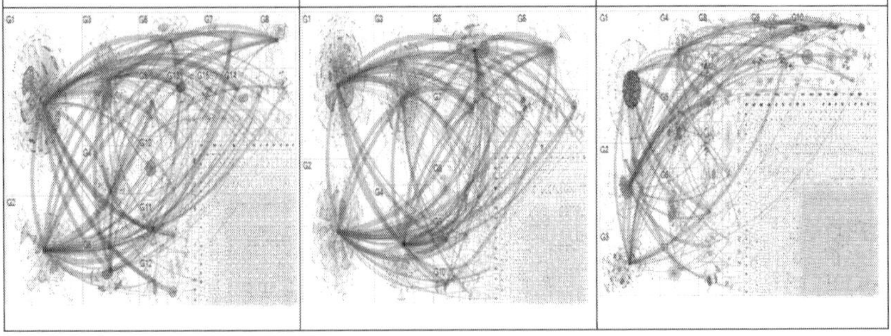

Figure 7.11. #Oxi Social Network (30 June 2015; 4 July 2015; 6 July 2015).

archetype. Looking at the evolution of the #oxi network and starting with an insight on the 30 June, the network consists of two large groups (G1 and G2) and a secondary one (G3), as well as from medium and small groups, leading to a number of disconnected users. On the 4th of July, the network is having the same characteristics in terms of structure, while there are some small changes on the 6th of July, with the network comprising one large group (G1), a secondary one (G2), followed by medium, and a higher number of small groups and many isolated users.

While the structure of the networks already suggests some characteristics and patterns about the formation of the networks, the calculation and the analysis of the top items support a more in-depth understanding of the issue. The top domains of the networks indicate the main sources of the transmitted information, while the hashtags and the top words support the analysis of meanings and discourse.

- #Menoumeevropi – top domains in tweet in entire graph/entire graph count:
  - Bailout expiration 30 June 2015
    - twitter.com: 629; skai.gr: 56; tovima.gr: 52; youtube.com: 48; blogspot.gr: 43; protothema.gr: 41; facebook.com: 41; gtp.gr: 26; netakias.com: 25; instagram.com: 24.
  - Referendum eve 4 July 2015
    - twitter.com: 734; youtube.com: 119; indymedia.org:67; thepressproject.gr: 56; gtp.gr:43; protothema.gr: 39; facebook.com: 34; athensvoice.gr: 32; google.com: 27; ohchr.org: 25.
  - Post-referendum 6 July 2015
    - twitter.com: 696; youtube.com: 111; indymedia.org: 67; thepressproject.gr: 56; facebook.com: 36; athensvoice.gr: 31; protothema.gr:27; google.com: 27; ohchr.org: 25; instagram.com: 23.

The top domains of the bailout expiration network consist of social media platform domains (Twitter, YouTube, Facebook and Instagram), mainstream

Greek media domains (Skai, To Vima and Protothema) as well as independent blog domains (netakias and blogspot) and portals of general interest (gtp – Greek Travel Pages). The second network's top domains follow the same trend as the first network and therefore what is observed here are social media platform domains (Twitter, YouTube and Facebook), Greek mainstream media domains (athensvoice and protothema) and general interest domains (gtp – Greek Travel Pages). It is interesting that among the top domains of this network, independent media projects and portals are included as well (Indymedia and thepressproject), while one of the top domains is the United Nations Human Rights domain (ohcrhr). It could be argued at this stage the #oxi campaign hijacked #menoumeevropi. The Indymedia URL leads to a post as regards direct actions against the #menoumeevropi demonstrations, while in a similar way, The Press Project published information to criticise the campaign. Additionally, the United Nations Human Rights made an announcement to welcome the Greek referendum and requested for international solidarity. On the other hand, on the last examined network, what is noticed is that the Greek Travel Pages' domain, which suggests that the #menoumeevropi campaign is associated and supportive to tourism in Greece, also noticed in the previous network, is now replaced by the Instagram domain, having some differences in the listing hierarchy. At the same time, the second and third network top domains are almost identical.

- #Oxi – top domains in tweet in entire graph/entire graph count:
  - Bailout expiration 30 June 2015
    - twitter.com: 885; youtube.com: 273; facebook.com: 198; theguardian.-com: 180; bbc.com123; indiegogo.com: 107; humanite.fr: 55; eldiario.es: 44; roarmag.org: 43; alterecoplus.fr: 38.
  - Referendum eve 4 July 2015
    - twitter.com: 841; youtube.com: 387; facebook.com: 95; elmundo.es: 58; eldiario.es: 49; newsit.gr: 47; co.uk: 6; zerohedge.com: 36; linkis.com: 35; tumblr.com: 32.
  - Post-referendum 6 July 2015
    - twitter.com: 407; avaaz.org: 267; youtube.com: 213; nytimes.com: 93; telegraaf.nl: 89; theguardian.com: 59; facebook.com: 58; bbc.com: 58; co.uk: 56; org.uk: 49.

In the top domains of the #oxi network, domains from different countries are included (e.g. .es, .gr, .uk, and .fr) in contrast to the #menoumeevropi top domains, which are composed mainly of Greek and international domains (e.g. .gr and .com). The first network's top domains are comprised of social media platform domains (e.g. Twitter, YouTube and Facebook), mainstream British media domains (e.g. The Guardian and BBC), Spanish (e.g. Eldiario) and French (e.g. Altercoplus and Humanite) media portals as well as the crowdfunding/fundraising site Indiegogo and the independent Roarmag, which focuses on politics. The second network's top domains include social media platform domains (e.g. Twitter, YouTube, Facebook and Tumblr), Spanish mainstream media (e.g. Elmundo Eldario), Greek mainstream media (newsit), as well as British domains (co.uk). While there are many mainstream media domains, only one independent portal is included (ZeroHedge). A very interesting observation on this network, though, is the Linkis.com domain, which belongs to a free link customisation service for social promotion. This domain is about services, which support online presence, especially on twitter, and encourage interaction with their readers. In the network, this domain is associated with a BBC article 'Joseph Stiglitz, Nobel Prize in Economics: "The conditions imposed on Greece are indignantes"' (Originally in Spanish; Fajardo, 2015). The third network has been created similarly to the previous two; therefore, what we see as top domains here are social media platforms (e.g. Twitter, YouTube and Facebook), while in a high position is the Avaaz.org, a global civil organisation promoting activism and supporting campaigns. Again, mainstream media domains from the UK (e.g. *The Guardian* and BBC), Netherlands (e.g. *Telegraaf*) and international media organisations are included too (e.g. *NYTimes*). The information transmitted in these networks comes mainly from mainstream media organisations and social media domains.

Therefore, what is suggested here is that the #menoumeevropi top domains are mainly social media platform domains and Greek mainstream media domains, while in contrast, more international and mainstream media organisations and social media domains are among the #oxi network top domains. The #menoumeevropi includes some independent media and political portals and blogs, while pages, which are used for civic organisation, activism and supporting the running of campaigns, are included in the #oxi top domains.

- #Menoumeevropi – top hashtags in tweet in entire graph/entire graph count:
  - Bailout expiration 30 June 2015
    - Menoumeevropi: 9,573; yeseurope: 1,201; dimopsifisma: 866; greferendum: 593; nai: 560; greece: 558; menoume_malakes: 501; ναι (yes): 438; grexit: 408; syntagma: 261.
  - Referendum eve 4 July 2015
    - Menoumeevropi: 10,045; dimopsifisma: 2,420; nai: 1,982; greferendum: 1,923; yeseurope: 1,762; oxi: 1,063; menoume_malakes: 819; greece: 647; ναι: 567; grineuro: 515.
  - Post-referendum 6 July 2015
    - Menoumeevropi: 10,017; dimopsifisma: 2,483; nai: 2,113; greferendum: 1,949; yeseurope: 1,506; oxi: 1,065; menoume_malakes: 701; ναι (yes): 643; greece: 564; grineuro: 516.

The dominant hashtags used in the #menoumeevropi network are related to the 'yes' campaign discourse (e.g. yeseurope, nai and grineuro) as well as to referendum-related events and debates (e.g. syntagma, Greece, no vs yes and Grexit), while there is a humourous approach to the issue as well (e.g. menoume_malakes). Similarly, the top words and pairs of words indicate the same features. What is interesting is that all the examined dates indicate a specific pattern in terms of discourse, without being strongly linked to the evolution of the events.

- #Menoumeevropi – top words in tweet in entire graph/entire graph count:
  - Bailout expiration 30 June 2015 (total words: 124,533)
    - Menoumeevropi: 9,572; rt: 6,511; να: 2,385; το: 2,233; και: 1,717.
  - Referendum Eve 4/7/2015 (Total Words: 139,279):
    - Menoumeevropi: 9,491; dimopsifisma: 2,330; ναι: 2,047; nai: 1,934; greferendum: 1,841.
  - Post-referendum 6 July 2015 (total words: 139,254):
    - Menoumeevropi: 9,514; rt: 7,661; το: 3,107; dimopsifisma: 2,385: να: 2,354.
- #Menoumeevropi – top word pairs in tweet in entire graph/entire graph count:
  - Bailout expiration 30 June 2015
    - yeseurope, menoumeevropi: 637; του, menoumeevropi: 432; οι, menoumeevropi: 425; menoumeevropi, menoume_malakes: 394; το, menoumeevropi: 344; menoumeevropi, nai: 304; στο, σύνταγμα: 284; στο, menoumeevropi: 282; rt, skaigr: 272; για, να: 268.
  - Referendum eve 4 July 2015
    - greferendum, menoumeevropi: 874; menoumeevropi, dimopsifisma: 809; yeseurope, menoumeevropi: 683; menoumeevropi, menoume_malakes: 674; dimopsifisma, nai: 641; menoumeevropi, yeseurope: 495; menoumeevropi, nai: 481; το, ναι: 395; του, menoumeevropi: 391; μένουμε, ευρώπη: 384.
  - Post- referendum 6 July, 2015
    - rt,paratiritirio: 1,065; greferendum,menoumeevropi: 1,023; menoumeevropi,dimopsifisma: 883; dimopsifisma,nai: 741; yeseurope,menoumeevropi: 641; menoumeevropi,menoume_malakes: 564; οι,menoumeevropi: 470; menoumeevropi,nai: 470; rt,akisdadais: 451; του,ναι: 442.

The top hashtags of the #oxi network indicate significant differences in comparison to the #menoumeevropi. While #oxi top hashtags do not indicate significant changes, focusing on the examined dates; still there are some interesting observations raised by the usage of different languages (l6ngreferéndum, Grecia, Greece) and the usage of hashtags expressing solidarity (aveclesgrecs, yovoycongrecia). In contrast to the #menoumeevropi hashtags and discourse, the #oxi network and discourse develops a multilayered discussion and meanings, linking the referendum campaign to the notion of solidarity, which in the crisis era is both related to solidarity among countries as well as solidarity initiatives in linkage to the anti-austerity movement. Therefore, instead of the evolution of meanings on the examined dates, there are more references to the evolution of the political campaign and debates, throughout the crisis period, concentrating on EU and the Greek context.

- #Oxi – top hashtags in tweet in entire graph/entire graph count:
  - Bailout expiration 30 June 2015
    - Oxi: 11,171; greferendum: 2,577; dimopsifisma: 1,712; greece: 1,590; yes-europe: 785; aveclesgrecs: 656; grexit: 578; oxi2015: 533; yovoycongre-cia: 446; grecia: 445.
  - Referendum eve 4 July 2015
    - oxi: 11,143; greferendum: 2,211; greece: 1,655; dimopsifisma: 1,019; oxi2015: 926; grecia: 670; yovoycongrecia: 549; freegreece: 481; l6ngreferéndum: 472; syntagma: 408.
  - Post-referendum 6 July 2015
    - oxi: 10,097; greece: 1,229; greferendum: 874; grefenderum: 840; greekre-ferendum: 680; grecia: 460; abilitatitfa: 409; tfalaresistenza: 393; grexit: 349; eurogroup: 288.

The top words and the pair of words appear similar to the hashtags of the network, suggesting a more intense change in the variation of languages and discourse. It is interesting that only in the last network the discourse developed in Greek, pointing to the referendum outcome understood as a potential rift between the EU and Greece.

- #Oxi – top words in tweet in entire graph/entire graph count:
  - Bailout expiration 30 June 2015 (total words: 153,693)
    - oxi: 10,093; rt: 6,932; greferendum: 2,377; greece: 1,601; dimopsifisma: 1,580.
  - Referendum eve 4 July 2015 (total words: 154,474):
    - oxi: 10,917; rt: 7963; de: 2,199; la: 2,140; greece: 2005.
  - Post-referendum 6 July 2015 (total words: 167,131):
    - oxi: 9,222; rt: 7,630; de: 2,824; la: 2,585; el: 1,903
- #Oxi – top word pairs in tweet in entire graph/entire graph count:
  - Bailout expiration 30 June 2015
    - oxi, oxi: 804; greferendum, oxi: 793; oxi, greferendum: 491; dimopsi-fisma,oxi: 473; dimopsifisma,greferendum: 426; rt,blacktom1961: 388; oxi,dimopsifisma: 353; greece,oxi: 272; oxi,oxi2015: 262; oxi,team_oxi: 262.
  - Referendum eve 4 July 2015
    - oxi, oxi: 1,289; oxi,greferendum: 598; rt,rcabrero75: 567; oxi,oxi2015: 544; de,la: 436; greece,oxi: 417; rt,tsipras_eu: 336; oxi,dimopsifisma: 317; rt,gsemprunmdg: 308; greferendum,oxi: 284.
  - Post-referendum 6 July 2015
    - rt,rcabrero75: 1009; de,la: 587; το,οχι: 533; οχι,σημαίνει: 523; σημαίνει,ρήξη: 523; oxi,http: 515; rcabrero75,el: 381; abilitatitfa,r: 378; r,esistono: 378; esistono,tfalaresistenza: 378.

Focusing on the top pair of words, a semantic network was formed, for both the examined hashtags and the examined dates, as follows (Figure 7.12).

Figure 7.12. #Menoumeevropi – Bailout Expiration Semantic Network (30 June 2015).

Starting with the #menoumeevropi hashtag and the bailout expiration network, the network consists of 144 edges and 180 vertices, based on which 13 groups were detected. In this network, the discussion developed mainly in Greek and provide a snapshot of some of the first reactions and discourse on the referendum debate. G1 suggests an insight into the development of #menoumeevropi and the referendum, signalling the use of Twitter for organising processes, as well as for transmitting information about the campaign (διαδώστε, πορείες, σύνταγμα – spread the information, demonstration and syntagma). At the same time, the criticisms of the referendum and the #menoumeevropi campaign are expressed through humorous or sarcastic comments (e.g. slavery_in_greece, menoume_malakes). G2, G3 and G4 develop in this context, commenting on the crisis frame, the new forms of slavery, as this is discussed in linkage to poverty, including comments on wages, linking this to the critics on the neoliberal and austerity policies. G5 and G6 concentrate on the last memorandum and the danger of Grexit. G4 makes a reference to A. Samaras and New Democracy the opposition party, while G8 discusses the issue of dignity and the unity of the Greek people during the referendum, mentioning that both the conflicting political and ideological sides should stay united (e.g. ταπείνωση, όλοι, ενωμένοι). I analyse the #menoumeevropi discourse in comparison to #oxi in Figure 7.13.

The #oxi semantic network develops differently in comparison to the #menoumeevropi network. The network comprised 110 vertices and 127 edges. In this network, discussion develops in English, Greek and Spanish, while a

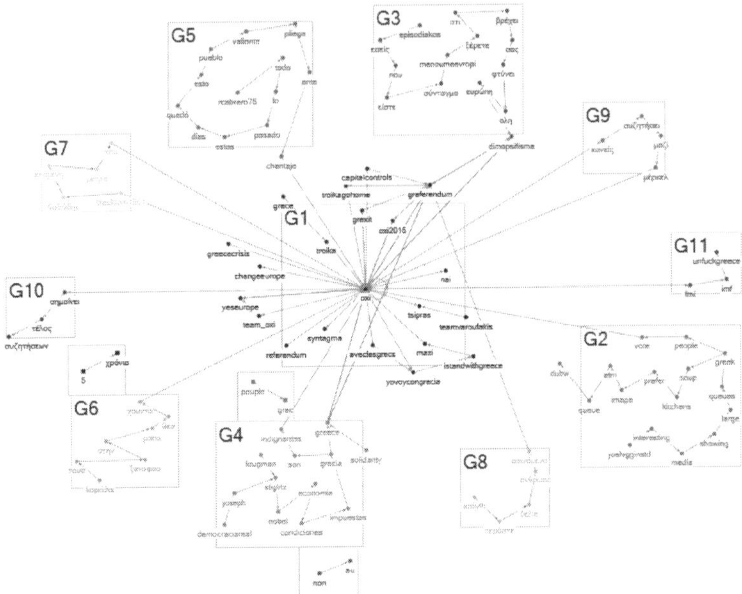

Figure 7.13. #Oxi Bailout Expiration Semantic Network (30 June 2015).

multitude of discussed themes that characterise the network is also observed. Starting with the first group, G1 is composed of three poles; the first one focuses on the greferendum debate, the second one focuses on the 'yes' campaign and the last one on Greek politics. More precisely, the central node, oxi, is directly linked to the referendum and the nodes' capital controls, troikagohome, oxi2015 and grexit. Thus, this cluster of nodes concentrates both on the evolution of the incident (capital controls), as well as on the EU debate and the danger of Grexit. The next cluster is concentrated on the yeseurope campaign, which in the graph, is presented as being in opposition to the node team_oxi. At the same time, another cluster is concentrated on the politicians who had a leading role in the referendum (e.g. Tsipras, teamvaroufakis) and the conflict between the troika, Greece and the potentiality or necessity for change in Europe (e.g. troika, Grece, changeeurope and greekcrisis).

G2 refers to the capital controls (e.g. atm, queues, showing, large and media) and the referendum vote. G3 heavily criticises the #menoumeevropi mobilisation (e.g. εσείς/you, που/that, είστε/you are, στο/at, σύνταγμα/syntagma, menoumeevropi, ξέρετε/you know, ότι/that, βρέχει/it's raining, σας φτύνει/spit on you, όλη/all and Ευρώπη/europe), while G3 is directly linked twice with G1 (e.g. greferendum and oxi). G4 is composed of words in Spanish including references to blackmail (e.g. chantaje), change and the braveness of people. G5 is comprised of English and Spanish words, which refer to Greece and the implementation of austerity measures (e.g. indignantes/outrageous, son/with, grecia/Greece, impuestas/imposed, condiciones/conditions and ecomia/economy). G7 refers to general comments and discussion on the referendum and the crisis making, while G6 makes a reference to the Greek Junta and G9 to Merkel and the negotiations. G10 emerges with words that are later used as hashtags of the so-called solidarity campaign, which alongside the #thisisacoup are used for the expression of opposition to the austerity politics and debate on the issue, on a national and transnational level. G10 and G11 develop focusing on the austerity measures and Greece (e.g. imf, unfuckgreece) and the negotiations (e.g. oxi, σημαίνει/means, τέλος/end and συζητήσεων/discussion) between the Greek government and the troika.

While both the examined hashtags and the examined dates could be analysed at multiple levels and at different depths, the already analysed material offers an insight into how Twitter is used, supporting the development of expressions of conflicting discourses as well as intensifying online political polarisation that interacts with offline polarisation. Before continuing the study of the evolution of hashtags, what is already suggested here is that before the referendum the #menoumeevropi and the 'yes' campaign developed mainly in Greek and did not manage to amplify political discussion on the referendum and, in extend, austerity policies. In contrast, #oxi users strongly criticise the 'yes' campaign and gain international attention, with participants tweeting in different languages, discussing the issue in different contexts. An interesting point is that, except for English, which is a dominant language online, languages from south European countries are strongly used in the networks, pointing out the interest in the issue, as well as linkages or similarities in politics and the hierarchical structures and power relations in the European political scene (e.g. Podemos, Austerity politics and PIGS) (Figure 7.14).

The semantic network of the hashtag #menoumeevropi, as shaped one day before the referendum, 4 July 2015, didn't indicate many differences in comparison to the network of the 30th June and the day of the bailout expiration. The network consists of 135 edges and 110 vertices. G1, the dominant group of the network created around the examined hashtag indicating an enriched discourse surrounding the 'yes' campaign, pointing out that Greece should accept the bailout conditions (e.g. yeseurope) and stay in Europe (e.g. grineuro and menoumeevropi), perceiving this is a 'yes' to Greece's' future (e.g. naistinellada/yes to Greece), while, at the same time, the danger of bankruptcy is also discussed. The name of the Olympic gold medallist and PASOK's former MP P. Dimas (Πύρρος Δήμας) is included in the group as he was among the supporters of the campaign, as many artists, athletes and public figures straightforwardly supported the campaign. However, this was among the strongest criticisms of the campaign. At the same time, hashtags such as SYRIZA_sano, SYRIZA_xeftiles are part of the main body of the network, in contrast to the 30 June 2015 #menoumeevropi network, in which these hashtags appeared isolated and linked together. These hashtags are used to criticise SYRIZA, mocking both the party and its policies; what is interesting is that these hashtags appear together online more than a year later, especially on Twitter conflicts between SYRIZA and the opposition party. Therefore, considering who was supporting the #menoumeevropi and their identification with mainstream politics a year later, this could

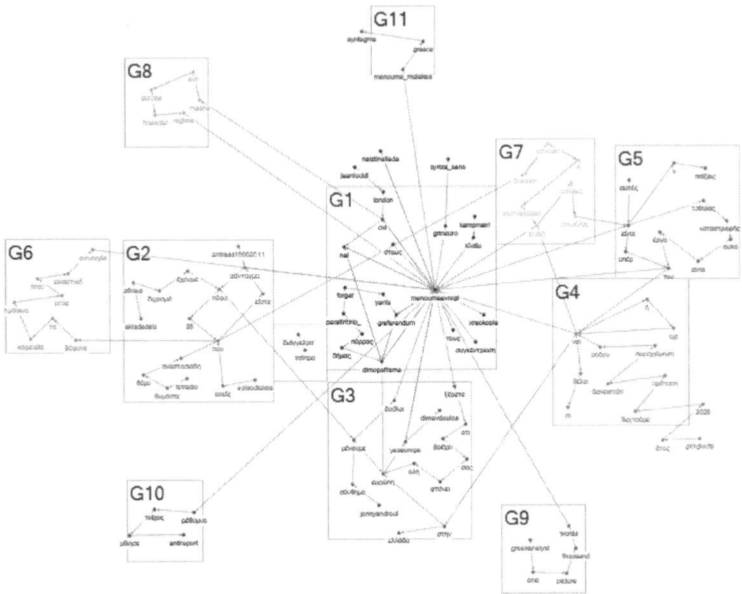

Figure 7.14. #Menoumeevropi Referendum Eve Semantic Network (4 July 2015).

suggest a continuity in terms of political and ideological conflict or opposition, online and offline.

In 2010, Josef Schlarmann, a senior member of Angela Merkel's Christian Democrats, and Frank Schaeffler, a finance policy expert in the Free Democrats gave an interview to the German tabloid Bild (BILD.de, 2010). The second group raised by the discussion originated from that article, criticising #menoumeevropi for compliance with the lenders' demands, even as that would mean questioning the sovereignty of the country. G3 develops in the same sarcastic spirit, very similar to the previous network, while G5 discusses the disastrous plans and ulterior goal of Tsipras, developing a discourse similar to the conspiracy theory discourses.

G2 criticises the #menoumeevropi and 'yes' campaign as well as public figures supporting it and connects to G7, which makes a reference on a financial and political scandal in Greece, in which Th. Anastasiadis, a Greek journalist and publisher was accused of tax evasion and money laundering but was vindicated by a decree in 2015 (Dima, 2015). Anastasiadis was among the 'menoumeevropi supporters, while this was also discussed in G2, linking this discussion to the issue of polarisation and division of Greek society (e.g. *εθνικό* national, *διχασμό* disunity, *έχουμε* have, *τώρα* now, *σύνταγμα* syntagma,). This discussion further develops in G6, making a reference to the politics and polarisation of the 1980s, focusing on the two dominant and antagonist parties, PASOK and ND

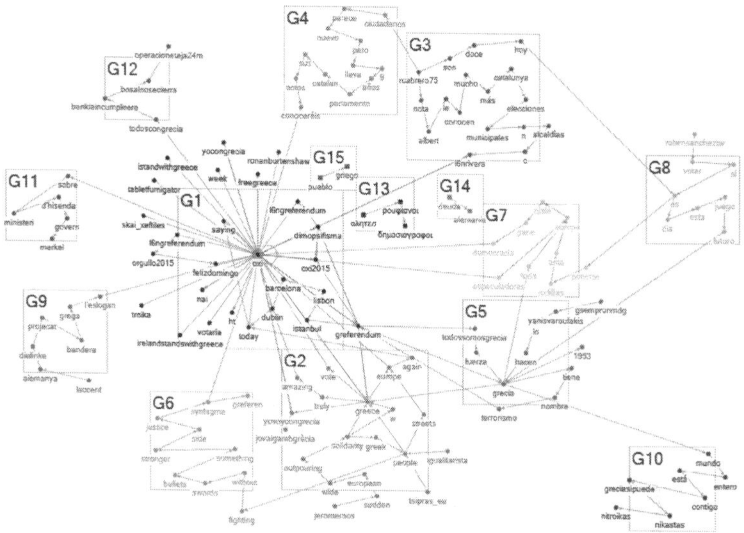

Figure 7.15. #Oxi Referendum Eve Semantic Network (4 July 2015).

(e.g. Giannarou, 2012), highlighting though, that what has happened during the period of the referendum is much more intense (e.g. *βάφανε* painting, *καφενεία* coffeehouse, πράσινα/green, μπλε/blue, ήταν/was, εικαστική/art and παρέμβαση/intervention). G4, developed around the tweet: Year 2015 Should we take lenders' proposal on conceding Rhodes island YES or No? Yes #menoumeevropi, it is not to risk that kind of things.

G9, G10 and G8 concentrate on the evolution of events, as well as on Europe and the crisis (e.g. financial, regime, Europe and means – G8). G11 reproduces the G3 group of the #menoumeevropi 30 June 2015 network, which criticises the #menoumeevropi mobilisation (e.g. *εσείς*/you, *που*/that, *είστε*/you are, *στο*/at, *σύνταγμα*/syntagma, menoumeevropi, *ξέρετε*/you know, *ότι*/that, *βρέχει*/it's raining, σας *φτύνει*/spit on you, *όλη* all and, Ευρώπη/europe) with the sarcastic comment 'it is not raining, it's europe spitting on you' (Figure 7.15).

The #oxi semantic network of 4 July 2015 is composed of groups developed in different languages, similarly to the network of 30 June 2015. The network comprised of 143 vertices and 178 edges. G1 focuses on the so-called greferendum (e.g. dimopsifisma, nai, and oxi2015), on the 'no' campaign and anti-austerity politics (e.g. freegreece, oxi2015 and troika), while solidarity is also expressed (e.g. istandwithgreece, irelandstandswithgreece, yocongrecia, Istanbul, Barcelona, Dublin, today and saying, oxi). Nodes that act as hubs in this groups (e.g. oxi, oxi2015, greferendum and dimopsifisma), suggest a strong linkage between the 'no' campaign and the referendum discourse. Throughout the crisis-era and especially during the referendum period, the dispute surrounding, and disgrace of the mainstream and traditional media institutions was strongly expressed, while the gap between the online and the offline discourse indicates strong points of consideration, both concentrating on the media institutions and its linkages to politics and society. While this will be examined later in depth, Skai_xeftiles refers to the disgrace regarding one of the most popular Greek TV channels, Skai, while this phrase/hashtag was widely used for months, referring to and commenting on all the Greek TV channels (e.g. mega_xeftiles, ant1_xeftiles and, skai_xeftiles), denoting mainstream corporate media industry corruption.

G2 develops around the nodes greece, people and europe, including general comments on the campaign, while solidarity is expressed too (e.g. solidarity, vote, streets, yocongrecia and tsipras_eu etc.). G6 concentrates on forms of struggle (e.g. fighting, without, swords and bullets) as well as on the Syntagma Square mobilisations, suggesting that the issue of justice is being directly linked to these points. G3 to G8 and G9 to G10 develop in Spanish and refer to Greece and Europe, to solidarity and banks (G10 and G12), as well as to the Catalan parliamentary elections of September 2015 (BBC 28 September 2015) (G3 and G4). G6 highlights that dignity is among the major concerns regarding the referendum (e.g. today/all, europa, ante/before, rodillas/knees, ojala/hopefully, especuladores/speculators, Democracia and gone/win), while the antagonistic relationship between Greece and the EU is indicated by G5, which is formed based on the tweet: '@yanisvaroufakis: Lo q hacen con #Grecia tiene un nombre: terrorismo/@yanisvaroufakis: What do with #Grecia has a name: terrorism'. Dignity and justice are keywords both in the #oxi campaign, as well as in the pre-election SYRIZA campaign. G8 highlights that the referendum should not be understood in the context of the Greek-EU negotiations, but in contrast, is indicative of and precludes the future of the EU.

G9 and G11 concentrate on the earlier tweet highlighting the online and offline political coalitions and solidarity. What is interesting here are the linkages between the European left parties and at the same time, the extent to which discourse develops in Spanish the night of the referendum, pointing out the political coalitions and polarisation in the EU context, both in regard to the division between south-north and the conflict between neoliberal politics and the left. While these suggest an insight into the pre-referendum discourse, the final examined date, 6 July 2015, aims to indicate changes in the discourse as shaped after the referendum's results (Figure 7.16).

The last examined semantic network of the #menoumeevropi develops with a similar pattern as the previous examples. The network comprised 120 edges and 101 vertices. G1 focuses on the referendum, although in this case the contrast between the yes and 'no' campaign (e.g. nai, oxi, naistinellada, grineuro ναι/yes, ή/or and όχι/no grexit) as well as criticisms of the #menoumeevropi (e.g. menoume_malakes and SYRIZA_sano) dominate the discourse, while the group forms around words/hubs both in Greek and English (e.g. yes, no, ναι, όχι). G2 is based on two different tweets, with the first criticising Tsipras' statement on the referendum as dividing society. This has been one of the strongest criticisms against the referendum and Tsipras, strongly expressed by the opposition party, both online and in the press

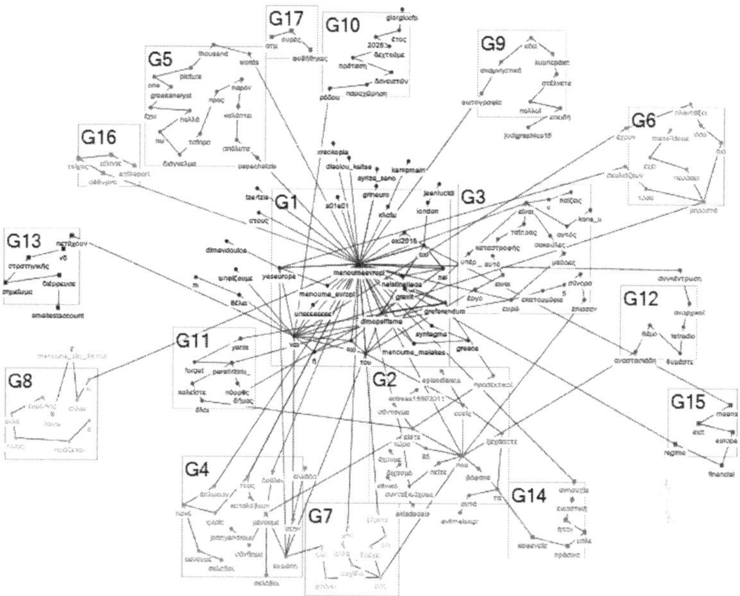

Figure 7.16. #Menoumeevropi Post-referendum Semantic Network (6 July 2015).

(Smith, 2015). G6 users comment on the reaction of the 'yes' campaign to the referendum results. G13 develops around the ND's leaked non-paper with the title *Strategy Curriculum on the Referendum*; the document was published online on an independent, left-wing affiliated portal, days before the referendum, and was supposed to have been circulated for ND internal communication purposes, as a guide on how to propagandise the 'yes' campaign, indicating the role of public figures supporting the campaign as well as the role of media (e.g. To Kouti tis Pandoras, 2015; TVXS, 2015). While this was published online before the referendum, it managed to dominate the #menoumeevropi discourse and Twitter discussion after the referendum. On the other hand, G3 suggests the merging of two groups and discourse already existed in previously examined #menoumeevropi networks, focusing on financial scandals and public figure supporters of the campaign, as well as on the debate regarding tsipras' secret plan and the referendum.

G8 highlights how the #menoumeevropi, which literally means we stay in Europe, was satirically and sarcastically converted to 'we stay slaves (e.g. μένουμε δούλοι and μένουμε σκλάβοι)', producing a counter-discourse and campaign against the 'yes' campaign. G10 repeats what is also observed in the #menoumeevropi semantic network and the 4 July 2015 discourse, concentrating on the 'yes' campaign's consent to lenders and the Troika's demands, sarcastically drawing on the Bild's original discussion about selling monuments, islands or national sovereignty and the debt. G8, G9 and G14, similarly,

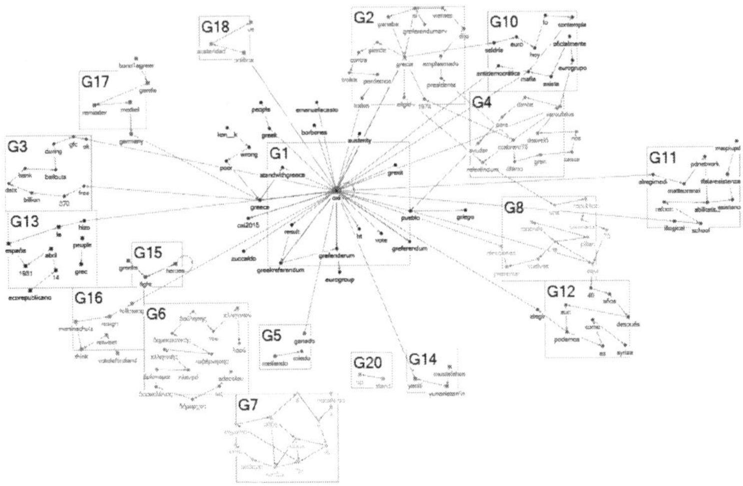

Figure 7.17. #Oxi Post-referendum Semantic Network (6 July 2015).

concentrate on financial scandals and the case of Anastasiadis as well as on the sociopolitical turmoil and polarisation making references to the 1980s (Figure 7.17).

The last examined #oxi semantic network develops in English, Spanish and Greek. The network consists of 217 vertices and 184 edges. G1 concentrates on the austerity debate and the solidarity campaign, as produced and expressed both online and offline (e.g. istandwithgreece, austeridad, grexit, troika and greferendum), pointing out the polarisation and the division between European countries and in Greece. G2 to G11, G13 and G12 develop in Spanish and focus on the austerity and referendum. Among the most interesting points in these groups is the discussion about the mafia, euro and antidemocracia (G10), the linkage between SYRIZA and Podemos (G12) and the political coalitions and solidarity (G6). At the same time, G4 and G13 refer to the elections of Catalonia.

Another interesting point in these groups is the historical references as observed in G2 and G13 which emerge from the tweets 'In 1974 in Greece, a referendum for democracy chooses 'no' to the crown (70%). Here 40 years later we still cannot choose #OXI'; on 14 April 1931, Spain vote #OXI for the Borbones', with both tweets supported by visual material of the referenced periods. These tweets point out historical references, linking the 1974 Greek referendum, the 1931 Spanish referendum and the 2015 Greek referendum, which in this context is understood to focus on the historical continuity of events, ideologies and conflict. At the same time, a parallelism between the cases of Greece and Spain is suggested focusing both on the historical events and the austerity politics. In contrast to the historical context in which the EU crisis and the neoliberal policies are often located, these tweets relocate the referendum and the crisis cases in a historical context and continuity.

#greferendum

Data collection was conducted on 27 June 2015, 30 June 2015 and 5 July 2015, collecting the last 10,000 tweets and relations for each of the examined hashtag. After the calculation of the overall graph metrics, the data were grouped by cluster using the Clauset-Newman-Moore algorithm (Clauset, Newman, & Moore, 2004) and resulted in the following network structures (Figure 7.18).

The examination of the #greferendum and the online networks as developed on Twitter during some of the most critical moments of the referendum period suggest an understanding relating to hierarchies, structures and communities. The referendum announcement network is composed of 5,793 vertices and 8,424 unique edges, and the collected material of 10,000 Tweets and relations includes data that evolved from 27 June 2015, 11:17:08 to 14:07:26. The bailout expiration network consists of 7,400 vertices and 9,400 unique edges, describing data produced from 30 June 2015, 18:24:57 to 1 July 2015, 00:23:59. Finally, the referendum network is composed of 8,194 vertices and 9,904 unique edges, covering the period from 5 July 2015, 23:07:57 to 6 July 2015, 01:24:43.

The examined network consists of one large and many small and medium groups, having many isolated users. Even if the examined networks do not indicate significant differences between the larger and the secondary groups, all the networks are characterised by strong linkages between groups and users, as well as by different characteristics and top items of the groups. However, there are also slight differences between the networks. The first network structure is designated by rich linkages between groups and users, in comparison to the later networks, which are characterised by a lower level of density.

Taking into consideration that this hashtag was used by both sides and campaigns, at this point, a major consideration focuses on whether the dominant actors are average users or accounts with media and political content. Also, is also of interest is to test whether the dominant users interact repeating the

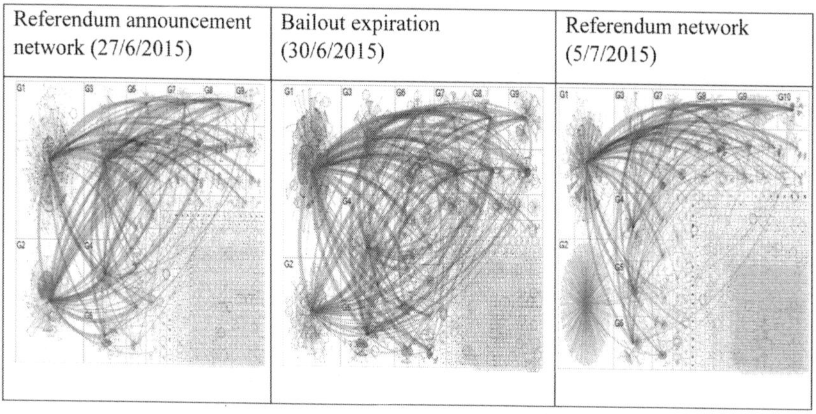

Figure 7.18. Referendum Announcement, Bailout Expiration and Referendum Network.

mainstream media's tweets and political material or produce alternative discourses and content. After the calculation of the graph metrics and especially concentrating on betweenness centrality, it is suggested that the nodes with a strong influence on the network, bridging different clusters and nodes, are as follow (Cherven, 2015, p. 195):

- #Greferendum influential nodes and actors according to betweenness centrality:
  - Referendum announcement network (27 June 2015)
    - Greekanalyst: 5,386,582.377; jodigraphics15: 2,548,635.424; j_dijsselbloem: 1,876,819.417; kkarkagiannis: 1,297,625.742; lilyinfidel: 1,295,131.207; atsipras: 1,218,250.532; traynorbrussels: 1,040,374.242.
  - Bailout expiration (30 June 2015)
    - Gmourout:.3,859,344.271; Manosgiakoumis:.3,081,082.932; jodigraphics 15:.2,917,609.984; joannap___:.2,890,669.594; Ertsocial:.2,044,886.148; Irategreek:.1,829,207.267; Prognosismedia:.1,663,936.887; Atsipras:. 1,582,314.108; Markospoulakis:.1,568,339.158.
  - Referendum network (5 July 2015)
    - Thereaibanksy: 9,566,801.754; aaronsidewhite: 2,993,516.158; harryslaststand: 2,845,342.945; suttonnick: 2,837,699.045; futiledemocracy: 2,389,302.762; georgemorina: 2,340,222.020; sickjew: 2,175,195.558.

In the examined network, the most influential nodes/actors are politicians (j_dijsselbloem, atsipras, gmourout, etc.) and media-related users (e.g. ertsocial, suttonick, kkarkagianis, traynorbrussels.), while only a few users are related to activism and independent or alternative media (e.g. lilyfindel, markopoulakis, jodihraphics15, joannap___, irategreek and sickjew), including political and media analysts (e.g. prognosismedia and greeknalysist). Most of the dominant nodes/actors are users/accounts from Greece (e.g. politicians, activists and media), although there are also dominant nodes/actors from other countries as well (e.g. UK). These were some of the most influential accounts that acted as hubs, around which groups and sub-networks developed. The examination of the dominant domains is an interesting point of analysis too, indicating the source of the transmitted information, giving an insight into how different platforms and media sources relate to the Twitter discourse.

- #Greferendum – top domains in tweet in entire graph/entire graph count:
  - Referendum announcement network (27 June 2015)
    - twitter.com: 739; naftemporiki.gr: 137; youtube.com: 94; newsit.gr: 72; piraeusview.gr: 62; facebook.com: 53; antenna.gr: 50; bloomberg.com: 47; ilfattoquotidiano.it: 45; protothema.gr: 38.
  - Bailout expiration (30 June 2015)
    - twitter.com: 699; referendum2015gov.gr: 147; theguardian.com: 144; youtube.com: 119; commonspace.scot: 86; facebook.com: 75; naftemporiki.gr: 61v instagram.com: 52; megatv.com: 50; ert.gr45.

- Referendum network (5 July 2015)
  - twitter.com: 292; trib.al: 203; youtube.com: 123; gu.com: 79; co.uk: 77; facebook.com: 64; nytimes.com: 63; bbc.com: 59; cnn.com: 50; theguardian.com: 46.

In all three examined networks, the dominant domains consist mainly of mainstream media platforms (e.g. antenna.gt, bloomberg.com, theguardian.com, naftemporiki.gr and bbc.com) and social media platforms (e.g. Twitter, YouTube, Facebook and Instagram). A comparison between the three networks suggests that the Greek domains appear mainly on the first and the second network; however, the international domains and platforms have a significant role in all the examined networks. It is quite interesting that, in contrast to the dominant actors, which are mainly from Greece, most of the dominant domains of the networks are international or from countries other than Greece. This is a point that draws attention to the considerations regarding the role of Greek and the international media, both online and offline, and their contribution/representation of the Greek referendum (e.g. announcement of the referendum and media representation, and exit polls) and the Greek crisis (e.g. Antoniadis, 2012; Mylonas, 2014). At the same time, such discussion should be situated within the wider debate regarding the Greek media system and the crisis, both in terms of structural characteristics (e.g. ownership, corruption and media crisis) (Doulkeri & Terzis 1997; Sims, 2003; Smyrnaios, 2010, 2013), as well as in terms of crisis representation (e.g. how crisis is mediated, Greek/EU representation and differences).

After developing an insight into the networks, it is also important to understand the kind of information, which was spread through these networks, including questions of ideology and over time, identities. This approach suggests a multidimensional analysis, although, at this stage it is important to develop an overall understanding of the semantic networks, as raised by the study of dominant hashtags, dominant words and pairs of words, suggesting an insight into the discourse as shaped online. The top hashtags of the network are as follows:

- #Greferendum – top hashtags in tweet in entire graph/entire graph count:
  - Referendum announcement network (27 June 2015)
    - Greferendum: 9,681; dimopsifisma: 2014; greece: 1,243; grexit: 733; vouli: 698; eurogroup: 531; yovoycongreciav225; tsipras: 221; topotami: 206; referendum: 205.
  - Bailout expiration (30 June 2015)
    - greferendum: 9,998 greece: 2,198; dimopsifisma: 1,784; grexit: 1,616; yeseurope: 1,217; oxi: 1,192; greececrisis: 838; oxi2015: 506; tsipras: 358; team_oxi: 338.
  - Referendum network (5 July 2015)
    - greekreferendum: 10,057 oxi: 1,711; greece: 1,116; grefenderum: 719; austerity: 508; grexit: 341; greeks: 323; greferendum: 236; greececrisis: 235; oxi2015: 222.

Considering that the collection of data was conducted by searching for the hashtag #greferendum, it is not surprising that this hashtag appears in all the examined networks, although on the last network it appears in a lower position than in the first two. Indeed, the political and social considerations, as well as, the media discourse indicate significant changes parallel to the evolution of the incident, while the day of the referendum could be perceived as being a turning point regards the political debates and discourse.

In the first network, the dominant hashtags are related to the referendum (e.g. Greferendum, dimopsifisma and referendum), the Eurogroup negotiations and the negotiations/debates of the Greek parliament (vouli). At the same time, the discussion and the hashtag #grexit are in a high position among the dominant hashtags and heavily used by the press, supporting the evolution of political turmoil. Focusing on Grexit, both the pro-/anti-austerity debates are established, as also, relevant political debates originating from the 2008 turmoil and the rapid development of the crisis (Vasilopoulou & Halikiopoulou, 2013).

The hashtag #yovoycongrecia is part of the online campaign #istandwithgreece, which was created based on this phrase translated into different languages, circulating on twitter for days, expressing solidarity with Greece. Later, this campaign was linked to another campaign and the trending hashtag #thisisacoup, expressing not only solidarity, but also opposition as regards the political turmoil and austerity politics. Even if these campaigns expressed solidarity, a more detailed study of the referendum hashtags could highlight who participated and supported the campaign, dominating the online discourse, revealing whether and how this developed as a bottom-up process. Hashtags related to the Greek political scene, such as #tsipras and #topotami, appear very often in the network, rapidly changing positions according to current affairs developments and incidents (e.g. parliament speech during the data collection).

On the second network, the debate and the contrast between the Yes/No campaigns is clear. This debate could be understood as a transformation of the anti-/pro-austerity debate, which before the referendum, was expressed through the anti-/pro-governmental mobilisations organised on 17 June–18 June 2015 (Fraser, 2015; Waerden & Fletcher, 2015). While the anti-austerity protests during the crisis era were not a rare phenomenon, after the elections of SYRIZA in January 2015, the context of such mobilisations changed from anti-austerity and anti-governmental mobilisations into pro-governmental, pro-SYRIZA mobilisations, which continued to express opposition to austerity.

After the anti-austerity protests, which took place on 17 June 2015, the first pro-European protest (menoumeevropi) took place on 18 June 2015 in Athens and other cities (Protothema.gr, 18 June 2015). The anti-austerity mobilisation and campaign, which was partially a pro-SYRIZA and pro-governmental campaign, was linked with keywords and hashtags such as #oxi (meaning no in Greek) and #oxi2015, which could be considered to suggest a symbolic parallelism to the historical usage of the words (e.g. WWII and the national celebration of 'OXI'). On the other hand, #yeseurope and #menoumeevropi, which means we stay in Europe, were among the keywords and hashtags representing the 'yes' campaign. These hashtags were also criticised in terms of symbolic meaning and historical continuity (e.g. the discussion on capitalism and neo-colonialism).

As expected, the dominant hashtags of the last network straightforwardly refer to the referendum and the result. Hashtags related to the #greekcrisis, the #grexit and #greferendum have been observed in the previously examined networks, although the hashtag #austerity appears again among the most dominant hashtags, pointing out the debate on austerity during the referendum period. After a brief discussion regarding the dominant hashtags, the examination of pairs of words will suggest a more detailed understanding of the meaning and ideas noticed in the examined networks. A major difference between the dominant hashtags and the dominant words, or pairs of words, is that the hashtags are used as descriptions or title, selected by the users, who themselves describe or categorise their statement/tweet. Even if each hashtag can be used and understood as having multiple content and purposes (e.g. usage of hashtag denoting irony, facts and humour), there is a specific direction in terms of meanings. In contrast, the dominant words or pairs of words reveal more information regarding meaning and discourse, without denoting or suggesting any direction in terms of understanding.

After the overall graph metrics' calculation and the calculation of the top items, then, the calculation of top words and top pairs of words supported the development of semantic networks. These networks developed through the examination of the most mentioned words and pairs of words, which were perceived as nodes and edges, suggesting an in-depth study into how meaning and discourse were produced (Figure 7.19).

The network consists of 166 edges and 147 vertices. The searched hashtag #greferendum is at the centre of the semantic network and the strongest connected node. This is clearer when the visualisation is not developed in groups and boxes; however, this approach highlights the differences between groups and discourse. The different languages noticed in the network pointed out the international interest regarding the referendum, highlighting the participation of countries which, directly or not, are involved in the political turmoil and the austerity debate, as well as the north-south debate/discussion (Freire, Lisi, Andreadis, & Leite-Viegas, 2014). Capital controls (G2, G3) and the banks (G3, G10) appeared on the graph, mainly due to users who insert up-to-date information on the issue as well as due to criticisms and comments regarding the issue. At the same time, the historical importance of the period is highlighted mainly through a humorous approach (G2, G7). While there are many groups, which developed politically oriented discussions and debates, Group 3 includes significant keywords, which denote the political debate of the time and the yes/no campaign (e.g. yesman, coup and drachma). G11 keywords are related to the discussion regarding austerity and democracy as well as the people who should rise, close to the SYRIZA rhetoric (Protothema.gr, 2015). This was close to the pre-election SYRIZA campaign rhetoric, as well as the rhetoric adopted by different left European parties, which in most cases highlighted the austerity effect on democracy and democratic values.

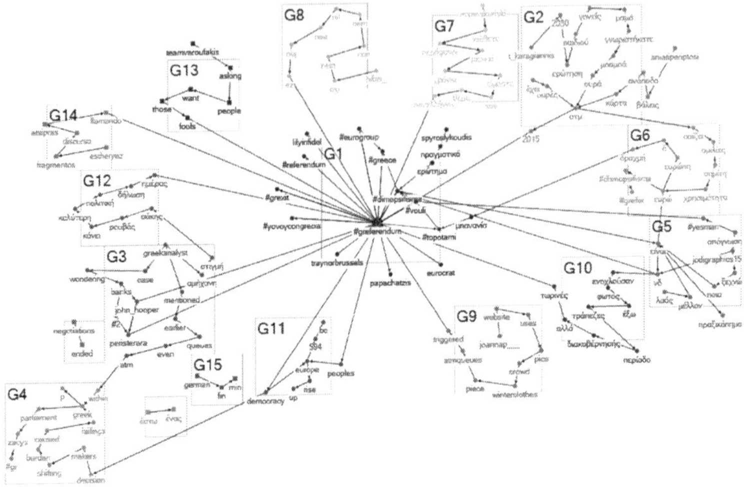

Figure 7.19. Greferendum – Referendum Announcement Semantic Network (27 June 2015).

An overall evaluation of the semantic network indicates that the discourse developing after the announcement of the referendum was characterised by a 'carnivalisque' and satirical sentiment (Kaika & Karaliotis, 2014, p. 10), in a way similar to the observed development of the case of the Greek Indignados. As often observed on Twitter, the political debates and the ideological division of the time are visible (Rieder, 2012), still the limited political discussion and the 'carnivalisque' character of the discourse indicate the danger of not having a revolutionary moment reinforcing democratic politics, but instead developing an urban fest similar to the example of the Greek Indignados (Rieder, 2012) (Figure 7.20).

The second date of the referendum developed in consequence and with many similarities to the previously examined semantic network. This network comprised 163 edges and 130 vertices. As expected, the searched hashtag #greferendum, has a central position in the graph (G2), although, on this network, the hashtag #dimopsifisma (referendum), also has a highly linked position in the graph too (G1). The larger group, G2 consists of words both in Greek and in English, while the content of the meanings developed in the group is related both to the development of the incident giving information and updates, as well as to the expression of solidarity. At the same time, hashtags in different languages (e.g. aveclesgrecs, yovoycongrecia and istandwithgreece) are used as a statement supporting Greece, indicating the way that the European solidarity campaign developed.

Throughout the graph, the division and the debate raised by the #yes and #no campaign are expressed much more strongly than in the previously examined semantic network (G5, G1, G3, G8 and G9). The #no campaign expressed strong critiques of the #yes campaign, indicating, once again, that the

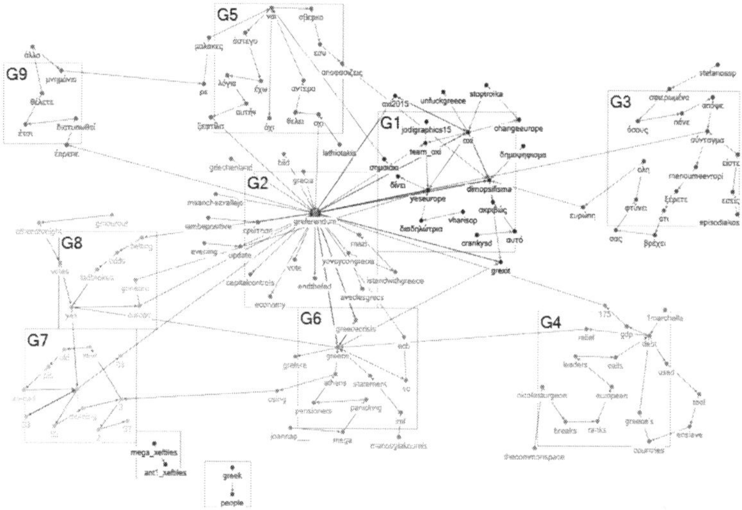

Figure 7.20. Greferendum – Bailout Expiration Semantic Network (30 June 2015).

referendum vote was an issue related to dignity (G5, G3). This is understood at a national level as regards the Greek government negotiations with the troika, as well as focusing on the impoverishment and the crisis era. At the same time, there is a strong linkage between the #no campaign and the discussion regarding the troika, European politics and the effect on Greece (e.g. G1, changeeurope, troika and unfuckgreece), which developed both in Greek and in English. Once again at this point, the nature of the crisis as problematic can be examined, focusing on austerity and the crisis as having both Greek, European or other dimensions (G1 and G4). The debt is discussed as a medium of controlling and enslaving countries (G4), while the necessity for changing Europe is also highlighted (G1), developing a parallelism to the contemporary political rhetoric and debates (e.g. Euroscepticism, change Europe and European left and SYRIZA).

Again, the #yes campaign did not manage to express specific ideas, critiques or considerations of the online discourse. Instead, its position in the graphs indicates that keywords related to the campaign are either points of critique or part of news and updates regarding the progress of the event (G1, G5 and G8). Another interesting point indicated by the graph is the strong linkage between the referendum and the so-called Grexit. One of the two dyads, mega_xeftiles/ant1_xeftiles, highlight the dispute in the mainstream media, pointing out the structural problems of the sector (e.g. ownership and corruption). At the same time, the role of the mainstream media as an institution and its contribution to democracy as well as its relationship to society, in terms of representation is arguably present throughout the crisis and the referendum era (Figure 7.21).

The evolution of the hashtag of the #greferendum on the examined dates shows that there are many more groups and themes of discussions as the events evolved. The graph of the semantic network, as shaped by data produced on the

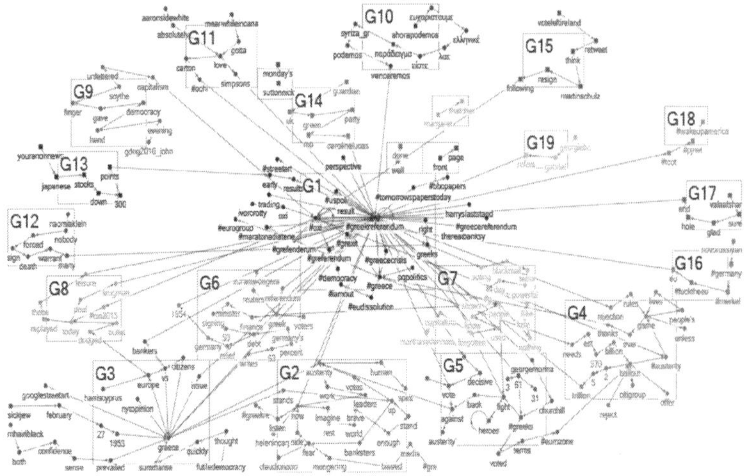

Figure 7.21. Greferendum – Referendum Semantic Network (5 July 2015).

day of the referendum, suggests a more plural and rich discourse, in comparison to the two previous semantic networks, developing a quite noisy graph with high density. The network consists of 279 edges and 232 vertices. Also, there is a change regarding the languages used in the discussion, where English and Spanish are the dominant languages in contrast to Greek, highlighting the international interest on the referendum at the actual day that it took place.

On this semantic network, the searched hashtag #greferendum is in the same group and strongly linked to the keywords Oxi, Grexit, Greek crisis and the No campaign (G1). At the same time, some of the topics raised are relevant to debates on capitalism and fear (G7and G9), on the significance of the vote (G3 and G16). Throughout the Greek crisis and especially during the referendum period, the discourse of fear was a dominant strategy, both for media and politics, justifying the implementation of austerity politics, now this is focusing beyond the national context.

In this network, terms such as 'EU dissolution' appeared for the first time in the graph (G1), while debates over Grexit or the implementation of anti-austerity politics are the main political debates since the beginning of the crisis, that directed the restructuring of the Greek political scene after the collapse of the two party system. This was a major point according to which the politics of the crisis developed in a national context, while and some of the parties that became popular in the crisis and after 2012 (e.g. SYRIZA, Golden Dawn, An. El.and Potami) developed according to their position within the pro-/anti-austerity debate and Euroscepticism. During the referendum, that was extended on concerns regarding the membership of Greece in EU, and in an extend, broader questions and debates on the future of the European Union and contemporary politics (G3 and G6).

Democracy, included both in G7 and G9, as well as, keywords/nodes, such as blackmailed, Europe vs citizens, stand up and rejection (G1, G9, G2, G7 and G4) are only some of the examples that highlight the tension regarding the referendum, the outcome and the impact that this will have in national and European context. Next, G16 includes nodes, such as oxi, oxi2015, eu, merkel and Germany, highlighting the dispute over the European project and austerity policies. Here, it is indicative that the #thisisacoup hashtag was trending during the days after the referendum (17 July–18 July 2015), raising strong debates and discussion, both within academia and in the press, regarding democratic values, the EU and austerity politics. Similar considerations are also expressed in G1, where the word oxi is in a central position in the sub-graph.

Discussion and Concluding Remarks

The examination of Twitter during the referendum era indicates some interesting points of consideration focusing on the usage of this platform both in relation to the two antagonistic campaigns as well as in relation to the online and offline evolution of the events. The selection of the examined hashtags develops an insight into the two antagonistic campaigns and the political and ideological conflict between them. Concentrating on the theoretical framework of cyberconflict, the conflict, or opposition, between the #yes and #no campaign is understood as a sociopolitical conflict, borrowing, to some extent, elements and characteristics that are also met in ethnoreligious cyberconflict (e.g. references on Greekness, Greeks vs others, EU, etc. and discourse of inclusion and exclusion)

After the social network and semantic analysis of the examined hashtags what is observed is that each of the two campaigns developed different attributes and characteristics, regarding the mobilising structure and the usage of Twitter, the framing processes, as well as the political opportunity structure (Karatzogianni, 2006, p. 88). Starting with the #syntagma and #17june hashtags and the mobilisations taking place before the announcement of the referendum, the issue of austerity and the danger of so-called Grexit are the main debates, which dominated the online discourse. In the #syntagma network, which is a prelude to what was later discussed as a #yes campaign, was developed mainly by mainstream and international media, which transmitted information and reports on the protest. In contrast, the #17junegr network, which was a prelude to the no campaign, developed via left-wing-oriented media as well as international and independent media. In terms of content and discourse, the #syntagma included key hashtags related to the #menoumeevropi rhetoric and to the austerity/anti-austerity debate. The #17junegr content and discourse indicated the SYRIZA – Podemos coalition, making references to the SYRIZA – Podemos – Venceremos slogan.

In both the examined hashtags, independent or alternative actors do not manage to dominate the networks and to challenge offline hierarchical structures, creating an alternative online public sphere. Instead, the two examined hashtags indicated that the frameworks relating to the crisis and the pro-referendum political turmoil had a different impact on the users' engagement and participation in the online discourse. The anti-austerity discourse attracted many more users than the pro-austerity discourse, developing a multi-themed discussion on the issue of austerity. At the same time, the high participation of users in the anti-austerity discourse pointed out the way the examined platform provided an alternative space for participation in the public debate, at the same time as mainstream media were concentrating on the pro-austerity debate.

The examination of the #antiausterity and #austerity hashtags indicated the way that the austerity debate manifested itself in different countries, pointing out that instead of concentrating at the national level, austerity should be understood in an EU context. The #antiausterity network was dominated by hashtags and keywords related to the UK labour party leadership elections and Corbyn, which took place during the same period as the Greek referendum. The semantic network of this hashtag includes considerations on Grexit, the IMF and the EU, as well as SYRIZA. At the same time, keywords on this network, such as communists, occupy and Greece, make historical references to the contemporary Greek history as regards the notion of the so-called communist peril, especially as this was understood during the civil war and, later, during the Cold War.

The examination of the #nai and #oxi hashtags highlighted the way in which the conflict between the two-antagonist campaign developed. While the mainframes and debates of the two-antagonist campaigns were already observed in the online discourse before the announcement of the referendum, the two-antagonist campaign, as shaped after the announcement of the referendum, reinforced the ideological and political conflict. It is quite interesting that the two-antagonist campaign didn't develop new frames or debates, but instead, these arose from the already existing ones, which were originally created through different procedures and during the crisis evolution (e.g. collective and direct actions, social movements, and so on).

The #nai network was dominated by Greek media and newspapers in contrast to the #oxi network, which included mainly domains of British and international newspapers. The #nai network pointed out the national and European character of the crisis, as well as the strong linkage between a potential Grexit and the greferendum. In contrast, the #oxi network concentrated more on propagating the goals and the rationale of the campaign. On the last examined network, the #nai network concentrated on the referendum results, while the #oxi network developed around the organisation of the mobilisation in Syntagma Square.

Following the already suggested characteristics of the two-antagonist campaigns, #menoumeevropi hashtag analysis indicated the strong contribution of social media platforms, of mainstream Greek media, as well as of some independent media and political actors. In the #oxi hashtag, international and mainstream media, as well as civic organisation groups supported the formation of the network. The discourse of the #menoumeevropi concentrated on the 'yes' campaign framework, while the evolution of the examined dates was not followed by an evolution of discourse, repeating the already existing debates on austerity. The semantic network of the #oxi hashtag indicated the international attention that the campaign gained, including expression of solidarity from different countries. In contrast, the #menoumeevropi discourse was limited to the national context, with users commenting mainly in Greek.

The #menoumeevropi discourse developed including sarcastic comments and criticisms of neoliberal policies, on poverty and on the crisis in both the European and Greek context. On the other hand, the #oxi campaign included more themes, raising a multilayered discussion and debate regarding austerity. A major limitation of the #menoumeevropi campaign is that it didn't manage to develop a narration before the referendum, but instead, it concentrated mainly on commenting on and criticising the antagonist campaign. Throughout the examination of the #oxi hashtag, the crisis effect on the division between the south and north in the EU is apparent, focusing on political coalitions, on austerity politics in the countries of the south as well as on the understanding of left-wing and neoliberal politics. Finally, concentrating on the Greek referendum (Greferendum), Grexit and the pro-/anti-austerity debate, which dominated the online discourse, while mainstream and social media platforms, as well as Greek actors, dominated the networks.

Chapter 8

Discussion and Concluding Remarks

This study explored the impact of digital media on contentious or radical politics in Greece during the period 2008–2015. This included the examination of four different online media platforms, concentrating on a seven-year period or in three different periods of political turmoil and mobilisations (2008; 2011–2012; 2015–2016). Here, I provide an overview of the most important findings of the three examined periods and the four examined online media platforms (Chapters 5–7). This chapter begins with a review of the main findings of the research and the digital media evolution and political transformation of the examined period. The next two sections provide an insight into how digital media was used in the crisis context, and on how *cyberconflict and digital activism evolve in* Greece (e.g. online networks, online coalitions to the offline world and vice versa). At the end, the project is completed with a discussion of the futures, the limitations and the contribution of the research.

Findings: Three Periods and Four Online Media Platforms

The impact of digital media in contentious politics in Greece between 2008 and 2015, as well as the influence of the political-economic sphere on the formation of the digital mediascape can be understood focusing on several points, some of which discussed below. At the same time, the findings of the research suggest an insight into the way that the digital media was used in the crisis context, as understood by the study of networks and discourses. In a final stage, the findings offer an understanding of how cyberconflict and digital activism evolve in Greece, focusing on the linkages of online networks, online coalitions to the offline world and vice versa.

Starting with the December Riots (Chapter 5), this was among the first examples that illustrated the importance of digital media in the emergence of collective actions and contentious politics in Greece. The research began with the examination of Indymedia and YouTube as the two most important platforms that associated with the outbreak of the so-called December Riots, in 2008. Looking at YouTube and Indymedia, the thematic analysis of the online data indicated that the December Riots denoted a new era on the use of new media and technology in collective action in Greece. Indymedia and YouTube were already used quite a lot of time before the December Riots in Greece; however, the way and the scale in which they used in the examined case, suggested that the two examined platforms provided a new space for political communication and debate, while at the same time, offered new tools and possibilities on the organisation of protests internally and externally. Starting with the internal communication and Indymedia, this platform was used to organise and coordinate actions, in a quicker and direct way than previous technologies and methods did in the past. Activists and politicised people who had access online started organising actions almost in a real-time with the actual, offline, development of the event. At the same time, in terms of communication in an external level, participants in the mobilisations had the opportunity to provide a self-representation of the protest, having a strong impact on the traditional media processes (i.e. representation of the event) and the state's reaction to the riots.

While digital media indicated a potential on communication and organisation processes (e.g. challenge mainstream media and dominant discourse), during the examined period, digital media in Greece were still at an early stage, and the issue of digital divide was still crucial. Digital media supported real-time communication among activists and participants of the protests, helping the coordination and organisation of solidarity actions across Greece and throughout Europe. At the same time, online media platforms used to spread the information and coordinate actions both online and offline, overcoming geographical or other limitations. The protests and the mobilisations were real-time reported online, while at a later stage, this was among the first times in which mainstream media adapted the online media representation and narratives (i.e. shooting video scene). However, as an overall, digital media did not dominate over mainstream media narratives, supporting the development of a new public sphere, but instead illustrated how digital media develop fragmented (online) sub-public spheres.

This period suggests that while the examined events developed on a pre-crisis era and discourse, still digital media used to express concerns and debates, which, a year later, shaped the crisis discourse and context both online and offline. In terms of cyberconflict, both sociopolitical and ethnic related debates were observed in the examined platforms. The sociopolitical cyberconflict concentrated on issues related to politics and social/cultural debates (i.e. inequality, youth and the state, capitalism and globalisation and others), while the ethnoreligious cyberconflict raised as an extension of sociopolitical conflict and is more related with far-right discourse. Issues and debates on ethnic/religious matters (i.e. migration and so on) were discussed in extension to sociopolitical debates (i.e. poverty, inequality, wages and so on) and further developed based on the division between left and right-wing politics. While the actual events of December Riots were characterised by sociopolitical debates, the way that these reflected and further developed online suggest that up to a very limited extent, the sociopolitical debates transformed to ethnoreligious debates and conflict. In the December Riots, the two examined platforms used to provide a space for debate and conflict on issues, which preexisted in the examined case, and were further developed online. Therefore, the remediation of issues/debates on migration, corruption and inequality, and state violence, was influenced by the December Riots context and the examined media platforms.

In terms of participation, this era was characterised by the digital divide debate and during the December Riots, online media users were mainly young, well-educated and living in urban centres. Online media provided a space for communication and participation in the public debate and sphere, developing further the gap among different audience's sub-groups and the fragmentation of public sphere. At the same time, because of the features of each platform, each of the examined online media platforms attracted online users with different characteristics. Indymedia, which already before December Riots was associated with the anti-globalisation movement and the Seattle protests, was used by users with specific political orientation in contrast to YouTube, which targeted the general public. Therefore, Indymedia was used for in-depth discussion and arguments over the development of the Riots in contrast to YouTube, which was used for more general discussion and various types of conflict, which were expressed in a more direct and conflictual way. In Indymedia, users interacted based on a common interest and similar ideological orientation, debating on more political and movement-oriented discussion. On the other hand, YouTube provides a space for conflict among users with various interests and ideologies. Therefore, while Indymedia provided more of a formation of a polarised online community, YouTube provided the space for general debate. In YouTube, the December Riots debates soon turned into conflict about other issues and events, indicating an association between sociopolitical and ethnoreligious cyberconflict, which shaped on the axis of the contrast between left and right-wing politics.

So, to sum up, this period denoted a new era on the use of digital media in collective actions and social movements in Greece, with protestors utilizing and taking advantage of new technologies. Internally they use that for organisation and real-time reports on the event, while externally they use digital media to develop their own representation, which in many cases was in contrast to mainstream media representations. While this indicated some significant change raised by the use of digital media, still digital media representations and narrations did not dominate over the mainstream media narratives. Therefore, digital media here did not contribute to the creation of a new public sphere, but instead to the development of a fragmented one. December Riots can be decoded through the motion of sociopolitical cyberconflict, with most of the debates having social and political context. However, already since 2008, discourses on inclusion/exclusion, historical references and debates on national identities and Greekness, could suggest some similarities to the ethnoreligious cyberconflict. At the same time, some of the issues, which later dominated the crisis in public discourse, were already debated online since the examined period (e.g. migration, corruption and inequality). While this period brought back traditional debates (e.g. state violence, corruption, left and right), still did not allow new debates or solutions to emerge, but recycled the already existed discussion. It is important to keep in mind that in this period the digital divide is decisive. Finally, Indymedia supported the in-depth discussion over the organisation of the protest, with users having common ideological background, while YouTube provided space for a more general discussion on various types of conflict, with users having various ideological backgrounds. These points suggest a contribution to the field, as these help us to understand in more depth and through a different approach the use of digital media during the examined period.

The second examined period concentrated on Facebook and the development of the anti-austerity movement in Greece (Chapter 6). Starting with the case of Aganaktismenoi and, then, the case of SYRIZA, what is discussed here is the association among EU and National context politics, as well as the association among mainstream and non-institutionalised politics. What is observed in this case is that there is both an ideological kinship between movements in national and EU context, as well as a clearly observed online kinship developed through networks. The different ways in which the anti-austerity movement emerged and manifested online and offline, in various EU countries, pointed out the multi-dimensional character of the examined period. The Aganaktismenoi mobilisations developed in hybrid mode (online and offline) as a form of resistance against austerity politics, which during the examined period was not discussed in a transnational context, but instead, focused on the 'P.I.G.S.' narration. According to Karatzogianni and Schandorf (2015), the order of dissent started from a national anti-corruption narrative, moved on to the regional anti-EU mode and ended up to jumpscale to an international anti-globalisation order of dissent. In Greece, this narrative constructed focusing on the Greek laziness and the division between the European north and south. At the same time, December Riots was one of the first cases in Greece, which illustrated how the mainstream media and the dominant discourse was possible to be challenged by the use of digital media. However, in the Aganaktismenoi case, the difference between the mainstream and digital media discourse is clearer and more intense, pointing out the digital media impact on public sphere, which now is in a more significant way fragmented.

The first examined network offered an understanding of how the Aganaktismenoi network developed, through online coalitions and sub-networks. This was decoded concentrating on cyberconflict and analysed in reference to the offline world and the debates indicated by the December Riots event. The historical continuity of the events and the debates was clear, while this platform indicated completely different attributes in comparison to the previously examined platforms. It should be noted that a full comparison across platforms could not be conducted, because of the different attributes and usages of each platform, the difference on the collected and analysed data, focusing both on networks and discourse. Thus, a full comparison of the examined platforms could only be conducted after a content-oriented analysis of Facebook pages, and other platforms.

The examination of networks developed an insight into how these platforms used from a more top-down and hierarchical development of the movement. What was analysed in this period was how Facebook used by social movements and mainstream, or semi-mainstream politics. Then, this was discussed in reference to the political turmoil resulting to the rise of SYRIZA, the far-right and populist politics. The examined networks and sub-networks pointed out the way that ideology and identity developed and differentiated, across networks and in the wider spectrum of politics, constructing the so-called 'politics of extreme'.

After the bankruptcy of the politics of the centre and the neoliberal mainstream political scheme, new actors dominated both the online and the offline networks/scene. Thus, what is observed online is that while there is some kinship between the Aganaktismenoi network and the December Riots, the debates and conflict were further developed and enriched through different political and ideological directions in juxtaposition to the development of the crisis. Then, focusing on the rise of SYRIZA and the analysis of the Facebook network, it is observed that this network developed based on the Aganaktismenoi network. Thus, there is a strong kinship between the two networks, in terms of structure and involved actors, as well as in terms of online coalition, both as regards the left and right-wing politics. The SYRIZA network developed based on the Aganaktismenoi network, riding the mobilisation wave, offering a platform and promising representation of all the included actors.

While in the case of Aganaktismenoi the network developed in extend to the December Riots debates (e.g. corruption, inequality and ideology), the SYRIZA network borrowed element of the Aganaktismenoi, and was strongly associated to the left-wing and to right/populist mainstream and institutionalised politics, as these emerged in the crisis context. The Aganaktismenoi network indicated strong linkages to the transnational social movements, in contrast to the SYRIZA network, which was linked to the transnational mainstream political scene and actors. The Aganaktismenoi network suggested an insight into how populist ideas adopted by both left and right-wing politics, filtering the relation between groups and sub-groups. At the same time, the SYRIZA network offered an insight into the EU crisis and its evolution. SYRIZA was strongly linked to the EU left-wing politics and academic circles, with both pointing out the necessity for a change in Europe (Podemos, Die Linke, etc.).

Focusing on the national context, SYRIZA's pre-election campaign of 2012 and 2015 developed in opposition to New Democracy rhetoric, which indicated the division between Us and the Them, as regards the pro-/anti-austerity debate. Therefore, SYRIZA's linkage to social movements and the European left, suggest the formation of a unitary political front with dynamic from 'below'. The evolution of social networks, from the Aganaktismenoi case to the case of SYRIZA highlights the evolution of the crisis. The contrast between the discourse and the themes discussed from the December Riots to the Greferendum period indicated the semantic and discursive transformation of the debt crisis of 2008 to the multi-layered crisis after 2015. At the same time, both the Aganaktismenoi and the SYRIZA network indicated strong linkages to the pre-crisis and international social movements, their association to contemporary collective actions and movements, such as environmental mobilisations (Skouries), solidarity initiatives (social clinics) and linkages to the antifascist movement. At the same time, the network of Aganaktismenoi suggested strong linkages between SYRIZA and An.El. parties online, which formed a coalition government in 2015.

In contrast to Indymedia and YouTube platforms, which suggested an insight into how digital media was used by politicised people and activists, Facebook showcased how digital media used in a more collective-based orientation, focusing not on the individual, but on the development of collective and social movements. Then, the examination of Twitter demonstrated how digital media was used both by individuals, collectives and social movements as well as mainstream actors. What was examined in this platform is both discourse and networks. Focusing on the Greferendum period, what was tested was how and up to which level, digital media challenged or shaped public sphere, hierarchical relations and online coalitions. At the same time, this platform offered an insight into the political and ideological polarisation as well as on the domination of actors, (i.e. political actors, media actors, or mainstream and non-institutionalised actors).

To sum up, the Aganaktismenoi and the SYRIZA network indicated an ideological kinship between movements in national and EU context, while both were associated with movements emerged before and during the so-called crisis. The Aganaktismenoi movement could be understood as being developed in a hybrid mode, both online and offline, as a form of resistance against austerity politics, similar to the anti-austerity and ant capitalist movements of those days (e.g. Occupy Movement and Indignados). Focusing on the order of dissent, what started here as a national anti-corruption narrative, soon moved on to the regional anti-EU mode and ended up to jumpscale to an international anti-globalisation order of dissent. Facebook supported the top-down and hierarchical development of the movement (as regards the framing process), which though is still rhizomatic (in terms of spatial online/offline organisation). The Aganaktismenoi network developed extended to the December Riots debates, while the SYRIZA network borrowed elements of the Aganaktismenoi, highlighting the continuity of movements and discourse. The SYRIZA network was clearly associated with the left-wing and with right/populist mainstream and institutionalised politics. The evolution of these two networks would describe the evolution of crisis, pointing out the discursive transformation of the debt crisis of 2008 to the multi-layered crisis after 2015. Again, these points should be understood as contributing to the field by helping us to understand the use of digital media during the examined period. This period indicated how the transition to the digital media completed. Here we understand the way that digital media became mainstream in juxtaposition to the evolution of the crisis.

The third examined period analysed focusing on the usage of Twitter. The examination of Twitter concentrated on the two antagonistic campaigns of the so-called Greferendum and developed through the analysis of keywords/hashtags and rending hashtags, illustrating the ideological and political conflict of the two antagonistic campaigns (#Menoumeevropi and #Oxi; 7.2.). Focusing both on social and semantic networks, what is suggested is that the conflict between the two campaigns was already formed online before the announcement of the referendum, preluding the greferendum debate and constructing the politics of fear (e.g. grexit and austerity vs anti-austerity). At the same time, already before the announcement of the referendum, the coalition between SYRIZA and Podemos, and the development of a left-wing coalition of the EU south and the countries affected by the crisis is observed through both the semantic and social networks.

In terms of discourse and public sphere, what is observed in the examined hashtags is that, in most of the cases, independent or alternative actors (e.g. domains, actors and URLs) did not manage to dominate the networks, challenging offline hierarchical structures and creating an alternative online public sphere. At the same time, looking on the contrast between social versus mainstream media and discourse, Twitter was dominated by the anti-austerity discourse, in contrast to mainstream media, which directly supported the pro-austerity campaign. Therefore, public participation and representation on Twitter was not only direct, but also more accurate and effective, in contrast to mainstream media. The pro-austerity discourse, which supported by mainstream media, developed in contrast to the online anti-austerity discourse. Thus, Twitter offered an alternative space for public engagement, developing a multi-themed discussion on the issue of austerity. The pro-/anti-austerity discourse online was shaped in an EU context rather than the national context, indicating the blurred boundaries on the national- EU crisis public sphere and the crisis context. In terms of historical references, the left and right-wing politics were discussed in reference to the 'communist peril' and the Civil War and Cold War narration.

The announcement of the referendum didn't develop debates, but instead, supported the further development of the already existing ones, which were originally created by different procedures (collective actions, social movements, etc.) and throughout the crisis evolution. The online networks indicated that the dominant media actors online on the pro-austerity campaign were mainly Greek media actors, while in contrast, the dominant media actors online in the anti-austerity campaign were mainly British and international media actors. The pro-austerity campaign developed focusing on the danger of Grexit, while the anti-austerity campaign concentrated on ideological and political debates, propagating the goals and the rationale of the campaign. A significant characteristic of the pro-austerity campaign is that it didn't manage to develop a narration before the referendum, but instead, alongside to the #grexit argument, it concentrated mainly on criticising the anti-austerity campaign. Throughout the greferendum period, the division between the south and north in the EU is apparent.

To sum up, the examination of Twitter indicated that the online conflict between the two antagonistic campaigns of the referendum was actually developed online before the announcement of the referendum, preluding the greferendum debate. Even before the referendum networks and discourse indicated a strong linkage between SYRIZA and Podemos, something which during the referendum was even stronger. In terms of discourse, Twitter had a contrasted narration in comparison to mainstream media and provided an alternative space for public engagement, but this didn't manage to dominate the media public discourse. At the same time, the pro-/anti-austerity discourse shaped in an EU rather than national context, pointing out the multidimensional linkages between the national–EU crisis, public sphere and the crisis context. The referendum debate was characterised by the historical references, (e.g. 'communist peril', Civil War and Cold War narration), in a similar way as observed in the previous examined platforms and periods. Therefore, the announcement of the referendum and the debates raised afterwards didn't suggest anything new but instead supported the further development of the already existing debates, as observed throughout the crisis evolution. Finally, while the pro-austerity campaign was mainly supported/discussed by Greek media actors, while in contrast the anti-austerity campaign was dominated by mainly British and international media actors. The pro-austerity campaign didn't develop a narration but concentrated only on criticising the anti-austerity campaign.

Overall, based on the significant characteristics of each online platform, each of these used was for different purposes supporting the sociopolitical transformation and turmoil of the period during 2008–2015. At the same time, the study of these platforms indicated question regards the evolution of social media platforms, the ephemeral nature of those, as well as the ephemerality of data.

Digital Media Evolutions and Political Transformations

The development of the Greek digital media occurred in juxtaposition to the evolution of the crisis. However, the development and the adaptation of digital media use in the Greek context followed the EU pattern. While at the beginning digital media were used by users, which for different reasons were familiar with technology, later digital media not only became mainstream, but were converted to a valuable tool for institutionalised communication (e.g. mainstream media, political actors and parties, and so on).

The research indicated that in the 2008 and the December Riots, Indymedia and YouTube attracted different types of users for different communication purposes and processes. In 2008, Indymedia attached users having a shared interest and ideology, and used the platform as a trustworthy source of information, or as a tool to organise and coordinate actions. On the other hand, YouTube attached the so-called general public, users who had access online and wanted to interact, exchange ideas and communicate. At that point of time, the Internet was not yet dominated by mainstream media and actors, but instead the online environment was yet to be explored and shaped. The development of the digital communication in Greece emerged in a point of transition, or in an end of an era, as this shaped in Greece after the Greek Olympic games and the promised prosperity, in EU after the French riots, and later in global scale with the 2007 US election campaign and then, the global recession. In a less mainstream environment, the Internet had already formed the Internet culture, focusing on the debate on commons, the right to information as well as the potentiality of digital media in journalism and politics (e.g. Iraq War).

In 2011–2012, the Greek online environment had significant differences in comparison to 2008. Again, the digital inequality and division is an important debate; however, the evolution of the digital communication in terms of infrastructure and cost had already made the Internet more attractive and accessible to the public. At the same time, the outbreak of the global recession and the emergence of social and resistance movements suggested the way that digital media could be used in the crisis context (OWS, Indignados, Arab Spring and so on). Social movements and collective actions, which at that point of time were much organised by activist and young people, took advantage of the digital media features, supporting the organisation of collective actions and protests. While this is a significant moment about the evolution of the crisis, this is also a significant moment for both the mainstream and traditional media too. The crisis deeply impacts the mainstream media through a variety of ways, including considerations on journalism and ethics, freedom of speech as well as regarding corruption. At that point of time, while the traditional sociopolitical structures in Greece collapsed, mainstream media acted in favour of the already existed system and politics, without managing to represent the people who were already reacting and organising alternative and new structures and initiatives, to resist and overcome the crisis limitations. At that point, the further development of digital media supported these initiatives and brought together people who shared the similar understanding on the new sociopolitical environment as this was shaped by the crisis. Digital media supported the development not only through online networks, but also most importantly offline networks, indicating the importance of an alternative structure in these new conditions. This had a strong impact on the fragmentation of the public sphere and, to a greater extent, on the emergence of alternative – shadow structures, which replaced the role and the limitations of the institutionalised actors (i.e. media, political parties and welfare state).

The development of social movements and collective actions, including initiatives and solidarity networks, or the so-called third sector, altogether with the evolution of digital media, created alternative structures, overlapping the inefficient response of the state and the institutionalised actors. In a way, digital media and the social movements of that era developed a shadow state, which for a while, not only overlapped the limitations of the state, but also indicated new political actors, challenged the public sphere offering the space for the development of anti-austerity narratives, and at the same time, provided actual solutions to problems raised by the collapse of the welfare state (e.g. social kitchens and social clinics). This is the point where the Aganaktismenoi network offered the base for the development of the SYRIZA network, which made these structures more mainstream and which later on made the party institutionalised. Therefore, indeed, the shadow state or the shadow structures filled the limitations of the crisis context and the state's incapability to efficiently respond to the new sociopolitical conditions. However, these alternative or shadow structures soon adapted the vulnerabilities of the mainstream and institutionalised structures (e.g. limitations on ideology and interrelated interests). SYRIZA is among the most indicative examples that illustrates the route that grassroots actions followed, before being transformed and incorporated into the mainstream and institutionalised structures.

Until 2015, digital media had been developed and the debates on the usage of digital media in crisis contexts, as raised by different cases (OWS, Indignados, etc.), had been started being relevant to the case of Greece. Following the EU trend, in the case of Greece, digital media supported the political polarisation, providing the opportunity for users to develop their opinion close to the echo chambers effect (Chater, 2016). This polarisation should be understood both in terms of conflict, as well as in terms of turmoil, with a potentiality to indicate new sociopolitical structures. In the case of the referendum, polarisation helped in the formation of less fluid identities online and offline, which further developed on the division between the political Us and Them. The platform based on which these identities developed were not politically or ideologically oriented, but instead it was shaped according to the conflict context. This is not related only to the rise of far-right and non-parliamentary left, but instead, it refers to any form of opposition, leading to ideological and political conflict. In this context, conflict did not manage to suggest alternatives or produce new debates and procedures, but instead, the conflict confined its cycle of action and impact over issues of domination (i.e. online and offline networks, networks with different ideologies and interests).

In the crisis context, and especially focusing on the three examined platforms, the Internet used a magnifying glass, pointing out conflict, opposition and supporting polarisation. While there were many opportunities and a strong potentiality on the Internet's impact on social movements, still the limitations of collective actions and social movements, which can be found on their origins and the historical background, did not manage to conclude to social or political change. Internet challenged mainstream media and dominant discourse, but still followed mainstream procedures on the production of narratives, on the development of semi and crypto-hierarchies, and at a later stage, on their association to institutionalised actors and structures. This resulted in two conflicted fronts, which both acted in terms of mainstream and institutionalised procedures and results. None of these two conflicted fronts supported the creation of new structures, but instead, conflicted the traditional limitations (i.e. hierarchies) and also, over the question of domination. Therefore, while the crisis supported the collapse of the already existed sociopolitical system and structures, the Internet supported the development of new ones, which though were not genuine in terms of ideology, goals or suggested solutions to current limitations, but, in contrast, they had identical characteristics and limitations with the collapsed ones.

Future, Limitations and Contribution

This project developed focusing both on the evolution of the crisis and on the digital media communications in Greece. While the research began in 2013, having slightly different in aims and purposes, finally it shaped following the development of both political transformation and digital media uses. That offered a great set of data and many research opportunities and this is a major element of both the strengths and the limitations of this study.

Starting with the digital media evolution, the research begun in September 2013, when, YouTube and Facebook were two of the most contemporary and popular social media platforms in Greece. At that point of time, the idea was to develop this study by concentrating on Blogs, as a sample of alternative online mediums, and then to focus on contemporary and popular social media platforms, as a sample of mainstream online media platforms. The evolution of the digital media communications though, indicated that apart from the contrast between alternative and mainstream online media, other points on the development of the digital media in Greece would also be interesting to be examined, looking into the power of networks and discourse. Thus, at the next stage, the research concentrated on the examination of various online media platforms, including Indymedia, YouTube, Facebook, and Twitter. The examination of online material from different online media platforms required a real-time collection of data parallel to the development of events. That was a complicated process, which required specific skills on the usage of software and apps, as well as, special skills as regards the research techniques, which were finally applied. Therefore, the research design was cultivated and reorganised throughout the research, and according to the events, evolution and data collection, reflecting the development of my research skills, and the limitations on researching online material. The unconventional development of the research design was indeed a very challenging process, which though helped to in-depth and in-practice understand the demands of researching the fast-changing online media environment.

Apart from the difficulties raised by the research of the online media environment, another set of limitations and difficulties raised by the evolution of the crisis, both in national, EU and global context. My keen interest was on researching the online media usages, focusing on what was then discussed and understood as Greek crisis. However, the different manifestation and evolution of the crisis throughout the years indicated additional considerations as regards the multiple crisis manifestations. Thereby, I tried to limit the research concentration on a specific time-frame (2008–2015), offering a snapshot of the digital media usage in key moments and events (e.g. December Riots, Aganaktismenoi and Greferendum). This project reflected the evolution of the sociopolitical debates and the political transformations emerged in the Greek crisis context, which in a few words, could be described as follows: the anti-/pro-austerity debate and the euro-vs-drachma/or grexit discussion, which soon transformed to the anti-/pro-governmental debate, and later expressed through the anti-/pro-European discourse. In a later stage, this transformation/evolution included the development of the far-right (GD trial), the refugees' crisis and other post-referendum debates. This project concentrated on the December Riots (2008), the Aganaktismenoi case and the rise of SYRIZA (2011–2012), as well as the Greferendum era (2015), pointing out the necessity for a follow-up research.

The December Riots signalled a new era for the autonomous initiatives and organisations, which, founded during that period and were further developed during the crisis evolution. Such initiatives included the creation of online and alternative media projects, the occupation of social public spaces and squats, as well as neighbourhood assemblies. These formed a conducive pre-existing environment of (offline and online) networked dissent, which at the crisis period supported the formation of alternative and solidarity structures and initiatives. For a moment, these initiatives and solidarity networks, formed a shadow state, providing a platform, based on which crisis' movements, initiatives and mobilisations emerged. A very critical and a turning point on the development of these initiatives was the Aganaktismenoi mobilisations supporting the formation of the so-called 'creative resistance' (2011–2012). During that period, more than 550 groups and collectivities (Petropoulou, 2013, pp. 73–76) were active in different sectors (e.g. education, welfare, health, housing squats and neighbourhood assemblies). Therefore, further research on the examined period could provide an in-depth examination and discussion on the usage of digital media by these initiatives (e.g. housing squats, social kitchens and clinics). Another important issue that was not in-depth examined in this project, but, still, was quite significant in the examined period is the development of the far-right, which in the future should be examined focusing both on the usage of online media platforms by far-right groups as well as, focusing on the usage of digital media and the formation of far-right discourse. These are some of the main issues that should be examined in follow-up researches.

Another limitation of this project raised by the examination of Twitter and the rich corpus of the collected data. The period 2015–2016, offered some very interesting political development of the crisis (e.g. elections 2015, GD trial, Skouries, #Wikileaks – #Ypoklopes – #Tsalikidis, #samesexmarriage, #idomeni, #refugeescrisis). While the collection of online data looked into many of these events, it was not possible to include in this project a more detailed examination of the post-referendum era and the multiple manifestations of the crisis (e.g. 2015 elections; refugees' crisis; Golden Dawn), as such an extended research would require more time, space and resources. Therefore, a follow-up research should concentrate on these latest manifestations of the crisis and at the same time, should also reflect the latest developments of the media and political environment, as this is still shaped in the crisis context. In terms of contribution to the field, this research offered a longitudinal study on the use of digital media during the Greek crisis, by providing snapshots of key event and platforms, of the digital media and crisis evolution. A follow up research should concentrate on different platforms (e.g. comparison among platforms, content and networks), events (e.g. refugees' crisis, the rise of far-right and networks) and uses (e.g. different actors, individuals and groups, organisation and communication).

In terms of research methods and the theoretical framework, this research employs the cyberconflict theory, which is used for the examination of various case studies (Karatzogianni, 2006; Olabode, 2016). This framework developed for the examination of digital media during the pre-social media era and as also explained earlier, here it was enriched with the theoretical element of connective action, so as to efficiently support the study of digital media and especially the examination of social media platforms. In other words, what was suggested here as an enriched version of Cyberconflict theory is the use of this theory in combination to the Bennett's connective action (2012). The outcome of this combination was a rich theoretical framework, which supported the in-depth study of conflict as this emerged in social media platforms, taking into consideration the impact of social media to the so-called personalised politics and their engagement to social networks, or event protest networks. Overall, the connective action helped the discussion as regards the organisational impact that social media are having to collective action and social movements. This was a great asset, taking into consideration that up to now Cyberconflict concentrated on social movements' theories and media theories, without looking in-depth on political engagement and personalised information through social networks.

The second innovative element of the use of cyberconflict was the use of digital research methods. Instead of using the CDA and interviews, which was traditionally used in this framework (Karatzogianni, 2006; Olabode, 2016), this research proposed a different approach to the analysis of digital material on online data in the examination of cyberconflict events. This study provided an example regarding the different options on using digital research methods for the study of cyberconflict, as well as a good start on exploring the multiple options as regards digital research methods (e.g. platforms, computational and analytical tools).

Therefore, this was the first time that the Cyberconflict was used for the study of social media, and by doing so, the theory enriched with additional theoretical elements. At the same time, this was the first time, that this theoretical framework was supported with the use of digital research methods. The use of digital research methods here, had both advantages and disadvantages, as discussed in the methodology and the empirical chapters, which should be under consideration in future studies. The use of the selected computational and analytical tools, for the study of four different online media platforms covering a seven-year period, indicated both strengths and limitations, suggested though how the selected software and app was used as supplementary, developing a rich corpus, which, based on the research aims and research questions each time, could be discussed and interpreted through different approaches. This research is an example of how the selected apps and software (e.g. NodeXL, Netvizz, Gephi, NVivo and NCapture) used to support the study of different online media platforms, and at the same time, a good example on their limitations (e.g. access on archive material, open/close access, small and big corpus – small and big data)

This study concentrated on the literature regards to Digital Media in Greece. Lately the literature on this topic is getting richer and richer, with many interesting studies, but still, most of the researches concentrate on either a case study (e.g. event) or an online media platform. Therefore, this research tried to combine some of these and provide an in-depth study of various platforms and events, starting from the transition to the digital era in media and communications in Greece, in 2008, and covering some of the most significant sociopolitical events raised in the so-called crisis, up to 2015. This project is a systematic research on the digital media in Greece, which developed through the examination of different online media platforms and focusing on key moments/events in the crisis. While there is already enough collected material for further research, I believe that the digital media usages in the Greek crisis should further be developed systematically, focusing on various platforms, actors and usages, as well as through a comparative approach of the Greek case to other crisis contexts and environments. Then, a better understanding of digital media in Greece should focus on regulatory frameworks and policies, which shapes digital communications in Greece.

Bibliography

Abelson, R. P., & Rosenberg, M. J. (1958). Symbolic psychologic: A model of attitude cognition. *Behavioral Science*, *3*, 1–13.

Abraham, A., Hassanien, A., & Snasel, V. (2012). *Computational social network analysis*. Dordrecht: Springer.

Afouxenidis, A. (2014). Social media and political participation: An investigation of small scale activism in greece. *Advances in Applied Sociology*, *4*(1), 1–4. doi:10.4236/aasoci.2014.41001

Agapidaki, I. (2016). *A seduction story* (Η ιστορία μιας αποπλάνησης, translated by the author). Retrieved from http://www.tovima.gr/opinions/article/?aid=838575

Albertazzi, D., & McDonnell, D. (2008). *Twenty-first century populism*. Basingstoke: Palgrave Macmillan.

Alevizopoulou, M., & Zenakou, A. (2013). *New democracy 'truth team': Forgers with the prime minister's approval*. Retrieved from https://borderlinereports.wordpress.com/2013/04/25/new-democracy-truth-team-forgers-with-the-prime-ministers-approval/

Allen, K. (2015). *Greece crisis timeline: The rocky road to another bailout*. Retrieved from https://www.theguardian.com/business/2015/aug/20/greece-crisis-timeline-rocky-road-another-bailout

Alston, K. (1962). Ziff's semantic analysis. *The Journal of Philosophy*, *59*(1), 5–20.

Altsantiri.gr. (2016). *ND's 'Truth's team' revealing its kids on Twitter* (Η "Ομάδα αλήθειας" της ΝΔ... αποκαλύπτει τα "παιδιά" της στο Twitter, translated by the author). Retrieved from http://www.altsantiri.gr/parapolitika/i-omada-alithias-tis-nd-dini-ta-pedia-tis-sto-tweeter/

Anastasakis, O. (2009). The new politics of the new century. In S. Economides & V. Monastiriotis (Eds.), *The return of street politics? Essays on the december riots on Greece*. London: The Hellenic Observatory, LSE.

Anderson, B. (2006). *Imagined communities: Reflections on the origins and spread of nationalism* (3rd ed.). London: Verso.

Anduiza, E., Cristancho, C., & Sabucedo, J. (2013). Mobilization through online social networks: The political protest of theindignadosin Spain. *Information, Communication & Society*, *17*(6), 750–764. doi:10.1080/1369118x.2013.808360

Argyrou, V. (2013). *Gift of European thought and the cost of living*. New York, NY: Berghahn Books.

Asimakoulas, D. (2009). Translating "self" and "others": Waves of protest under the Greek Junta. *The Sixties*, *2*(1), 25–47. doi:10.1080/17541320902909532

Askitas, N. (2015). Calling the greek referendum on the nose with Google trends. *SSRN Electronic Journal*. doi:10.2139/ssrn.2633443

Athanasiadis, H. (2008). *Three aspects of the Greek labour movement* (Τρες πτυχές του Ελληνικού εργατικού κινήματος, translated by the author). Retrieved from http://pep.uoi.gr/prosopiko/CVs/athanasiades/docs/ptyxes.pdf

AthensVoice.gr. (2017). *From SYRIZA's troll and against memorandum, with Tsipras in Cuba, posting Maduro* (Από τρολ του ΣΥΡΙΖΑ και αντιμνημονιακός, με τον Τσίπρα στην Κούβα και ποστάρει Μαδούρο, translated by the author). Retrieved from http://www.athensvoice.gr/politiki/apo-trol-toy-SYRIZA-kai-antimnimonia-kos-me-ton

Bamford, J. (2015). *Did a rogue NSA operation cause the death of a Greek telecom employee?* Retrieved from https://theintercept.com/2015/09/28/death-athens-rogue-nsa-operation/

BBC News. (2007). *BBC NEWS | Europe | Greek forest fire close to Athens.* [online] Retrieved from http://news.bbc.co.uk/2/hi/europe/6252676.stm. Accessed on February 15, 2017.

BBC News. (2010). *BBC News – Three dead as Greece protest turns violent.* [online] Retrieved from http://news.bbc.co.uk/1/hi/8661385.stm?ls. Accessed on February 15, 2017.

BBC News. (2015). *Catalonia vote: Pro-independence parties win elections – BBC News.* [online]. Retrieved from http://www.bbc.co.uk/news/world-europe-34372548. Accessed on February 15, 2017.

Benford, R., & Snow, D. (2000). Framing processes and social movements: An overview and assessment. *Annual Review of Sociology*, *26*(1), 611–639.

Bennett, W. (2003). Communicating global activism. *Information, Communication & Society*, *6*(2), 143–168.

Bennett, W. (2012). The personalization of politics: Political identity, social media, and changing patterns of participation. *The Annals of the American Academy of Political and Social Science*, *644*(1), 20–39.

Bennett, W. (2014). Response to Sidney Tarrow's review of the logic of connective action: Digital media and the personalization of contentious politics. *Perspectives on Politics*, *12*(2), 470–471.

Bennett, W., & Segerberg, A. (2012). The logic of connective action. *Information, Communication & Society*, *15*(5), 739–768.

Bernard, R. (2006). *Research methods in anthropology: Qualitative and quantitative approaches* (4th ed.). Lanham, MD: AltaMira Press.

Berghel, H. (2018). Malice domestic: The Cambridge analytica dystopia. *Computer*, *51*(5), 84–89.

BILD.de. (2010). *Griechenland: Verkauft doch eure Inseln, ihr Pleite-Griechen!* (Translation by the author: Sold but your islands, you bankrupt Greeks… And do with Acropolis the same!) [online]. Retrieved from http://www.bild.de/politik/wirtschaft/griechenland-krise/regierung-athen-sparen-verkauft-inseln-pleite-akropolis-11692338.bild.html. Accessed on February 15, 2017.

Billig, M. (1995). *Banal nationalism* (1st ed.). London: Sage.

Bistis, G. (2013). Golden Dawn or democratic sunset: The rise of the far right in Greece. *Mediterranean Quarterly*, *24*(3), 35–55.

Blalock, H. M. (1964). *Causal inferences in non-experimental research.* Chapel Hill, NC: University of North Carolina Press.

Blalock, H. (1975). *Causal inferences in non-experimental research.* Chapel Hill, NC: University of North Carolina Press.

Blumer, H. (1969). Collective behaviour. In A. McClung-Lee (Ed.), *Principles of sociology*. New York, NY: Barnes & Noble.

Borgatti, S., & Halgin, D. (2011). On network theory. *Organization Science*, 22(5), 1168–1181.

Botetzagias, I., & Karamichas, J. (2009). Grassroots mobilisations against waste disposal sites in Greece. *Environmental Politics*, *18*(6), 939–959.

Boukala, S., & Dimitrakopoulou, D. (2016). The politics of fear vs. the politics of hope: Analysing the 2015 Greek election and referendum campaigns. *Critical Discourse Studies*, *14*(1), 39–55.

Boyd, D., & Crawford, K. (2012). Critical questions for big data. *Information, Communication & Society*, *15*(5), 662–679.

Braun, V., & Clarke, V. (2006). Using thematic analysis in psychology. *Qualitative Research in Psychology*, *3*(2), 77–101.

Breiger, R. (2004). The analysis of social networks. In M. Hardy & A. Bryman (Eds.), *Handbook of data analysis*. London: Sage.

Buechler, S. (1993). Beyond resource mobilization? Emerging trends in social movement theory. *The Sociological Quarterly*, *34*(2), 217–235.

Buechler, S. (1995). New social movement theories. *The Sociological Quarterly*, *36*(3), 441–464.

Cammaerts, B., & Carpenter, N. (2007). *Reclaiming the media* (1st ed.). Bristol: Intellect.

Carnoy, M. (1984). *The state and political theory* (1st ed.). Princeton, NJ: Princeton University Press.

Carringhton, P. (2014). Social network research. In S. Dominguez & B. Hollstein (Eds.), *Mixed methods social networks research: Design and applications* (1st ed.). New York, NY: Cambridge University Press.

Carringhton, P., & Wasserman, S. (2005). *Models and methods in social network analysis* (1st ed.). Cambridge: Cambridge University Press.

Castells, M. (2000a). *The rise of the network society* (1st ed.). Oxford: Blackwell.

Castells, M. (2000b). Materials for an exploratory theory of the network society. *British Journal of Sociology*, *51*(1), 5–24.

Castells, M. (2004a). *The network society* (1st ed.). Cheltenham: Edward Elgar.

Castells, M. (2004b). Informationalism, networks, and the network society: A theoretical blueprint, the network society: A cross-cultural perspective. In M. Castells (Ed.), *The network society: A cross-cultural perspective* (1st ed.). Northampton, MA: Edward Elgar.

Castells, M. (2011). A network theory of power. *International Journal of Communication*, *5*, 773–787.

Castells, M. (2015). *Networks of outrage and hope* (1st ed.). Cambridge: Polity.

Castells, M., & Cardoso, G. (2005). *The network society: From knowledge to policy* (1st ed.). Washington, DC: Johns Hopkins Center for Transatlantic Relations.

Castoriadis, C. (1987). *The imaginary institution of society*. Cambridge, MA: MIT Press.

Charalambous, G. (2012). *European integration and the communist dilemma: Communist party responses to Europe in Greece, Cyprus, and Italy* (1st ed.). Farnham: Ashgate Publishing.

Chater, J. (2016). What the EU referendum result teaches us about the dangers of the echo chamber. [online] *Newstatesman.com*. Retrieved from http://www.newstatesman.com/2016/07/what-eu-referendum-result-teaches-us-about-dangers-echo-chamber. Accessed on June 5, 2017.

Cheliotis, L., & Xenakis, S. (2010). What's neoliberalism got to do with it? Towards a political economy of punishment in Greece. *Criminology and Criminal Justice*, *10*(4), 353–373.
Cherven, K. (2015). *Mastering Gephi network visualization* (1st ed.). Birmingham: Pakt Publishing.
Chiotis, V. (2011). *The square wants a permanent movement*, To Vima (Μόνιμο κίνημα θέλει η πλατεία. Σύμφωνα με δημοσκόπηση, οι εξεγερμένοι πολίτες αυτοχ αρακτηρίζονται κίνημα ειρηνικό και όχι ανατροπής, το βήμα). [Online] Retrieved from http://www.tovima.gr/politics/article/?aid=406882. Accessed on December 20, 2013.
Choudhury, S., & Breslin, J. (2010). User sentiment detection: A YouTube use case. In The *21st National Conference on Artificial Intelligence and Cognitive Science*, 30 August – 1 September 2010, Galway, Ireland.
Chouliaraki, L. (2008). Discourse analysis. In T. Bennett & J. Frow (Eds.), *The Sage handbook of cultural analysis* (1st ed., pp. 674–698). London: Sage.
Christensen, C. (2011). Twitter revolutions? Addressing social media and dissent. *The Communication Review*, *14*(3), 155–157.
Clarke, J., Huliaras, A., & Sotiropoulos, D. (2016). *Austerity and the third sector in Greece* (1st ed.). London: Routledge.
Clarke, V., & Braun, V. (2013). Teaching thematic analysis: Overcoming challenges and developing strategies for effective learning. *The Psychologist*, *26*(2), 120–123.
Cohen, J. (1985). Strategy or identity: New theoretical paradigms and contemporary social movements. *Social Research*, *52*(4), 663–716.
Coleman, S., & Blumler, J. (2009). *The Internet and democratic citizenship* (1st ed.). Cambridge: Cambridge University Press.
Conover, M., Ratkiewicz, J., Francisco, M., Goncalves, B., Flammini, A., & Menczer, F. (2011). *Political polarization on Twitter*. Barcelona: 5th International AAAI Conference on Weblogs and Social Media.
Cooley, C. H. (1902). *Human nature and the social order*. New York, NY: Scribner.
Correa, E., & Girón, A. (2013). Credit and capital formation: Lessons of Mexican migrant entrepreneurs in the U.S. financial crisis. *Journal of Economic Issues*, *47*(2), 555–560.
Coursaris, C., & Papagiannidis, S. (2009). Online political marketing in Greece: An evaluation of the 2007 national elections and two case studies. *Computers in Human Behavior*, *25*(4), 853–861.
Coyer, K., Dowmunt, T., & Fountain, A. (2007). *The alternative media handbook*. London: Routledge.
Crossley, N. (2002). *Making sense of social movements* (1st ed.). Buckingham: Open University Press.
Crisis-scape.net. (n.d). *The city at a time of crisis, crisis-scape*. [online] Retrieved from http://crisis-scape.net/index.php and http://www.tiki-toki.com/timeline/entry/128759/Athens-and-the-Crisis/. Accessed on March 16, 2017.
Cukier, W., Ngwenyama, O., Bauer, R., & Middleton, C. (2009). A critical analysis of media discourse on information technology: Preliminary results of a proposed method for critical discourse analysis. *Information Systems Journal*, *19*(2), 175–196.
Curran, J. (1990). The new revisionism in mass communication research. *European Journal of Communication*, *5*(2–3), 135–164.

D'Andrade, R. (1991). The identification of schemas in naturalistic data. In M. J. Horowitz (Ed.), *Person schemas and maladaptive interpersonal patterns* (pp. 279–301). Chicago, IL: University of Chicago Press.

D'Andrade, R. (1995). *The development of cognitive anthropology* (1st ed.). Cambridge: Cambridge University Press.

Dahlberg, L. (2001). The Internet and democratic discourse: Exploring the prospects of online deliberative forums extending the public sphere. *Information, Communication & Society*, *4*(4), 615–633.

Dahlberg, L. (2006). Computer-mediated communication and the public sphere: A critical analysis. *Journal of Computer-Mediated Communication*, *7*(1), 0–0.

Dalakoglou, D. (2012). Beyond spontaneity. *City*, *16*(5), 535–545.

Dalakoglou, D. (2016). Europe's last frontier: The spatialities of the refugee crisis. *City*, *20*(2), 180–185.

Dalton, R. J., Kuechler, M., & Burklin, W. (1990). 'The challenge of new movements'. In R. J. Dalton & M. Kuechler (Eds.), *Challenging the political order: New social and political movements in Western democracies*. Cambridge: Polity Press.

Daskalopoulou, D., & Droukas, G. (2015). *Duel in...'El' Internet (Μονομαχία στο... Ελ Διαδίκτυο)*. [online] Efimerida ton Syntakton/Η Εφημερίδα των Συντακτών. Retrieved from http://www.efsyn.gr/arthro/monomahia-sto-el-diadiktyo. Accessed on February 24, 2017.

Davidson, L. (2015). *#ThisIsACoup: Greece bailout demands spark social media backlash against Germany*. [online] Telegraph.co.uk. Retrieved from http://www.telegraph.co.uk/finance/economics/11735388/ThisIsACoup-Greece-bailout-demands-spark-social-media-backlash-against-Germany.html. Accessed on February 23, 2017.

Dawson, C. (2002). *Practical research methods* (1st ed.). Oxford: How To Books.

Dearden, L. (2015). Why Angela Merkel has been pictured with Nazis on this magazine cover. [online] *The Independent*. Retrieved from http://www.independent.co.uk/news/world/europe/angela-merkel-pictured-with-nazi-commanders-in-greece-as-war-reparation-dispute-continues-10127488.html. Accessed on February 15, 2017.

Della Porta, D., & Diani, M. (2006). *Social movements* (2nd ed.). Malden, MA: Blackwell Publishing.

Deleuze, G., & Guattari, F. (1987). *A thousand plateaus: Capitalism and schizophrenia* (1st ed.). Minneapolis, MN: University of Minnesota Press.

Diani, M., & McAdam, D. (2003). *Social movements and networks* (1st ed.). New York, NY: Oxford University Press.

Diaz Romero, L. (2013). Enhancing civic engagement in the digital age: Global activism, new media and the virtual public sphere, Actas del I Congreso Internacional Comunicación y Sociedad. UNIR. Logroño 2013.

Dijck, J. (2013). *The culture of connectivity* (1st ed.). New York, NY: Oxford University Press.

Dima, M. (2015). *Vaccinated by decree for the 5 million euro* («Καθάρισε» με βούλευμα για τα 5 εκατ. Ευρώ) [online] Η Εφημερίδα των Συντακτών. Retrieved from http://www.efsyn.gr/arthro/katharise-me-voyleyma-gia-ta-5-ekat-eyro. Accessed on February 15, 2017.

Dimokidis, A. (2016). *Who are the three left stunners of the Greek Twitter* (Ποιες είναι στην πραγματικότητα οι τρεις αριστερές κουκλάρες του ελληνικού Twitter). [online] LiFO. Retrieved from http://www.lifo.gr/articles/mikropragmata/121124. Accessed on February 23, 2017.

Dinas, E. (2008). The Greek general election of 2007: You cannot lose if your opponent cannot win. *West European Politics*, *31*(3), 600–607.

Dinas, E. (2010). The Greek general election of 2009: PASOK – The third generation. *West European Politics*, *33*(2), 389–398.

Doulkeri, T., & Terzis, G. (1997). Changing television in Greece the commercialization of creek TV and the historical, legal, economic and social environment. *Asian Journal of Communication*, *7*(2), 118–131.

Douzinas, C. (2013). Athens rising. *European Urban and Regional Studies*, *20*(1), 134–138.

Economides, S., & Monastiriotis, V. (2009). *The return of street politics? Essays on the December riots in Greece*. London: The Hellenic Observatory, LSE.

Edwards, B., & Gillham, P. (2017). Resource mobilization theory. In S. Snow (Ed.), *The Wiley-Blackwell encyclopedia of social and political movements* (1st ed.). Malden, MA: Willey.

Edwards, B., & McCarthy, D. (2004). Resources and social movement mobilization. In D. Snow, S. Soule, & S. Kristi (Eds.), *The Blackwell companion to social movements* (1st ed.). Oxford: Blackwell Publishing.

Eleftheros Typos/Ελεύθερος Τύπος. (2016). *Theodorakis: There is a linkage between KKE listening-in with right-wing websites and documents* (Θεοδωράκης: Υπάρχει σύνδεση των «συνακροάσεων» του ΚΚΕ με ακροδεξιά σάιτ και έντυπα) | Ελεύθερος Τύπος. [online] Retrieved from http://www.eleftherostypos.gr/politiki/58388-theodorakis-yparxei-syndesi-ton-synakroaseon-toy-kke-me-akrodexia-sait-kai-entypa/. Accessed on February 23, 2017.

Ellinas, A. (2010). *The media and the far right in Western Europe* (1st ed.). Cambridge: Cambridge University Press.

Ellinas, A. (2013). The rise of Golden Dawn: The new face of the far right in Greece. *South European Society and Politics*, *18*(4), 543–565.

Ellinas, A. (2014). Neo-Nazism in an established democracy: The persistence of Golden Dawn in Greece. *South European Society and Politics*, *20*(1), 1–20.

EL.STAT. – National Statistical Service of Greece – Hellenic Statistical Authority (2010). *Research on households' usage of information technology and communication: 2013* (Έρευνα Χρήσης Τεχνολογιών Πληροφόρησης και Επικοινωνίας από τα Νοικοκυριά, 2010) (In Greek). [online] Retrieved from http://www.statistics.gr/portal/page/portal/ESYE/BUCKET/A1901/PressReleases/A1901_SFA20_DT_AN_00_2010_01_F_GR.pdf. Accessed on February 15, 2017.

EL.STAT. – National Statistical Service of Greece – Hellenic Statistical Authority, (2013). *Research on households' usage of Information Technology and Communication: 2013* (Έρευνα χρήσης τεχνολογιών Πληροφόρησης και Επικοινωνίας από τα Νοικοκυριά, 2013) (In Greek). [online] Retrieved from http://www.statistics.gr/portal/page/portal/ESYE/BUCKET/A1901/PressReleases/A1901_SFA20_DT_AN_00_2012_01_F_GR.pdf. Accessed on February 15, 2017.

EL.STAT. – National Statistical Service of Greece – Hellenic Statistical Authority. (2014). *Research on households' usage of Information Technology and Communication: 2014* ('Έρευνα Χρήσης Τεχνολογιών Πληροφόρησης και Επικοινωνίας από τα Νοικοκυριά – 2014). [online] Retrieved from http://www.statistics.gr/portal/page/portal/ESYE/BUCKET/A1901/PressReleases/A1901_SFA20_DT_AN_00_2014_01_F_GR.pdf. Accessed on May 30, 2017.

EL.STAT. – National Statistical Service of Greece – Hellenic Statistical Authority. (2015). *Research on households' usage of Information Technology and Communication: 2014* ('Έρευνα Χρήσης Τεχνολογιών Πληροφόρησης και Επικοινωνίας από τα Νοικοκυριά – 2015). [online] Retrieved from http://www.statistics.gr/portal/page/portal/ESYE/BUCKET/A1901/PressReleases/A1901_SFA20_DT_AN_00_2015_01_F_GR.pdf. Accessed on May 30, 2017.

ELTRUN. (2014). *Annual study of Greek social media users.* [online] Retrieved from https://www.eltrun.gr/wp-content/uploads/2013/10/EthsiaEreynaKoinonikhsDiktyoshs2013-4.pdf. Accessed on March 2, 2017.

Eleytherotupia. (2014). *Geron Paisions convinced* (Καταδικάστηκε ο «Γέροντας Παστίτσιος»). [online] Retrieved from http://www.enet.gr/?i=news.el.article&id=410044. Accessed on May 29, 2017.

Eleytherotupia. (2014). *Geron Paisions convinced (Καταδικάστηκε ο «Γέροντας Παστίτσιοςς»)*. Retrieved from http://www.enet.gr/?i=news.el.article&id=410044. Accessed on May 29, 2017.

Enikos.gr. (2013). *Samaras: 'Greece is Europe' s Success Story'* (Σαμαράς:"Η Ελλάδα είναι το success story της Ευρώπης") | www.enikos.gr – Πολιτική/Politics. [online] Retrieved from http://www.enikos.gr/politics/150789/samarasi-ellada-einai-to-success-story-tis-evropis. Accessed on March 27, 2017.

EU Commission, Digital Agenda for Europe. (2017). *EU Commission, Digital Agenda for Europe.* [online] Retrieved from http://digital-agenda-data.eu/. Accessed on May 27, 2017.

Euronews. (2015). *Thousands of citizens gathered in Syntagma square to send a message against austerity* (Χιλιάδες πολίτες συγκεντρώθηκαν στο Σύνταγμα για να στείλουν μήνυμα κατά της λιτότητας). [online] Retrieved from http://gr.euronews.com/2015/06/17/greeks-rally-ahead-of-eurozone-crunch-talks. Accessed on March 10, 2017.

Eurostat. (n.d.). *Eurostat.* [online] Retrieved from http://appsso.eurostat.ec.europa.eu/nui/show.do. Accessed on May 30, 2017.

Evripidou, A., & Drury, J. (2013). This is the time of tension: Collective action subjective power in the Greek austerity movement. *Contention: The Multidisciplinary Journal of Social Protest Peer Reviewed Journal, 1*, 31–51.

Exadaktylos, T. (2011). *Whither the Indignados of Athens?* [online] Greece@LSE. Retrieved from http://blogs.lse.ac.uk/greeceatlse/2011/07/12/whither-the-indignados-of-athens/. Accessed on February 15, 2017.

Eyerman, R., & Jamison, A. (1991). *Social movements: A cognitive approach.* Cambridge: Polity Press.

Fairclough, M. (1992). *Discourse and social change* (1st ed.). Cambridge: Polity Press.

Fairclough, N. (2013). *Analysis discourse, textual analysis for social research* (1st ed.). London: Routledge.

Fajardo, L. (2015). *Joseph Stiglitz, Nobel de Economía: 'Las condiciones impuestas a Grecia son indignantes' – BBC Mundo. [online] BBC Mundo.* Retrieved from http://linkis.com/www.bbc.com/mundo/no/mDAvA. Accessed on May 9, 2017.

Featherstone, K. (1982). Elections and parties in Greece. *Government and Opposition, 17*(2), 180–194.

Featherstone, K. (2009). Street protests in 'Une Société Bloquée'. In S. Ecomomides & V. Monastiriotis (Eds.), *The return of street politics? Essays on the December riots in Greece* (1st ed.). London: The Hellenic Observatory, LSE.

Fenton, N. (2007). Contesting global capital, new media, solidarity, and the role of a social imaginary. In B. Cammaerts & N. Carpentier (Eds.), *Reclaiming the media, communication rights and democratic media roles* (1st ed.). Bristol: Intellect.

Fenton, N. (2008). Mediating hope: New media, politics and resistance. *International Journal of Cultural Studies*, *11*(2), 230–248.

Ferra, I. (2016). Understanding the Greek crisis and digital media. A cyberconflict approach. In A. Karatzogianni, D. Nguyen, & E. Serafinelli (Eds.), *The digital transformation of the public sphere. Conflict, migration, crisis and culture in digital networks*. London: Palgrave Macmillan.

Ferra, I., & Karatzogianni, A. (forthcoming). A tale of cyberconflict in Greece: Polarization and mobilization for the Greek referendum on Twitter. In Th. Stathopoulou (Ed.), *Transformations of protest in Greece*. Athens: Papazisis Publishers & EKKE.

Financial Times. (2016). *Highest Greek court blocks Syriza media law*. [online] Retrieved from https://www.ft.com/content/c8d5347e-9bd0-11e6-8f9b-70e3cabccfae. Accessed on January 16, 2018.

Flick, U. (2004). Design and process in qualitative research. In U. Flick, E. Von Kardorff, & I. Steinke (Eds.), *A companion to qualitative research*. London: Sage.

Flynn, S. (2011). *Sociology reference guide*. Pasadena, CA: Salem Press.

Focusbari.gr. (2015). *Focus on tech life: Web*. [online] Retrieved from https://www.focusbari.gr/en/media-research-en/internet-web-id-en.html. Accessed on May 29, 2017.

Forchten, B. (2010). Jürgen Habermas' language-philosophy and the critical study of language. *Critical Approaches to Discourse Analysis across Disciplines*, *4*(1), 18–37.

Fouskas, V. (2009). *The inglorious end of the Third Hellenic Republic, 1974–2008*. RIEAS Research Institute for European and American Studies [online]. Retrieved from http://rieas.gr/images/FOUSKAS.pdf. Accessed on March 6, 2012.

Fouskas, V., & Dimoulas, C. (2012). The Greek workshop of debt and the failure of the European project. *Journal of Balkan and Near Eastern Studies*, *14*(1), 1–31.

Fraser, I. (2015). *Bank of Greece issues grave warning of Grexit as British government prepares for fallout – as it happened 17 June 2015*. [online] Telegraph.co.uk. Retrieved from http://www.telegraph.co.uk/finance/11680077/Bank-of-Greece-issues-grave-warning-of-Grexit-as-British-government-prepares-for-fallout-as-it-happened-17-June-2015.html. Accessed on February 15, 2017.

Fraidaki, K., & Pramatari, K. (2013). *Social media usage from the Greek Internet users*. [online] ELTRUN. Retrieved from https://www.eltrun.gr/wp-content/uploads/2013/01/social-media_2012_final.pdf. Accessed on March 2, 2017.

Freire, A., Lisi, M., Andreadis, I., & Leite Viegas, J. (2014). Political representation in bailed-out Southern Europe: Greece and Portugal compared. *South European Society and Politics*, *19*(4), 413–433.

Friemel, T. (2008). *Why context matters* (1st ed.). Wiesbaden: VS Verlag für Sozialwissenschaften/GWV Fachverlage GmbH, Wiesbaden.

Fuchs, C. (2008). *Internet and society* (1st ed.). London: Routledge.

Fuchs, C. (2011). *Foundations of critical media and information studies* (1st ed.). London: Routledge.

Fuchs, C. (2012). *The right-wing European mainstream media campaign against SYRIZA and the need to end neoliberalism | Christian Fuchs*. [online] Fuchs.uti.at. Retrieved from http://fuchs.uti.at/825/. Accessed on February 23, 2017.

Fuchs, C. (2014a). *Digital labour and Karl Marx* (1st ed.). New York, NY: Routledge.

Fuchs, C. (2014b). *Social media: A critical introduction*. London: Sage.

Fuller, M. (2019). Big data and the Facebook scandal: Issues and responses. *Theology*, *122*(1), 14–21.

Gainous, J., & Wagner, K. (2014). *Tweeting to power. The social media revolution in American politics* (1st ed.). Cary, NC: Oxford University Press.

Galpin, R. (2006). *Death muddies Greek spy probe*|BBC NEWS | World | Europe. [online] News.bbc.co.uk. Retrieved from http://news.bbc.co.uk/1/hi/world/europe/4838552.stm. Accessed on March 21, 2017.

Gamson, W. (1990). *The strategy of social protest* (2nd ed.). Homewood, IL: Dorsey Press.

Garner, R., & Zald, N. M. (1981). Social movement sectors and systemic constraint, towards a structural analysis of social movements, Center of Research on Social Organization, Working Paper No. 238.

Geiger, R. (2009). *Does Habermas understand the Internet? The algorithmic construction of the blogo/public sphere* | gnovis. [online] Gnovisjournal.org. Retrieved from http://www.gnovisjournal.org/2009/12/22/does-habermas-understand-internet-algorithmic-construction-blogopublic-sphere/. Accessed on February 15, 2017.

Gemenis, K. (2008). The 2007 parliamentary election in Greece. *Mediterranean Politics*, *13*(1), 95–101.

Georgopoulou, P. (2014). The digital divide profile of Greece: One step further. *National Centre for Social Research*, *136*(136), 97–110.

Gerbaudo, P. (2012). *Tweets and the streets: Social media and contemporary activism* (1st ed.). London: Pluto Press.

Gerbaudo, P. (2015). Populism 2.0: Social media activism, the generic internet user and interactive direct democracy. In D. Trottier & C. Fuchs (Eds.), *Social media, politics and the state*. New York: Routledge.

Giannarou, L. (2012). Η πολιτική πόλωση του '80 με χρώματα του 2012 (Translated by the author: The political polarization of the 80s, with the colors of 2012). [online] Kathimerini. Retrieved from http://www.kathimerini.gr/459784/article/epikairothta/politikh/h-politikh-polwsh-toy-80-me-xrwmata-toy-2012. Accessed on February 15, 2017.

Golbeck, J. (2013). *Analyzing the social web* (1st ed.). Amsterdam: Elsevier.

Gould-Wartofsky, M. (2015). *The occupiers*. New York, NY: Oxford University Press.

Graeber, D. (2013). *The democracy project* (1st ed.). New York, NY: Penguin.

Graeber, J. (2016). Citizenship in the shadow of the Euro crisis: Explaining changing patterns in naturalisation among intra-EU migrants. *Journal of Ethnic and Migration Studies*, *42*(10), 1670–1692.

Granovetter, M. (1983). The strength of weak ties: A network theory revisited. *Sociological Theory*, *1*, 201.

Guba, E., & Lincoln, S. (1994). Competing paradigms in qualitative research. In N. Denzin & S. Lincoln (Eds.), *Handbook of qualitative research* (1st ed.). Thousand Oaks, CA: Sage.

Habermas, J. (1984). *The theory of communicative action*. Boston, MA: Beacon Press.

Habermas, J. (1991). *The structural transformation of the public sphere* (1st ed.). Cambridge, MA: Massachusetts Institute of Technology.

Hafner, K., & Lyon, M. (1998). *Where wizards stay up late* (1st ed.). New York, NY: Simon & Schuster.

Hansen, D., Shneiderman, B., & Smith, M. (2011). *Analyzing social media networks with NodeXL* (1st ed.). Amsterdam: Elsevier/Morgan Kaufmann.

Harary, F., Norman, R., & Cartwright, D. (1966). *Structural models – An introduction to the theory of directed graphs*. New York, NY: John Wiley & Sons.

Hardt, M., & Negri, A. (2000). *Empire* (1st ed.). Cambridge, MA: Harvard University Press.

Hardy, M., & Bryman, A. (2004). Handbook of data analysis. In *The analysis of social networks* (1st ed.). London: Sage.

Harvey, D. (2010). *A companion guide to Marx's capital*. London: Verso.

Held, D. (1992). Democracy: From city-states to a cosmopolitan order? *Political Studies*, *40*(1_suppl), 10–39.

Hensby, A. (2014). Networks, counter-networks and political socialisation – Paths and barriers to high-cost/risk activism in the 2010/11 student protests against fees and cuts. *Contemporary Social Science*, *9*(1), 92–105.

Hesmondhalgh, D. (2013). *The cultural industries*. London: Sage.

Hope, K. (2013). Greek police 'infiltrated' by Golden Dawn. [online] *Financial Times*, Ft.com. Retrieved from https://www.ft.com/content/e5046b8c-3261-11e3-b3a7-00144feab7de. Accessed on March 24, 2017.

Hughes, N. (2011). Young people took to the streets and all of a sudden all of the political parties got old: The 15M movement in Spain. *Social Movement Studies*, *10*(4), 407–413.

Hunt, S., & Benford, R. (2004). Collective identity, solidarity and commitment. In S. Snow, S. Soule, & H. Kriesi (Eds.), *The Blackwell companion to social movements* (1st ed.).

Inglehart, R. (1990). *Culture shift in advanced industrial society*. Princeton, NJ: Princeton University Press.

Ioannou, C. (1999). *Trade unions in Greece: Development, structures & prospects/ Christos A. Ioannou*. – [Electronic ed.]. – Athens, 1999. – 40 S. = 183 Kb, TextElectronic ed.: Bonn: FES Library, 2000© Friedrich-Ebert-Stiftung. [online] Fes.de. Retrieved from http://www.fes.de/fulltext/bueros/athen/00740toc.htm. Accessed on February 15, 2017.

Iosifidis, P. (2013). *The closure of the Greek ERT: What is really at stake for PSB in Austere Times?* [online] Media Policy Project, LSE. Retrieved from http://blogs.lse.ac.uk/mediapolicyproject/2013/07/03/the-closure-of-the-greek-ert-what-is-really-at-stake-for-psb-in-austere-times/. Accessed on March 27, 2017.

Iosifidis, P., & Boucas, D. (2015). *Media policy and independent journalism in Greece*. Open Society Foundations.

Janicka, A., & Kaczmarczyk, P. (2016). Mobilities in the crisis and post-crisis times: migration strategies of Poles on the EU labour market. *Journal of Ethnic and Migration Studies*, *42*(10), 1693–1710.

Jasper, J. (1997). *The art of moral protest* (1st ed.). Chicago, IL: The University of Chicago Press.

Jasper, J. M. (2015). *The art of moral protest: Culture, biography, and creativity in social movements*. Chicago, IL: University of Chicago Press.

Jauregul, A. (2012). Facebook page mocking eastern orthodox monk leads to blasphemy arrest in Greece. [online] *The Huffington Post*. Retrieved from http://www.huffingtonpost.com/2012/09/24/gerontas-pastitsios-pastafarian-facebook-greece-elder-paisios_n_1909511.html. Accessed on February 5, 2017.

Jenkins, C., & Form, W. (2005). Social movements and social change. In T. Janoski (Ed.), *The handbook of political sociology: States, civil societies, and globalization*. New York: Cambridge University Press.

Joyce, M. (2010). *Digital activism decoded: The new mechanism of change* (1st ed.). New York, NY: International Debate Education Association.

Kaika, M., & Karaliotas, L. (2014). The spatialization of democratic politics: Insights from Indignant Squares. *European Urban and Regional Studies*, *23*(4), 556–570.

Kaitatzi-Whitlock, S. (2014). Greece, The Eurozone crisis and the media: The solution is the problem. *Javnost – The Public*, *21*(4), 25–45.

Kallivretakis, L. (2006). Georgios Papadopoulos: Security Battalions and 'X': An attempt to gather and reevaluate earlier and more recent evidence (Γεώργιος Παπαδόπουλος, Τάγματα Ασφαλείας και 'Χ': Μια απόπειρα συγκέντρωσης και επανεκτίμησης του παλαιότερου και νεότερου τεκμηριωτικού υλικού). *Archiotaxio*, *8*, 109–147.

Karamesini, M. (2005). European strategies for employment dealing the financial crisis, (Η Ευρωπαϊκή Στρατηγική για την Απασχόληση Αντιμέτωπη με την Οικονομική Κρίση). *Hellenic Social Policy Association*, 2.

Karamichas, J. (2007). The impact of the Summer 2007 forest fires in Greece: Recent environmental mobilizations, cyber-activism and electoral performance. *South European Society and Politics*, *12*(4), 521–533.

Karamichas, J. (2009). The December 2008 riots in Greece. *Social Movement Studies*, *8*(3), 289–293.

Karatzogianni, A. (2005). 'Social Movement Theory and Sociopolitical Cyberconflict', Tenth International Conference on ALTERNATIVE FUTURES and POPULAR PROTEST, Manchester Metropolitan University, Manchester.

Karatzogianni, A. (2006). *The politics of cyberconflict* (1st ed.). New York, NY: Routledge.

Karatzogianni, A. (2012). WikiLeaks affects: Ideology, conflict and the revolutionary virtual. In A. Karatzogianni & A. Kuntsman (Eds.), *Digital cultures and the politics of emotion: Feelings, affect and technological change* (1st ed., pp. 52–73). Basingstoke: Palgrave Macmillan.

Karatzogianni, A. (2015). *Firebrand waves of digital activism 1994–2014* (1st ed.). Basingstoke: Palgrave Macmillan.

Karatzogianni, A., & Robinson, A. (2013). *Power, resistance and conflict in the contemporary world* (1st ed.). London: Routledge.

Karatzogianni, A., & Schandorf, M. (2015). Surfing the revolutionary wave 2010–12: A technosocial theory of agency, resistance, and orders of dissent in contemporary social movements. In A. Ornella (Ed.), *Anthropotechnologies – Making humans. Religious, technological, and aesthetic perspectives* (1st ed.). Oxford: Inter-Disciplinary Press.

Karyotis, G. (2007). Securitization of Greek terrorism and arrest of the 'revolutionary organization November 17'. *Cooperation and Conflict*, *42*(3), 271–293.

Kassam, A. (2015). Spain's Podemos inspired by SYRIZA's victory in Greek elections. [online] *The Guardian*. Retrieved from https://www.theguardian.com/world/2015/jan/26/spain-podemos-SYRIZA-victory-greek-elections. Accessed on February 15, 2017.

Kassimeris, G. (1995). Greece: Twenty years of political terrorism. *Terrorism and Political Violence*, *7*(2), 74–92.

Kassimeris, G. (2004). The 2004 Greek Election: PASOK's Monopoly Ends. *West European Politics*, *27*(5), 943–953.

Kassimeris, G. (2005). Junta by another name? The 1974 Metapolitefsi and the Greek extra-parliamentary left. *Journal of Contemporary History*, *40*(4), 745–762.

Kassimeris, G. (2013a). Greece: The persistence of political terrorism. *International Affairs*, *89*(1), 131–142.

Kassimeris, G. (2013b). *Inside Greek terrorism*. New York, NY: Oxford University Press.

Kassimi, A. (2015). *Half of Greeks engage in social media* | Kathimerini. [online] Ekathimerini.com. Retrieved from http://www.ekathimerini.com/201228/article/ekathimerini/community/half-of-greeks-engage-in-social-media. Accessed on February 15, 2017.

Kathimerini.gr. (2015). *Pro-EU protest at Syntagma Square* (Συγκέντρωση υπέρ της παραμονής στο ευρώ στην πλατεία Συντάγματος) | Kathimerini. [online] Retrieved from http://www.kathimerini.gr/819580/article/epikairothta/ellada/sygkentrwsh-yper-ths-paramonhs-sto-eyrw-sthn-plateia-syntagmatos. Accessed on March 10, 2017.

Katsikas, D. (2012). The Greek crisis and the search for political leadership. *The International Spectator*, *47*(4), 49–56.

Katsoridas, D., & Lampousaki, S. (2012). Strikes in 2011. In A. Stamati & E. Kousta (Eds.), *Restructures in Greece* (Αναδιαρθρώσεις στην Ελλάδα, Οι Απεργίες το 2011, 1st ed). Athens: Institute GSEE.

Kegley, C., & Blanton, S. (2009). *World politics* (12th ed.). Wadsworth: Cengage Learning.

Kelly Garrett, R. (2006). Protest in an information society: A review of literature on social movements and new ICTs. *Information, Communication & Society*, *9*(2), 202–224.

Kelly, M., Mazzoleni, G., & McQuail, A. (2004). *The media in Europe: The Euromedia research group* (1st ed.). London: Sage.

Khan, M. (2015). *Desperation forces Greeks back out on to the streets in Athens anti-austerity protests*. [online] Telegraph.co.uk. Retrieved from http://www.telegraph.co.uk/news/worldnews/europe/greece/11682338/Desperation-forces-Greeks-back-out-on-to-the-streets-in-Athens-anti-austerity-protests.html. Accessed on May 29, 2017.

Khasnabish, A., & Haiven, M. (2014). *The radical imagination: Social movement research in the age of austerity* (1st ed.). London: Zed Books.

Klandermans, B. (1994). Mobilization and participation: Social-psychological expansisons of resource mobilization theory. *American Sociological Review*, *49*(5), 583.

Klandermans, B. (1992). The social construction of protest and multiorganizational fields. In A. D. Morris & C. M. Mueller (Eds.), *Frontiers in social movement theory* (pp. 77–103). New Haven, CT: Yale University Press.

Knoke, D. (1994). *Political networks* (1st ed.). Cambridge: Cambridge University Press.

Kollia, E. (2012). *The Square was full of Indignados* (Η πλατεία ήταν γεμάτη... αγανακτισμένους). [online] To Vima. Retrieved from http://www.tovima.gr/society/article/?aid=467898. Accessed on June 7, 2017.

Korizi, S., & Vradis, A. (2012). From innocence to realisation. *City*, *16*(1–2), 237–242.

Kornetis, K. (2010). No more heroes? Rejection and reverberation of the past in the 2008 events in Greece. *Journal of Modern Greek Studies*, *28*(2), 173–197.

Koronaiou, A., Lagos, E., Sakellariou, A., Kymionis, S., & Chiotaki-Poulou, I. (2015). Golden Dawn, austerity and young people: The rise of fascist extremism among young people in contemporary Greek society. *The Sociological Review*, *63*(2_suppl), 231–249.

Kostopoulou, M. (2015). *SYRIZA – Podemos – Venceremos!* [online] Avgi.gr. Retrieved from http://www.avgi.gr/article/10842/5249004/SYRIZA-podemos-venceremos. Accessed on May 11, 2017.

Kothari, C. R., (2004). *Research methodology: Methods & techniques*. New Delhi: New Age International.

Kounenaki, P. (1995). The magic of radio (in Greek). Kathimerini, *Epta Imeres*, 31 December 1995, Retrieved from http://wwk.kathimerini.gr/kath/7days/1995/12/31121995.pdf. Accessed on March 3, 2014.

Kretsos, L. (2012). Greece's neoliberal experiment and working class resistance. *WorkingUSA*, *15*(4), 517–527.

Kriesi, H. (1989), New social movements and the new class in the Netherlands. *American Journal of Sociology*, *94*(5), 1078–1116.

Kriesi, H. (2004). Political context and opportunity. In D. Snow, S. Soule, & H. Kriesi (Eds.), *The Blackwell companion to social movements* (1st ed.). Oxford: Blackwell Publishing.

Krippendorff, K. (2004). *Content analysis* (1st ed.). London: Sage.

Kyriakopoulos, L. (2010). December's riots as mediated by the image of mass media. In A. Schwarz & T. Sagris (Eds.), *We are an image from the future* (1st ed.). Edinburgh: AK Press.

Lampropoulos, V. (2012). *One out of two police officers voted for Golden Dawn* (Ενας στους δύο αστυνομικούς ψήφισαν «Χρυσή Αυγή»). [online] To Vima. Retrieved from http://www.tovima.gr/afieromata/elections2012/article/?aid=457088. Accessed on March 24, 2017.

Laraña, E., Johnston, H., & Gusfield, J. (Eds.) (1994). *New social movements: From ideology to identity*. Philadelphia, PA: Temple University Press.

Lauk, T. (2014). *The triple crisis of western capitalism: Democracy, banking, and currency* (1st ed.). Basingstoke: Palgrave Macmillan.

Lavdas, K. (1997). *Europeanization of Greece* (1st ed.). Basingstoke: Palgrave Macmillan.

Left.gr. (2015). #stopausterity #change4all #mazi: Mobilizations in Syntagma and across the country (updates – photos), left.gr. (#stopausterity #change4all #mazi: Συγκεντρώσεις στο Σύνταγμα & όλη τη χώρα (ενημέρωση – φωτογραφίες), left.gr.) [online] Retrieved from https://left.gr/news/sygkentrosi-tin-tetarti-sto-syntagma-pairnoyme-ti-diapragmateysi-sta-heria-mas#sthash.4f116jF3.dpuf. Accessed on March 10, 2017.

LeVine, P., & Scollon, R. (2004). *Discourse and technology* (1st ed.). Washington, DC: Georgetown University Press.

Likic-Brboric, B. (2011). EU enlargement, migration, and asymmetric citizenship: Political economy of inequality and the demise of the European social model? *Globalizations*, *8*(3), 277–294.

Lincoln, Y. (2004). Life in transit. In U. Flick, E. vod Kardoff, & I. Steinke (Eds.), *A companion to qualitative research* (1st ed.). London: Sage.

Loulis, J. (2001). *The twenty years that transformed Greece: Winners and losers* (Τα είκοσοι χρόνια που άλλαξαν την Ελλάδα: Κερδισμένοι και Χαμένοι), Livanis, Athens.

Luben. (2016). *Asinines' war: All the fake ND trolls and SYRIZA (that we know) on Twitter* (Ο πόλεμος των χαζών: Όλα τα ψεύτικα τρολ της ΝΔ και του ΣΥΡΙΖΑ (που γνωρίζουμε) στο twitter (PHOTOS). [online] Retrieved from http://luben.tv/politix/96685. Accessed on February 23, 2017.

Lusher, D., Koskinen, J., & Robins, G. (2012). *Exponential random graph models for social networks* (1st ed.). Cambridge: Cambridge University Press.

Lyrintzis, C. (2007). The changing party system: Stable democracy, contested 'modernisation'. *West European Politics*, *28*(2), 242–259.

Lyrintzis, Ch. (2011). *Greek politics in the era of economic crisis: Reassessing causes and effects*. Hellenic Observatory Papers in Southeast Europe, GreeSE Paper No 45, The Hellenic Observatory, London School of Economics and Political Science, London, UK. [online] Retrieved from http://eprints.lse.ac.uk/33826/1/GreeSE_No45.pdf. Accessed on August 5, 2016.

Madden, D., & Vradis, A. (2012). From Athens to occupy and back. *City*, *16*(1–2), 235–236.

Madden, A., Ruthven, I., & McMenemy, D. (2013). A classification scheme for content analyses of YouTube video comments. *Journal of Documentation*, *69*(5), 693–714.

Malkoutzis, N. (2011). *Greece – A year in crisis examining the social and political impact of an unprecedented austerity programme*. Occasional Paper, International Policy Analysis Unit (IPA), Friedrich Ebert Stiftung, June. Retrieved from https://library.fes.de/pdf-files/id/ipa/08208.pdf

Maltezou, R., & Koutantou, A. (2015). *Greek parliament approves bailout measures as Syriza fragments*. [online] Reuters. Retrieved from https://www.reuters.com/article/us-eurozone-greece-idUSKBN0P40EO20150716. Accessed on May 29, 2017.

Mandrou, I. (2017). *The lawsuit against G. Papandreou for the 'Money Exists', was examined today at the General Court* (Συζητήθηκε στο Πρωτοδικείο η αγωγή κατά Γ. Παπανδρέου για το «λεφτά υπάρχουν») | Kathimerini. [online] Kathimerini.gr. Retrieved from http://www.kathimerini.gr/892413/article/epikairothta/ellada/syzhth8hke-sto-prwtodikeio-h-agwgh-kata-g-papandreoy-gia-to-lefta-yparxoyn. Accessed on March 20, 2017.

Maniadakis, D., & Kountrias, T., (2006). *Broadband in Greece, infrastructures and services* (Ευρυζωνικότητα στην Ελλαδα, Υποδομή και Υπηρεσίες) (In Greek). National and Kapodistrian University of Athens, Dept. of Informatics and Telecommunications. online: Retrieved from http://cgi.di.uoa.gr/~mop07195/maniadakis_broadband.pdf. Accessed on March 1, 2014.

Manolopoulos, J. (2011). *Greece's 'odious' debt* (1st ed.). London: Anthem Press.

Marres, N. (2015). Why map issues? On controversy analysis as a digital method. *Science, Technology, & Human Values*, *40*(5), 655–686.

Maruyama, M. (1963). The second cybernetics: Deviation-amplifying mutual causal processes. *American Scientist*, *51*, 164–179.

Marx, K. (1956). In T. B. Bottomore (Trans.), *Karl Marx: Selected writings in sociology and social philosophy*. New York, NY: McGraw-Hill.

Marx, G. T., & Wood, J. (1975). Strands of theory and research in collective behaviour. *Annual Review of Sociology*, *1*, 363–428.

Mason, P. (2015). 'Hope begins today': The inside story of SYRIZA's rise to power. [online] *The Guardian*. Retrieved from https://www.theguardian.com/world/2015/jan/28/greek-people-wrote-history-how-SYRIZA-rose-to-power. Accessed on February 23, 2017.

Mavroudeas, S. (2015). *The Greek saga: Competing explanations of the Greek crisis*. (Discussion Paper). 38 p. (Economics Discussion Papers, no. 2015-01). Kingston upon Thames, UK: Faculty of Arts and Social Sciences, Kingston University.

McAdam, D., Tarrow, C., & Tilly, C. (1996). Comparative perspectives on contentious politics. In M. Lichbach & A. Zuckerman (Eds.), *Comparative politics: Rationality, culture, and structure: Advancing theory in comparative politics* (1st ed.). Cambridge: Cambridge University Press.

McCarthy, J. D., & Zald, M. N. (1973). *The trend of social movements in America: Professionalization and resource mobilization*. Morristown, NJ: General Learning Press.

McCarthy, J., & Zald, M. (1977). Resource mobilization and social movements: A partial theory. *American Journal of Sociology*, *82*(6), 1212–1241.

McChesney, R. (2013). *Digital disconnect* (1st ed.). New York, NY: New Press.

McChesney, R., Wood, M., & Foster, B. (1998). *Capitalism and the information age: The political economy of the global communication revolution* (1st ed.). New York, NY: Monthly Review Press.

McElroy, D., & Anast, P. (2010). *Greece crisis: Three bank workers killed in street protests*. [online] Telegraph.co.uk. Retrieved from http://www.telegraph.co.uk/travel/destinations/europe/greece/7682628/Greece-crisis-three-bank-workers-killed-in-street-protests.html. Accessed on February 15, 2017.

Melucci, A. (1980). The new social movements: A theoretical approach. *Social Science Information*, *19*(2), 199–226.

Melucci, A. (1996). *Challenging codes: Collective action in the information age* (1st ed.). Cambridge: Cambridge University Press.

Merton, R. (1975). Thematic analysis in science: Notes on Holton's concept. *Science*, *188*(4186), 335–338.

Michael-Matsas, S. (2010a). Greece and the world capitalist crisis. *Critique*, *38*(3), 489–502.

Michael-Matsas, S. (2010b). The Greek revolt, the world crisis and freedom of expression. *Critique*, *38*(1), 51–59.

Michaletos, I. (n.d.). *Wildfires in Greece*. [online] Research Institute for European and American Studies (Rieas.gr). Retrieved from http://www.rieas.gr/research-areas/greek-studies/384.html. Accessed on March 28, 2017.

Milioni, D. (2009). Probing the online counterpublic sphere: The case of Indymedia Athens. *Media, Culture & Society*, *31*(3), 409–431.

Milioni, D. (2012). Between 'identity politics' and 'politics of influence': The role of alternative media in the Greek protests in 2008. *Estudos em Comunicação nº*, *11*, 1–28.

Milioni, D., & Panos, D. (2011). New media and radical protest: Reflections from the 'Greek 2008 riots'. *International Journal of Media & Cultural Politics*, 7(2), 233–240.

Ministry of Interior, ypes.gr. (n.d.). *Ministry of interior – Elections results*. [online] Retrieved from http://www.ypes.gr/en/Elections/NationalElections/Results/. Accessed on May 29, 2017.

Ministry of Interior, Hellenic Republic. (2015). *Declaratory Act, Political Parties Support on the Referendum Questions and the constitution of commissioners of the article 10 of d. 4023/2011* (In Greek, translated by the author: Υποστήριξη των πολιτικών κομμάτων στα ερωτήματα του δημοψηφίσματος και στην συγκρότηση Επιτροπών του άρθρου 10 του ν. 4023/2011). Athens: General Directorate of E-government and Elections, Ministry of Interior.

Mitchell, A., Simmons, K., Matsa, K., & Silver, L. (2018). *Publics globally want unbiased news coverage, but are divided on whether their news media deliver*. Pewresearch.org. Retrieved from https://www.pewresearch.org/global/wp-content/uploads/sites/2/2018/01/Publics-Globally-Want-Unbiased-News-Coverage-but-Are-Divided-on-Whether-Their-News-Media-Deliver_Full-Report-and-Topline-UPDATED.pdf. Accessed on Aug 27, 2019.

Monastiriotis, V. (2011). *London burning, stock markets melting… time for structural change!*. [online] Greece@LSE. Retrieved from http://blogs.lse.ac.uk/greeceatlse/2011/08/11/london-burning/. Accessed on May 29, 2017.

Morozov, E. (2012). *The net delusion* (1st ed.). New York, NY: Public Affairs.

Morrow, R., & Brown, D. (1996). *Critical theory and methodology*. London: Sage.

Morris, A., & Herring, C. (1988). Theory and research in social movements: A critical review. In S. Long (Ed.), *Annual review of political behaviour* (Vol. 2, pp. 137–198). Boulder, CO: Westview Press.

Moschonas, G. (2013). A new left in Greece: PASOK's fall and SYRIZA's rise. *Dissent*, *60*(4), 33–37. Retrieved from http://muse.jhu.edu/journals/dissent/v060/60.4.moschonas.html

Mosco, V. (2014). *To the cloud: Big data in a turbulent world*. London: Routledge.

Moustaka, M. (2008). *Zahopoulos gives away Tsekou* (Ζαχόπουλος «καίει» Τσέκου). [online] Ta Nea Online. Retrieved from http://www.tanea.gr/news/greece/article/63568/?iid=2. Accessed on March 21, 2017.

Mouzelis, N. (2009). On the December events. In S. Economides & V. Monastiriotis (Eds.),. *The return of street politics? Essays on the december riots in Greece*. London: The Hellenic Observatory LSE, 2009.

Mowbray, M. (2010). *Blogging the Greek riots: Between aftermath and ongoing engagement*. In Kullenberg, Ch. & Hiller P. (Eds.), *Resistance Studies Magazine*, Issue 1–2010.

Mpintelas, L. (2009). 70 years on air (70 Χρόνια στον α-E.P.A.) (In Greek). *Ethnos*. 9 January 2009. Retrieved from http://www.ethnos.gr/article.asp?catid=22733&subid=2&pubid=2144911. Accessed on March 3, 2014.

Mueller, J. (1994). *Policy and opinion in the Gulf war*. Chicago, IL: University of Chicago Press.

Mylona, I. (2008). SMS in everyday political marketing in Greece. *Journal of Political Marketing*, *7*(3–4), 278–294.

Mylonas, Y. (2014). Crisis, austerity and opposition in mainstream media discourses of Greece. *Critical Discourse Studies*, *11*(3), 305–321.

Nasioulas, I. (2012). *Greek social economy revisited* (1st ed.). Frankfurt: Peter Lang GmbH, Internationaler Verlag der Wissenschaften.

Naughton, J. (1999). *A brief history of the future: Origins of the Internet*. London: Weidenfeld & Nicolson.

Nevradakis, M. (2012). When both sides are wrong.... [online] *The Huffington Post*. Retrieved from http://www.huffingtonpost.com/michael-nevradakis/when-both-sides-are-wrong_b_1912498.html. Accessed on February 5, 2017.

Newman, N., Fletcher, R., Kalogeropoulos, A. L., Levy, D., & Kleis Nielsen, R. (2017). *Digital News Report 2017*. [online] Reuters Institute for the Study of Journalism. Retrieved from https://reutersinstitute.politics.ox.ac.uk/sites/default/files/Digital%20News%20Report%202017%20web_0.pdf. Accessed on November 12, 2017.

Newman, J. (2006). Modularity and community structure in networks. *Proceedings of the National Academy of Sciences of the United States of America*, *103*(23), 8577–8696.

Nikolaidis, A. (2017). The impact of austerity on the Greek news media and public sphere. In *The Death of Public Knowledge?: How Free Markets Destroy the General Intellect* (pp. 33–44). London: Goldsmiths Press.

Nguyen, D. (2016). Anaysing transnational web spheres. The European example during the eurozone crisis. In A. Karatzogianni, D. Nguyen, & E. Serafinelli (Eds.), *The digital transformation of the public sphere. Conflict, migration, crisis and culture in digital networks*. London: Palgrave Macmillan.

Niaoti, I. (2011). *The slogan that only the Greek media heard* (Το σύνθημα που άκουσαν μόνο τα ελληνικά MME). [online] Eleytherotypia. Retrieved from http://www.enet.gr/?i=news.el.kosmos&id=278406. Accessed on May 29, 2017.

Nomikos, J. (2007). Terrorism, media, and intelligence in Greece: Capturing the 17 November Group. *International Journal of Intelligence and CounterIntelligence*, *20*(1), 65–78.

Ntelis, M. (2015). *Opinion: The class No and the future of inequality* (Αποψη: Το ταξικό ΟΧΙ και το μέλλον της ανισότητας), | Kathimerini. [online] Kathimerini.gr. Retrieved from http://www.kathimerini.gr/823210/article/oikonomia/ellhnikh-oikonomia/apoyh-to-ta3iko-oxi-kai-to-mellon-ths-anisothtas. Accessed on March 10, 2017.

Observatory for Digital Greece (ODG). (2010). *Internet users' identity in Greece* (Ταυτότητα χρηστών Internet στην Ελλάδα) (In Greek). Online: Retrieved from http://www.observatory.gr/files/meletes/InternetUsers2007_FINAL.pdf. Accessed on March 1, 2014.

Osgood, E. C. (1959). The representation model and relevant research methods. In I. de Sola Pool (Ed.), *Trends in content analysis* (pp. 33–88). Urbana, IL: University of Illinois Press.

Offe, C. (1985). New social movements: Challenging the boundaries of institutional politics. *Social Research, 52*(4), 817–868. Retrieved from http://search.proquest.-com/docview/1297285517/

O'Hare, L. (2015). *How SYRIZA won the media war and overcame 'project fear'.* [online] CommonSpace. Retrieved from https://www.commonspace.scot/articles/107/how-SYRIZA-won-media-war-and-overcame-project-fear. Accessed on February 23, 2017.

Olabode, Sh. (2016). Veterans of diaspora activism: An overview of ICT uses among Nigerian migrant networks. In A. Karatzogianni, D. Nguyen, & E. Serafinelli (Eds.), *The Digital transformation of the public sphere. Conflict, migration, crisis and culture in digital networks*. London: Palgrave Macmillan.

Olson, M. (1965). *The logic of collective action* (1st ed.). Cambridge, MA: Harvard University Press.

Oliver, P., Marwell, G., & Teixeira, R. (1985). A theory of the critical mass. I. Interdependence, group heterogeneity, and the production of collective action. *American Journal of Sociology, 91*(3), 522–556.

Opp, K. (2009). *Theories of political protest and social movements*. London: Routledge.

O'Sullivan, F. (2016). *Europe's open borders are crumbling*. [online] CityLab. Retrieved from http://www.citylab.com/politics/2016/02/european-union-open-border-belgium-checks-syrian-refugee-isis/470733/. Accessed on March 19, 2017.

Ovenden, K., & Mason, P. (2015). *SYRIZA* (1st ed.). London: Pluto Press.

Owens, L., & Palmer, L. (2003). Making the news: Anarchist counter-public relations on the world wide web. *Critical Studies in Media Communication, 20*(4), 335–361.

Panourgia, N. (2009). *Dangerous citizens* (1st ed.). New York, NY: Fordham University Press.

Papacharissi, Z. (2002). The virtual sphere. *New Media & Society, 4*(1), 9–27.

Papadaki, L. (2012). *Reportage: SYRIZA's Admins* (Ρεπορτάζ: Οι admins του ΣΥ.ΡΙΖ.Α). [video] Retrieved from https://www.youtube.com/watch?v=eQeyNCPUvCI. Accessed on February 23, 2017.

Papadimitriou, L. (2013). *Ioannis Voulpiotis: The Greek who Hitler liked* (Ιωάννης Βουλπιώτης: Ο Ελληνας που συμπάθησε ο Χίτλερ). [online] To Vima. Retrieved from http://www.tovima.gr/vimagazino/views/article/?aid=508041. Accessed on May 27, 2017.

Papagiannidis, S., Coursaris, C., & Bourlakis, M. (2012). Do websites influence the nature of voting intentions? The case of two national elections in Greece. *Computers in Human Behavior, 28*(2), 300–307.

Papagiannidis, S., & Manika, D. (2016). Political participation and engagement via different online and offline channels. *International Journal of E-Business Research, 12*(4), 1–22.

Papathanassopoulos, S. (1990). Broadcasting, politics and the state in socialist Greece. *Media, Culture & Society, 12*(3), 387–397.

Papathanassopoulos, S. (1997). The politics and the effects of the deregulation of Greek television. *European Journal of Communication, 12*(3), 351–368.

Papathanassopoulos, S. (1999). The effects of media commercialization on journalism and politics in Greece. *The Communication Review, 3*(4), 379–402.

Pappas, T. (2008). Political leadership and the emergence of radical mass movements in democracy. *Comparative Political Studies*, *41*(8), 1117–1140.

Pappas, T. (2010). Winning by default: The Greek election of 2009. *South European Society and Politics*, *15*(2), 273–287.

Pappas, T. (2014). *Populism and crisis politics in Greece* (1st ed.). Basingstoke: Palgrave Macmillan.

Pappas, T., & Dinas, E. (2006). From opposition to power: Greek conservatism reinvented. *South European Society and Politics*, *11*(3–4), 477–495.

Parut, B., & Parut, M. (2014). *Social media in politics: Case studies on the political power of social media* (1st ed.). Cham: Springer.

Passy, F. (2003). Social networks matter. But how? In M. Diani & D. McAdam (Eds.), *Social movements and networks: Relational approaches to collective action* (1st ed.). Oxford: Oxford University Press.

Patton, M. (1990). *Qualitative evaluation and research methods* (2nd ed.). London: Sage.

Pentaraki, M. (2012). The class impact of post disaster restoration policies: The example of Ilia, Greece and the need for a politics of disaster. *International Social Work*, *56*(6), 761–774.

Petmezas, S. (n.d.). *History of modern Greece*. [online] Secretariat of General Information and Communication. Retrieved from http://video.minpress.gr/wwwminpress/aboutgreece/aboutgreece_history.pdf. Accessed on May 27, 2017.

Petrakis, E. (1999). *The mass structure of electronic mass media in Greece (Η διάρθρωση της αγοράς των τηλεοπτικών μέσων στην Ελλάδα)*. Athens: National & Kapodistrian University of Athens.

Petropoulos, A. (2015). *Americans and Greeks started the 2004 wiretaps together| Kathimerini*. [online] ekathimerini.com. Retrieved from http://www.ekathimerini.com/202026/interactive/ekathimerini/special-report/americans-and-greeks-started-the-2004-wiretaps-together#firstPage. Accessed on March 21, 2017.

Petropoulou, Ch., (2013). Alternative networks of collectivities and solidarity-cooperative economy in Greek cities: Exploring their theoretical origins. *Journal of Regional Socio-Economic Issues*, *3*(2), 61–86.

Phillips, B. (n.d.). *High police support for Greece's Golden Dawn*. [online] Aljazeera.com. Retrieved from http://www.aljazeera.com/blogs/europe/2012/12/52586.html. Accessed on March 24, 2017.

Pickerill, J. (2006). Radical politics on the net. *Parliamentary Affairs*, *59*(2), 266–282.

Plender, J. (2003). *Going off the rails*. West Sussex: John Wiley & Sons.

Pleios, G. (2013). *Crisis and the media (Η Κρίση και τα ΜΜΕ; in Greek)*. Athens: Papazisi Publications.

Porta, D., & Diani, M. (2006). *Social movements: An introduction* (2nd ed.). Oxford: Blackwell.

Posner, R. (2011). *A failure of capitalism*. Cambridge, MA: Harvard University Press.

Pourgouris, M. (2010). The phenomenology of Hoods: Some reflections on the 2008 violence in Greece. *Journal of Modern Greek Studies*, *28*(2), 225–245.

Pradella, L., & Cillo, R. (2015). Immigrant labour in Europe in times of crisis and austerity: An international political economy analysis. *Competition & Change*, *19*(2), 145–160.

Protothema.gr. (2015). *Pro-Europe rally day after anti-austerity (and pro-SYRIZA) protest held.* [online] Retrieved from http://en.protothema.gr/pro-europe-rally-day-after-anti-austerity-and-pro-SYRIZA-protest/. Accessed on May 27, 2017.

Psacharopoulos, G., & Kazamias, A. (1980). Student activism in Greece: A historical and empirical analysis. *Higher Education*, *9*(2), 127–138.

Psimitis, M. (2011a). The protest cycle of Spring 2010 in Greece. *Social Movement Studies*, *10*(2), 191–197.

Psimitis, M. (2011b). Collective identity versus social exclusion: The December 2008 Greek youth movement. *The Greek Review of Social International Research (Επιθεώρηση Κοινωνικών Ερευνών)*, Special Issue (136C), 111–133.

Publicissue.gr. (2015). *Public Issue – Referendum 2015: Analysis of the «NO» voters* (Public Issue – Δημοψήφισμα 2015: Η ακτινογραφία των ψηφοφόρων του «ΟΧΙ»). [online] Retrieved from http://www.publicissue.gr/11719/referendum-2015-no/. Accessed on March 10, 2017].

Ravanos, A. (2012). *'Independent Greek' the name of the new* «Ανεξάρτητοι Ελληνες» το όνομα του νέου κόμματος υπό τον Πάνο Καμμένο. [online] To Vima. Retrieved from http://www.tovima.gr/politics/article/?aid=445342. Accessed on April 29, 2017.

Quillian, M. R. (1968). Semantic memory. In M. L. Minsky (Ed.), *Semantic information processing* (pp. 216–270). Cambridge, MA: MIT Press.

Rakopoulos, T. (2015). The solidarity economy in the Greek crisis: Movementality, economic democracy and social reproduction. In K. Hart, (Ed.), *Economy for and against democracy* (1st ed.). London: Berghahn.

Reuters. (2018). *Six media groups submit bids for Greek TV licences.* [online] Retrieved from https://www.reuters.com/article/greece-media/six-media-groups-submit-bids-for-greek-tv-licences-idUSL8N1P62ZG. Accessed on January 16, 2018.

Rheingold, H. (2000). *The virtual community* (1st ed.). Cambridge, MA: MIT Press.

Rice, R., & Richards, W., Jr. (1985). An overview of network analysis methods and programs. In D. Brenda & J. V. Melvin (Eds.), *Progress in communication sciences* (Vol. 6, pp. 105–165). Norwood, NJ: Ablex.

Richards, W., Jr., & Rice, R. (1981). NEGOPY network analysis program. *Social Networks*, *3*, 215–223.

Richards, L. (1999). *Using NVivo for qualitative research* (1st ed.). London: Sage.

Rieder, B. (2012). The refraction chamber: Twitter as sphere and network. *First Monday*, *17*(11).

Rieder, B. (2013). *Studying Facebook via data extraction: The Netvizz application.* 5th annual ACM web science conference, pp. 346–355.

Rieder, B., & Röhle, T. (2012). Digital methods: Five challenges. In D. Berry (Ed.), *Understanding digital media humanities* (pp. 66–84). London: Palgrave Macmillan.

Rigos, A. (2007). *The Skiadika accelerate the anti-ruler struggle.* [online] Avgi.gr. Retrieved from http://www.avgi.gr/NavigateActiongo.action?articleID=305682. Accessed on June 7, 2017.

Rosenberg, S., Schnurr, P., & Oxman, T. (1990). Content analysis: A comparison of manual and computerized systems. *Journal of Personality Assessment*, *54*(1), 298–310.

Rogers, R. (2009). *The end of the virtual.* Amsterdam: Amsterdam University Press.

Rogers, E., & Kincaid, D. L. (1981). *Communication networks: Toward a new paradigm for research.* New York, NY: Free Press.

Rucht, D., (1988). Themes, logics, and arena of social movements: A structural approach. *International Social Movement Research*, *1*, 305–328.

Rüdig, W., & Karyotis, G. (2013). Who protests in Greece? Mass opposition to austerity. *British Journal of Political Science*, *44*(3), 487–513.

Rüdig, W., & Karyotis, G. (2014). Who protests in Greece? *Mass Opposition to Austerity*, *44*(3), 487–513.

Ryan, J. (2010). *A history of the Internet and the digital future* (1st ed.). London: Reaktion Book.

Samara, V. (2013). *The internet Taliban of Samaras* (Οι ιντερνετικοί «ταλιμπάν» του Σαμαρά). [online] Eleftherotypia/Ελευθεροτυπία. Retrieved from http://www.enet.gr/?i=news.el.article&id=338966. Accessed on February 24, 2017.

Samatas, M. (2015). "Austerity surveillance" in Greece under the austerity regime (2010 – 2014). *Media and Communication*, *3*(3), 68.

Sarup, M. (1993). *An introductory guide to post-structuralism and postmodernism* (2nd ed.). Hemel Hempstead: Harvester Wheatsheaf.

Schank, R., & Abelson, R. (1977). *Scripts, plans, goals, and understanding: An inquiry into human knowledge structures*. Hillsdale, NJ: Lawrence Erlbraum.

Schwarz, A., & Sagris, T. (2010). *We are an image from the future* (1st ed.). Edinburgh: AK Press.

Scott, J. (2000). *Social network analysis* (2nd ed.). London: Sage.

Snee, H., Hine, C., Morey, Y., Roberts, S., & Watson, H. (2016). *Digital methods for social science*. London: Palgrave Macmillan.

Siani-Davies, P., & Katsikas, S. (2009). National reconciliation after civil war: The case of Greece. *Journal of Peace Research*, *46*(4), 559–575.

Siapera, E., & Veikou, M. (2016). The digital Golden Dawn: Emergence of the nationalistic-racist digital mainstream. In A. Karatzogianni, D. Nguyen, & E. Serafinelli (Eds.), *The digital transformation of the public sphere. Conflict, migration, crisis and culture in digital networks*. London: Palgrave Macmillan.

Simcox, R. (2013). Greece's ERT TV station symbolises what is happening to the country | Rich Simcox. [online] *The Guardian*. Retrieved from https://www.theguardian.com/commentisfree/2013/nov/11/greece-ert-closure-austerity-government. Accessed on March 27, 2017.

Simiti, M. (2014). *Rage and protest: The case of the Greek Indignant movement*. Hellenic Observatory Papers on Greece and Southeast Europe, GreeSE Paper No. 82.

Simon, H. (1987). *Models of man*. New York, NY: Garland.

Sims, J. (2003). Politicians and media owners in Greek radio: Pluralism as Diaplokí. *Journal of Radio Studies*, *10*(2), 202–215.

Sklair, L. (1995). Social movements and global capitalism. *Sociology*, *29*(3), 495–512.

Smith, H. (2012). 'Friend of Greece' François Hollande gives bailout ultimatum. [online] *The Guardian*. Retrieved from https://www.theguardian.com/world/greek-election-blog-2012/2012/jun/14/greece-bailout-hollande-ultimatum-eurozone. Accessed on March 21, 2017.

Smith, H. (2013a). Greeks protest against Golden Dawn attack on Communists. [online] *The Guardian*. Retrieved from https://www.theguardian.com/world/2013/sep/13/greeks-protest-golden-dawn-attack-communists. Accessed on February 24, 2017.

Smith, H. (2013b). Greek police 'battered four terrorist suspects then launched cover-up'. [online] *The Guardian*. Retrieved from https://www.theguardian.com/world/2013/feb/04/greece-police-local-terrorist-arrests. Accessed on March 24, 2017.

Smith, H. (2015). Greece fiercely divided as referendum campaign gets under way. [online] *The Guardian*. Retrieved from https://www.theguardian.com/world/2015/jun/29/greece-fiercely-divided-as-referendum-campaign-gets-under-way. Accessed on March 16, 2017.

Smith, P. (2008). *Motivation and personality: Handbook of thematic content analysis* (1st ed.). Cambridge: Cambridge University Press.

Smith, C., Atkinson, J., McClelland, D., & Veroff, J. (1992). *Motivation and personality* (1st ed.). Cambridge: Cambridge University Press.

Smith, M., Raine, L., Hemelboim, I., & Shneiderman, B. (2014). *Mapping Twitter topic networks: From polarized crowds to community clusters*. Numbers, facts and trends shaping the world, PewResearchCenter in association with the Social Media Research Foundation.

Smith, M., Shneiderman, B., Milic-Frayling, N., Rodrigues, E., Barash, V., Dunne, C., … Gleave, E. (2009). *Analyzing (social media) networks with NodeXL*. International Conference on Communities and Technologies (C&T).

Smyrnaios, N. (2010). Financial aggregation and institutional framework in Greek private television. In I. Vovou (Ed.), *The world of television: Theoretical approaches, program's analysis and Greek reality*. Athens: Herodotos.

Smyrnaios, N. (2013). *Financial power and Media: An exercise of Mapping* (Οικονομική εξουσία και ΜΜΕ στην εποχή της κρίσης : μια άσκηση χαρτογράφησης). [online] Ephemeron. Retrieved from http://ephemeron.eu/943. Accessed on May 29, 2017.

Smyrnaios, N. (2015). *How did the electoral victory of SYRIZA in Greece become a worldwide trend on Twitter*. [online] Ephemeron. Retrieved from http://ephemeron.eu/1553. Accessed on February 23, 2017.

Smyrnaios, N. (2017). *How the mainstream media created the Macron phenomenon*. [online] Ephemeron. Retrieved from http://ephemeron.eu/1981. Accessed on May 16, 2017.

Snow, D., & Oliver, P. (1995). Social movements and collective behavior: Social psychological dimensions and considerations. In K. Cook, G. Fine, & J. House (Eds.), *Sociological perspectives on social psychology* (pp. 57l–599). Boston, MA: Allyn and Bacon.

Snow, D. (2013). *The Wiley-Blackwell encyclopedia of social and political movements* (1st ed.). Malden, MA: Wiley.

Sotirakopoulos, N., & Sotiropoulos, G. (2013). 'Direct democracy now!': The Greek indignados and the present cycle of struggles. *Current Sociology*, *61*(4), 443–456.

Sotiris, P. (2010). Rebels with a cause: The December 2008 Greek youth movement as the condensation of deeper social and political contradictions. *International Journal of Urban and Regional Research*, *34*(1), 203–209.

Sowa, J. (2014). *Principles of semantic networks* (1st ed.). Burlington: Elsevier Science.

Sputniknews.com. (2015). *Protesters gather for anti-austerity rallies in Greece prior to bailout*. [online] Retrieved from https://sputniknews.com/europe/201506171023498909/. Accessed on March 10, 2017.

Stavrakakis, Y. (2014). The return of 'the people': Populism and anti-populism in the shadow of the European crisis. *Constellations*, *21*(4), 505–517.

Stekelenburg, J., & Klandermans, B. (2009). Social movement theory. In S. Ellis & I. Kessel (Eds.), *Movers and shakers, social movements in Africa* (1st ed.). Boston, MA: Brill.

Stiglitz, J. (2002). *Globalization and its discontents* (1st ed.). London: Penguin Books.

Stoecker, R., (1995). Community, movement, organization: The problem of identity convergence in collective action. *Sociological Quarterly*, *36*, 111–130.

Sweney, M. (2016). Greece cuts TV channels from eight to four in controversial licence auction. [online] *The Guardian*. Retrieved from https://www.theguardian.com/media/2016/sep/02/greece-tv-channels-licence-auction. Accessed on January 16, 2018.

Ta Nea Online. (2015). *Parallel mobilizations supporting yes and no campaigns completed the short pre-election period of the referendum* (Παράλληλες συγκεντρώσεις υπέρ του «ναι» και του «όχι» στην Αθήνα ολοκλήρωσαν τη σύντομη προεκλογική περίοδο για το δημοψήφισμα). [online] Retrieved from http://www.tanea.gr/news/politics/article/5255147/arxizoyn-oi-parallhles-sygkentrwseis-yper-toy-nai-kai-toy-oxi-sthn-athhna/. Accessed on March 16, 2017.

Tadeo, M., & Penty, C. (2015). *Greek deal shows limitations facing SYRIZA Ally Podemos in Spain*. [online] Bloomberg.com. Retrieved from https://www.bloomberg.com/news/articles/2015-07-13/greek-deal-shows-limitations-facing-SYRIZA-ally-podemos-in-spain. Accessed on March 11, 2017.

Tarrow, S. (1998). *Power in movement*. Cambridge: Cambridge University Press.

Tarrow, S. (2011). *Power in movement* (3rd ed.). Cambridge: Cambridge University Press.

Tarrow, S. (2014). Critical dialogue. The logic of connective action: Digital media and the personalization of contentious politics. In W. L. Bennett & A. Segerberg (Eds.), *Perspectives on Politics* (Vol. 12(2), pp. 468–470). New York, NY: Cambridge University Press, 2013.

Terranova, T. (2004). *Network culture* (1st ed.). London: Pluto Press.

The Guardian. (2011). *George Papandreou: An all too final stand* | Editorial. [online] Retrieved from https://www.theguardian.com/commentisfree/2011/nov/01/george-papandreou-final-stand-editorial. Accessed on March 20, 2017.

Thelwall, M., Sud, P., & Vis, F. (2011). Commenting on YouTube videos: From guatemalan rock to El Big Bang. *Journal of the American Society for Information Science and Technology*, *63*(3), 616–629.

Theocharis, Y. (2011). Young people, political participation and online postmaterialism in Greece. *New Media & Society*, *13*(2), 203–223.

Theocharis, Y., Lowe, W., & Van Deth, J. (2014). Using Twitter to mobilise protest action: Transnational online mobilisation patterns and action repertoires in the occupy wall street, Indignados and Aganaktismenoi movements. In 41st ECPR Joint Sessions of Workshops Johannes Gutenberg Universität. Mainz.

Theodoropoulou, I. (2014). *Sociolinguistics of style and social class in contemporary Athens (Discourse approaches to politics, society and culture)* (1st ed.). Amsterdam: John Benjamins Publishing.

Theofilopoulos, A. (2008). *Social discrimination in Greece: The case of far-right groups and political parties 1975–2007* (Κοινωνικός αποκλεισμός στην Ελλάδα: η περίπτωση των οργανώσεων και των κομμάτων της άκρας δεξιάς 1975–2007). MA in Sociology. The Panteion University of Social and Political Sciences.

Tilly, C. (1973). *Revolution and collective actions.* Center for Research on Social Organization, University of Michigan, Working Paper #83.

Toch, H. (1965). *The social psychology of social movements.* Indianapolis, IN: Bobbs-Merrill.

To Kouti tis Pandoras. (2015). *ND strategy curicculum to support yes leaked: It is proved that they rig polls* (Διέρρευσε το σημείωμα στρατηγικής της ΝΔ για να πετύχουν το ΝΑΙ – Αποδεικνύει ότι στήνουν δημοσκοπήσεις) To Kouti tis Pandoras | To Κουτί της Πανδώρας. [online] Retrieved from http://www.koutipandoras.gr/article/dierreyse-simeioma-stratigikis-tis-nd-gia-na-petyhoyn-nai-apodeiknyei-oti-stinoyn. Accessed on March 16, 2017.

To Vima International. (2014). *Witnesses unable to identify any of the Velvento robbery suspects.* [online] Retrieved from http://www.tovima.gr/en/article/?aid=564278. Accessed on March 16, 2017.

Tornes, A. (2015). *Instant and complete access to every historical public Tweet |* Twitter Blogs. [online] Blog.twitter.com. Retrieved from https://blog.twitter.com/2015/full-archive-search-api. Accessed on May 16, 2017.

Touraine, A. (1985). An introduction to the study of social movements. *Social Research, 52*(4), 749–787.

Touri, M., & Rogers, S. (2013). Europe's communication deficit and the UK press: Framing the Greek financial crisis. *Journal of Contemporary European Studies, 21*(2), 175–189.

Triliva, S., Varvantakis, C., & Dafermos, M. (2014). YouTube, young people, and the socioeconomic crises in Greece. *Information, Communication & Society, 18*(4), 407–423.

Trottier, D., & Fuchs, C. (2015). *Social media, politics and the state: Protests, revolutions, riots, crime and policing in the age of Facebook, Twitter and YouTube.* New York: Routledge.

Tsakatika, M., & Eleftheriou, C. (2013). The radical left's turn towards civil society in Greece: One strategy, two paths. *South European Society and Politics, 18*(1), 81–99.

Tsakiroglou, T. (2015). *They vote for no on the instititions' proposal* (Ψηφίζουν «όχι» στην πρόταση των θεσμών). [online] Efsyn/Η Εφημερίδα των Συντακτών. Retrieved from http://www.efsyn.gr/arthro/psifizoyn-ohi-stin-protasi-ton-thesmon. Accessed on March 10, 2017.

Tsaliki, L. (2010). Technologies of political mobilization and civil society in Greece: The wildfires of summer 2007. *Convergence: The International Journal of Research into New Media Technologies, 16*(2), 151–161.

Tsaliki, L. (2012). *The Greek 'Indignados': The Aganaktismenoi as a case study of the 'new repertoire of collective action'.* Retrieved from http://www2.media.uoa.gr/people/tsaliki/wp-content/uploads/2010/07/Tsaliki_The_Greek_Indignados.pdf. Accessed on March 10, 2017.

Tsatsou, P. (2014). *Internet studies* (1st ed.). London: Ashgate Publishing.

Tsimitakis, M. (2009). Revolt and the Internet (Εξέγερση και Διαδίκτυο). *Sýnchrona Thémata, 103*, 29–33.

Tsiras, E. (2011). *The new far right in Greece: Organizational evolution, electoral influence and political speech of the People's Orthodox Rally (LAOS).* (Διατριβή: Η νέα άκρα δεξιά στην Ελλάδα: οργανωτική εξέλιξη, εκλογική επιρροή και πολιτικός λόγος του Λαϊκού Ορθόδοξου Συναγερμού). Ph.D. University of Macedonia. [online] National Archive of Ph.D. Theses, Thesis.ekt.gr. Retrieved from http://thesis.ekt.gr/thesisBookReader/id/28119#page/1/mode/2up. Accessed on March 31, 2017.

Tsiras, St. (2012). *Nation and LAOS: New far right and populism ('Έθνος και ΛΑΟΣ: νέα άκρα δεξιά και λαϊκισμός)*. Thessaloniki: Epikentro.

Turkle, S. (1997). *Life on the screen: Identity in the age of the Internet* (1st ed.). New York, NY: Touchstone.

Turner, R. (1969). The public perception of protest. *American Sociological Review*, *34*(6), 815.

TVXS. (2011). *Siemens' scandal in numbers* (Το σκάνδαλο Siemens σε αριθμούς). [online] Retrieved from http://tvxs.gr/news/%CE%B5%CE%BB%CE%BB%CE%AC%CE%B4%CE%B1/%CF%84%CE%BF-%CF%83%CE%BA%CE%AC%CE%BD%CE%B4%CE%B1%CE%BB%CE%BF-siemens-%CF%83%CE%B5-%CE%B1%CF%81%CE%B9%CE%B8%CE%BC%CE%BF%CF%8D%CF%82. Accessed on March 21, 2017.

TVXS. (2015). *ND's non-paper with instructions: this is how to propagandate the 'yes' guide* (Non-paper με οδηγίες από τη ΝΔ: Έτσι να προπαγανδίζετε το «ναι»). [online] Retrieved from http://tvxs.gr/news/ellada/non-paper-me-odigies-apo-ti-nd-etsi-na-propagandizete-nai. Accessed on March 16, 2017.

Tzogopoulos, G. (2013). *Greek crisis in the media* (1st ed.). New York, NY: Routledge.

Uldam, J., & Askanius, T. (2013). Online civic cultures: Debating climate change activism on YouTube. *International Journal of Communication*, *7*(2013), 1185–1204.

Van Aelst, P., & Walgrave, S. (2002). New media, new movements? The role of the internet in shaping the 'anti-globalization' movement. *Information, Communication & Society*, *5*(4), 465–493.

Van Dijk, T. (2008). Critical discourse analysis and nominalization: Problem or pseudo-problem? *Discourse & Society*, *19*(6), 821–828.

Vasilopoulou, S., & Halikiopoulou, D. (2013). In the shadow of Grexit: The Greek election of 17 June 2012. *South European Society and Politics*, *18*(4), 523–542.

Vatikiotis, P. (2011). Networking activism: Implications for Greece. *Estudos em Comunicação*, *10*, 169–185.

Voutyras, S. (2016). This radicalisation which is not one: contentious politics against the backdrop of the Greek crisis. *Journal of Contemporary European Studies*, *24*(2), 223–239.

Vovou, I. (Ed.) (2010). Financial aggregation and institutional framework in Greek private television. In *The world of television: Theoretical approaches, program's analysis and Greek reality* (1st ed., pp. 141–174). Athens: Herodotos.

Vradis, A. (2009). Greece's winter of discontent. *City*, *13*(1), 146–149.

Vradis, A., & Dalakoglou, D. (2011). *Revolt and crisis in Greece* (1st ed.). Edinburgh: AK Press & Occupied London Collective.

Vulliamy, E., & Smith, H. (2014). Athens 1944: Britain's dirty secret. [online] *The Guardian*. Retrieved from https://www.theguardian.com/world/2014/nov/30/athens-1944-britains-dirty-secret. Accessed on March 31, 2017.

Wallace, A. F. C. (1961). *Culture and personality*. New York, NY: Random House.

Wasserman, S., & Faust, K. (1994). *Social network analysis* (1st ed.). Cambridge: Cambridge University Press.

Wearden, G., & Fletcher, N. (2015). Greek crisis: Protesters demand end to austerity, with EU future in doubt – As it happened. [online] *The Guardian*. Retrieved from http://www.theguardian.com/business/live/2015/jun/17/greek-crisis-austria-default-ecb-banks-live?page=with%3Ablock-5581a4a1e4b06ca1215f272a. Accessed on May 29, 2017.

Weisenthal, J. (2012). 27-year old in Greece arrested for blaspheming a monk on Facebook. [online] *Business Insider*. Retrieved from http://www.businessinsider.com/geron-pastitsios-2012-9?IR=T. Accessed on May 29, 2017.

Wellman, B., & Berkowitz, S. (1998). *Social structures*. Cambridge: Cambridge University Press.

Williams, S., Terras, M., & Warwick, C. (2013). What do people study when they study Twitter? Classifying Twitter related academic papers. *Journal of Documentation*, *69*(3), 384–410.

Wodak, R., & Busch, B. (2004). Approaches to media texts. In J. Downing (Ed.), *The Sage handbook of media studies* (1st ed.). London: Sage.

Wood, E. (1995). *Democracy against capitalism* (1st ed.). Cambridge: Cambridge University Press.

Xenakis, S. (2012). A new dawn? Change and continuity in political violence in Greece. *Terrorism and Political Violence*, *24*(3), 437–464.

Zafiropoulos, K. (2012). Connectivity practices and activity of Greek political blogs. *Future Internet*, *4*(4), 719–736.

Zaharopoulos, T. (2002). The evolution of public service radio broadcasting in Greece: From authoritarianism to anarchy and irrelevance. *Global Media Journal*, [online] *1*(1). Retrieved from http://lass.purduecal.edu/cca/gmj/fa02/gmj-fa02-zaharopoulos.htm

Zald, M., & Ash, R. (1966). Social movement organizations: Growth, decay and change. *Social Forces*, *44*(3), 327–341.

Zald, M., McCarthy, J., & McAdam, D. (1996). *Comparative perspectives on social movements* (1st ed.). Cambridge: Cambridge University Press.

Žižek, S. (2012). *The year of dreaming dangerously* (1st ed.). London: Verso.

Zoulas, C. (2016). *The birth of the Menoume Evropi protest movement*, Constantinos Zoulas | Kathimerini. [online] Ekathimerini.com. Retrieved from http://www.ekathimerini.com/209844/article/ekathimerini/community/the-birth-of-the-menoume-evropi-protest-movement. Accessed on March 8, 2017.

Index